Feminist Social and Political Theory

D1290416

Feminist Social and Political Theory

Contemporary Debates and Dialogues

Janice McLaughlin

First published 2003 by
PALGRAVE MACMILLAN
Houndmills, Basingstoke, Hampshire RG21 6XS and
175 Fifth Avenue, New York, N.Y. 10010
Companies and representatives throughout the world

PALGRAVE MACMILLAN is the global academic imprint of the Palgrave Macmillan division of St. Martin's Press, LLC and of Palgrave Macmillan Ltd. Macmillan® is a registered trademark in the United States, United Kingdom and other countries. Palgrave is a registered trademark in the European Union and other countries.

ISBN 0–333–96810–7 hardback
ISBN 0–333–96811–5 paperback

This book is printed on paper suitable for recycling and made from fully managed and sustained forest sources.

A catalogue record for this book is available from the British Library.

Library of Congress Cataloging-in-Publication Data
McLaughlin, Janice, 1968–
    Feminist social and political theory : contemporary debates and dialogues / Janice McLaughlin.
        p. cm.
    Includes bibliographical references and index.
    ISBN 0–333–96810–7—ISBN 0–333–96811–5 (pbk.)
    1. Feminist theory. 2. Feminist criticism. I. Title.

HQ1190 .M388 2003
305 .42'01—dc21   2003049820

10 9 8 7 6 5 4 3 2 1
12 11 10 09 08 07 06 05 04 03

Printed and bound in Great Britain by
Creative Print & Design (Wales), Ebbw Vale

To Katie Ash
(just as well)

Contents

Acknowledgements

In some ways this text has been a relatively lonely affair, in other ways a variety of people, often without their knowing, became part of the production of the end product; of course without having responsibility for the ideas found within. Overall, producing the book has been an enjoyable exercise, partly because I must confess it has been a solitary affair (maybe it is my age), but also because it has been a reasonable excuse to spend some time reading ideas. I still can't figure out why I feel guilty about spending some of my work-time reading, but explaining it is leading to a book always seems to calm those concerned (friends and colleagues alike).

The last stages of the book coincided with a period of personal and academic turmoil, so my acknowledgements focus on those who helped through that difficult time. I begin by providing the reader with two important tips about what not to do when just about to submit the final manuscript:

1 Do not move house, particularly if the builders will be moving in with you;
2 Do not take on a major new administrative role, particularly if your university is going through a period of restructuring.

My biggest thanks go to the people who dealt with the consequences of me not following these two straightforward suggestions. To the builders who finished on time and did just about everything we asked them. To my parents and Helen who came to help with the house and stayed away when asked. To the electrician who got our electricity back on, after a mere five hours of ripping out newly reclaimed flooring. To the administrative support staff (particularly Nicki, Sue and Brad) who helped with student induction and put up with a fair degree of angst, even if they transferred to other areas not long after. To Colin for providing musical gems that saw me through the last few weeks. To students who obeyed the do not disturb sign on my door, to staff who did not.

Apart from the immediate mechanics of the production of the text I would like to thank Catherine Gray at Palgrave Macmillan for her understanding about the slight fluidity in the final deadline and word limit. In addition, both Catherine and the reviewers produced invaluable comments which have been incorporated into the final text. Thank you for your careful attention and proposals. I would also like to thank colleagues at Newcastle and my last department, Sociology and Social Policy, at the University of Leeds for providing input and contexts for the ideas in the text.

Finally, Katie, thank you for lots more than your proof-reading expertise.

JANICE M^CLAUGHLIN

Introduction

CONTENTS

Feminist activism is often divided into two periods; the late nineteenth century (known as the first wave) and the 1960s and 1970s (the second wave). Both periods led to important changes in the levels of rights and freedoms women now have (at least in some countries), and in how issues of gender are understood in different societies. The first wave was a political movement aimed at challenging the lack of rights for women in the public sphere. The right to vote, own property and obtain an education were vital demands of the first feminist movement. The campaigns of this period were based on important feminist theoretical texts, which captured the incompatibility of modern democracy with the confinement of women into the private sphere. Second-wave feminism, in different ways, connected the continued gaps in the rights and opportunities women suffered in the public realm to the roles they played in the private sphere. The focus on the private sphere brought a new range of issues into activism and the development of feminist ideas. The new areas included sexuality, reproduction, domestic labour and domestic violence. Again, during the second wave a rich body of feminist theoretical ideas developed, closely linked to the activities of the Women's Liberation Movement.

Both periods led to an increased presence for the 'woman question' in wider social and political thought (Jackson, 1998; Okin, 1992). An important target in each wave was highlighting the inability of established social and political thought to respond to the oppression of women. Feminist thought has always sought to engage with and reinterpret the foundations of the theoretical frameworks it coexists with and at times draws from. First-wave feminists challenged women's apparent failure to display the values associated with human nature; the excuse used at the time to justify the lack of rights women had in areas such as property and suffrage. Second-wave feminists went on to challenge the masculine values embedded in how social and political thought approached many issues. They fundamentally challenged theory's lack of interest in the private sphere. They argued that much of social and political thought simply saw the division between the private and public as a given; an assumption that could only happen because of the association made between the private and women. Once the private came under investigation, feminists were able to identify patterns of power, harm and abuse women suffered in this sphere and push for legislation to challenge such abuse. This last point highlights an important criterion that has always been an element in the formulation of feminist ideas. The object of feminist theorizing should be the production of ideas and strategies that can feed into (as well as learn from) feminist activism aiming to change things.

In first and second-wave feminism, Marxism, socialism and liberalism were reconfigured in order to apply them to the position of women in society. In the second wave, radical feminism emerged as a political framework focused on constructing theory from women's life experiences and collective consciousness. Each of these different frameworks have produced important approaches to understanding the processes and structures that lie behind the oppression of women and the role of gender in shaping society in different areas of the globe and in different periods. Over time these groupings of feminist thought have changed and new ideas have continued to emerge beyond the second-wave period in order to continue to reflect on 'the woman question'. The work produced in these frameworks means that it is harder (although it is still possible) to introduce the major debates in social and political thought without discussing feminist contributions. However, the idea for this book came from noting how feminist ideas are represented in theory modules and in examining the resources lecturers have available to introduce students to the scope of those ideas.

What I have realized is that there is a significant limitation in how feminist theories are taught. Feminist ideas continue to be taught and represented through discussion of Marxist/socialist feminism, liberal feminism and radical feminism, occasionally with postmodern and perhaps psychoanalytic feminism added on at the end. My claim is that this approach to teaching or writing about feminist theory does little to reflect the priorities and frameworks of contemporary feminist work. Therefore, my main aim in writing this book is to fill the gap by detailing the current priorities and concerns of feminist social and political thought. Without denying the importance of these existing perspectives I seek to capture contemporary dynamics and concerns in feminist thought in such a way that both students and academics can reflect on the continued importance and vitality of feminist thinking.

There is a need for a new text surveying contemporary feminist ideas for a number of reasons. First, it is important to give testimony to the continued importance of and developments within feminist ideas. The continued focus on second-wave feminist ideas in teaching and textbooks leads to the impression that feminist writing ended around 1977. Feminist thought has continued to reflect on its own frameworks and develop new concerns, partly because changing empirical and theoretical contexts have altered the environment in which its ideas are produced. Second, the new directions and anxieties developing in feminism are indicative of wider processes in social and political thought. It is not just feminist thought that is reflecting on its own practice and approaches; wider social and political thought is also in an important period of self-reflection. How bodies of theoretical work conceptualize rights, democracy, citizenship, identity and knowledge is under debate. Third, my assertion is that feminist writings are important sites for the ongoing developments currently shaping contemporary social and political thought. If current teaching and resources are to reflect on contemporary theoretical tensions, feminist contributions must have a strong presence. This book is an important resource in enabling that presence in sociology, political science and philosophy.

The role of this opening chapter is to indicate some important contexts and issues that will be fully developed within the book itself. I begin by indicating empirical and theoretical contexts that are important backgrounds to both shifts in theoretical discussion and to the book itself. In particular I discuss the increased importance given to issues of difference and recognition in theoretical debates in general and feminism in particular. The Introduction then goes on to look at the dilemmas that feminists have raised with how difference and recognition are being incorporated into theoretical writing and debate. I then go on to indicate how these dilemmas have led some to question the current health of feminist theorizing. The last section is a description of the structure of the book and the themes of the individual chapters.

Current contexts

Before discussing important theoretical developments let's begin by considering the empirical context to contemporary feminist writing.

For particular groups of Western women the quality of life and the choices available are distinctly better than was the case in the 1970s. Liz Stanley comments that it 'must be nearly impossible for younger generations to understand the wall of silence – and silencing – that surrounded women's lives in the early and mid 1970s' (1997: 174). In the UK one can point to equal pay, anti-discrimination legislation, increased numbers of women in higher education, the improved performance of girls in schools, the acknowledgement of feminist approaches in the academy and women in senior positions in commerce, the arts and politics as evidence of better times. Looking to the future, due to the increased importance of the service economy, changes in family living and in people's attitudes, we have been promised that life for women will continue to improve.

Alongside the important victories, there are significant problems that continue to directly effect the lives and life chances of many women. Women make up a significant and disproportionate segment of the poor in the UK and the USA. The double burden remains an everyday reality for many working mothers. In the UK women who try to manage this dilemma by working part-time face lower pay, less rights and protection and significant barriers to any kind of career advancement. Sylvia Walby (1997) argues that this is producing increased polarization amongst women. On the one side is a group of white, professional, middle-class young women who are reaping the benefits of changing conditions in the labour market and in wider society. On the other there are women who are often older, from ethnic minorities and working in the less glamorous areas of the service economy, who face difficult futures in a context of an ever-reducing welfare system and a deregulated global economy.

If we look outside the West, many of the basic rights now accorded to women in the West are still actively denied, particularly in countries where religious fundamentalism and nationalism are on the increase. Globalized patterns of trade and manufacturing are creating new patterns of exploitation at a time when in many areas organizations that seek to protect workers are in a less able position to respond to these new forms of capitalist organization. The overall picture can be summarized as 'one of confused, uneven, erratic and reversible changes through which many women have gained but many have also lost' (Bryson, 1999: 5). Regardless of the extent or scope of improvement, the lives and issues women face today are different from those in previous decades. These changes shift the context of feminist theorizing and make it seem less obvious and certain what its main objectives should be.

These empirical changes imply a period of uncertainty; that uncertainty is matched in theoretical debates and agendas. In wider social and political thought and feminism itself uncertainty about what theory can say and on whose behalf it speaks is marked. This uncertainty is a product of recognition that the structures of theoretical writing in the Enlightenment and in feminism have sought to ignore or deny the importance of difference. In this book I aim to indicate how existing social and political frameworks, for example liberalism and Marxism, are responding to the demand for recognition of difference. In addition I will show how difference issues are leading to the production of new frameworks. In each area it will be clear that feminists are important participants in critique, rearticulation and the production of new ideas. Just now, I will highlight the critique in relation to the Enlightenment before indicating how this critique is effecting feminist theorizing.

Deconstructing the Enlightenment

The Enlightenment saw the development of a body of work, particularly in liberalism and contract theory, which has given us the core terms and perspectives of democracy and rights in Western political thought. Writers such as Immanuel Kant, John Locke and John Stuart Mill have in their importantly different ways set the values that lie at the heart of social and political thought in modernity. For each of them the individual sits at the centre of their political framework. A sovereign individual, in light of 'his' ability to act with reason and rationality, has the right to make judgements about 'his' property, body and actions. The state, if democratic and based on a model of rights, treats all its citizens in the same way. This framework is premised on certain assertions about human nature. In particular, that we think rationally and that we are similar in terms of need and attitude. Contracts between individuals, and between the state and the individual, are the main means to offer protection against one individual exerting their desires over the rights of others. A shared morality maintains the contract; where that fails, the sanction of law provides penalties for those who are judged to have broken society's rules and norms. For the law to be just it must be blind to the interests of particular individuals, and treat everyone in the same way. The progress of society is tied to the pursuit of knowledge. Scientific knowledge enables society to be built and governed by truth (about man and nature) rather than folk tales and tradition.

Contemporary critics of Enlightenment ideas argue that particular exclusions had to occur in order for the pretence of universality and truth to appear attainable in its ideals. To define a universal standard for the good life and the good citizen, 'mis-recognition' had to occur (Fraser, 2001). When the values of the good citizen were laid down they were thought to be available only to a select few. Others – women, colonial subjects, and the poor – were constructed as incapable of such modes of thought and wisdom. The twentieth century was marked by demands from these groups to be afforded the rights put in place by Enlightenment writers – to be recognized as fully human. However, the more different kinds of groups and individuals have demanded such rights, the less feasible it has appeared for the existing model of abstract individualism and universal rights to cover the variety of human condition. In more recent times, marginalized groups have changed their demand from being about **acceptance** or **tolerance** to a call for

recognition. Rather than demand the right to be thought of as capable of the same things as Western Man, they push for wider recognition of different ways to be a subject and a good citizen.

There are two areas where groups are pressing for recognition of difference:

- Differences in identity and cultural values – groups argue that recognition of their cultural traditions and values cannot occur in frameworks that consider human beings as relatively similar in needs and wants.
- Differences in social position – groups argue that historical and contemporary patterns of inequality that have left them marginalized and oppressed cannot be responded to by an approach that 'brackets off' (Fraser, 1997b) consideration of people's different background and social position.

It has proved difficult for Enlightenment ideas to incorporate recognition, which has led some to argue that the existing models of political and social thought were designed to exclude important issues of differences in identity and social position – that is, that the promise of universality could only be achieved through pretending that differences between us do not matter. The principles of the Enlightenment require that truth, knowledge, power and morality can be separated from their social and political context. The difference debates produce a 'loss of innocence' (Flax, 1992b) regarding the feasibility of making such a separation, and this loss is being particularly felt in debates about achieving rights and justice.

The more the differences amongst citizens are recognized, the less legitimate it is to think of rights being protected through a universal set of rules. If there are differences amongst us and these differences relate to identity as well as social position, then is it not possible that the way we define rights, justice, fairness and morality will be influenced by who we are and where we are? Without recognition of difference, the application of rights secures the values of those who were allowed to participate in their formulation. Behind the myth of universality lies a system that maintains the values and perspective of a narrow group. Access to rights appears to be dependent on fitting prescribed norms in society, norms that explicitly deny the legitimacy of particular groups and individuals. For example, in most Western countries same-sex marriage is not allowed. Citizens only have the right to marry if they fit the cultural norm of heterosexuality. In defining marriage as a monogamous relationship between two people of the opposite sex, sanctioned by the Church, the right of lesbians and gay men for full recognition and citizenship rights is denied. Barriers such as this can be thought of as 'a serious violation of justice' (Fraser, 2001: 26).

Recognition has become a matter of rights, a demand for a response to previous harm and denial. Cultural plurality and the space for the expression of varied identities are now seen as valid components to rights discussions, and sit alongside analyses of material inequality and division. With the shift away from universal truth comes a new language about the situatedness of any claim to what is valuable, a right or the human condition (Hekman, 1997; Quillen, 2001). Impartiality is replaced by a stress on 'the importance of grounding one's theories of justice in the value structures of the surrounding world' (Phillips, 1993: 56).

To sum up, the foundations of social and political thought are slowly being chipped away by calls for recognition that challenge its concepts of human nature and individuality. The values and claims of the Enlightenment have been repositioned as contestable and contingent in the ways shown in Box 1. Feminists are important participants in the deconstruction of the Enlightenment. However, the same gaps and exclusions identified in the Enlightenment's founding ideas have also been identified in feminist social and political thought.

Deconstructing feminism

The second wave of feminism focused in varied ways on the differences – political, material, cultural or essential – between women and men. This is

---

Box 1 Repositioning Enlightenment claims

Enlightenment Claim

- Theorists can identify universal truths, which are beyond the particularity of their own position.
- Thought can transcend the particularity of time and space via the use of reason and rationality.
- Science is neutral, a producer of true knowledge that frees society from the false myths of religion and folk tales.
- False knowledge is the result of the corruption of power.

Contemporary Response

- Any claim to truth is influenced by the position from which the author looks upon the world.
- Reason and rationality are the products of particular modes of thinking, which develop in particular historical and social contexts.
- Science maintains its own myths and folk tales within its claims to truth and knowledge.
- All knowledge is the product of particular power relations.

now seen as having been at the cost of fully considering differences amongst women. In second-wave claims about the foundations of power, or the experience of oppression, or the solution to transform society, there was at times less care taken to identify, acknowledge and respond to differences in women's experiences, social position and culture.

The interrogation of the dangers of universality within feminist theorizing began with a consideration of its founding subject: **woman**. In identifying the oppression women faced, their values, and the difference they could make to a better society, feminism presumed an identity and perspective shared by all women. An essentialist underpinning to discussion of 'woman' led to her being given a 'substance, as a kind of entity in which some specific attributes inhere' (Young, 1995: 207). In this way the category hid a variety of important areas of both identity and division. The main problem is that hierarchies amongst women influenced the type of woman feminism spoke of. Elizabeth V. Spelman (1988: 4) argues that 'the focus on women "as women" addressed only one group of women – namely, white middle-class women of Western industrialized countries'. Where other cultures and ways of life were discussed in second-wave feminism, at times it only served to validate ethnocentric values. Audre Lorde (1984c) commented when she read Mary Daly's work (1978) that 'I began to feel my history and my mythic background distorted by the absence of any images of my foremothers in power' (1984c: 67).

The next interrogation stage involved identifying the dangers of universality within particular feminist analyses and agendas. Strategies, which were aimed at removing the inequalities between women and men, kept hidden recognition that significant inequalities between women exist. Marxist feminism equated gender to class, and in doing so presented exploitation as a universal process experienced by all women. Nancy Hartsock, in acknowledging silences in her own work, argues that 'efforts to overcome discrimination against women took the form of attempts to create what could only be a false universality and a concomitant refusal to recognize the economic and social underpinnings of power differences' (1998: 59). Talk about patriarchy and its effects on women hid the variety of ways in which women are exploited and oppressed (Acker, 1989). Radical feminism argued that 'women as a social group are oppressed by men as a social group and that this oppression is the *primary* oppression for women' (Rowland and Klein, 1996: 11, original emphasis). This claim appears to rule out that for some women, 'race' or class may be the oppression they consider their primary barrier. The focus on the nuclear family as the locus of female oppression has been challenged for its insensitivity to different forms of family found in different communities and cultures. In short, other aspects of a woman's identity and social position influence the type and form of oppression she will suffer.

'Race' is one of the most significant challenges to key perspectives of the second wave. 'Race' is a socially produced category, rather than biological; in contemporary debates the inverted commas placed around 'race' are used to flag this approach to understanding its meaning. Feminism charged existing social theories with bias when they did not consider the significance of gender. The same charge can be made against some second-wave feminist work. If 'race' and ethnicity are not mentioned, the white experience becomes the norm. If feminists who are white do not confront the benefits and privileges they have, then they remain part of racist structures (Bhavnani and Coulson, 1997). There is significant evidence of white lives and experiences shaping the priorities and perspectives of much of the second wave:

> Thus the perception white middle-class feminists have of what they need liberating from has little or no relevance to the day to day experience of the majority of Black women in Britain and the ways in which they determine the political choices which have to be made. (Amos and Parmar, 1984: 5)

A vital text of second wave feminism in the USA was Betty Friedan's *The Feminine Mystique* (1965). Friedan outlined the 'disease with no name', which she argued afflicted American women. This was a disease of confinement, unhappiness and loss, a product of seclusion in the home and a life centred on children and husbands. In reality this disease was unheard of by many African American women – yet the text made no mention of 'race'. The plight she described was of the married housewife. At the same time many African American women were the single breadwinners for their families, working as the maids of Friedan's angst-ridden housewives. For bell hooks (1982, 1984, 1995), Friedan is symbolic of this era of feminism's lack of interest in African American women's lives:

> Feminism in the United States has never emerged from the women who are the most victimised by sexist oppression; women who are daily beaten down, mentally, physically, and spiritually – women who are powerless to change their condition in life ... Betty Friedan's *The Feminine Mystique* is still heralded as having paved the way for the contemporary feminist movement – it was written as if these women did not exist. (hooks, 1995: 270)

Difference is now on the agenda for feminist approaches, and varied strategies have developed to respond to it. The first has been to acknowledge differences and then to make a claim to something women share beyond it. At various times feminists have stipulated that they will 'lay aside the important differences among women across "race" and class boundaries and instead search for central commonalties' (Hartsock, 1998: 112). Sonia Johnson asserts that 'One of the basic tenets of radical feminism is that any woman in the world has more in common with any other woman regardless of class, race, age, ethnic group, nationality – than any woman has with any man' (quoted in Rowland and Klein, 1996: 18). Susan Moller Okin argues that it is important that feminism maintains an ability to separate the effects of gender from other categories of difference:

> Some feminists have been criticised for developing theories of gender that do not take sufficient account of difference among women especially race, class, religion, and ethnicity … Many injustices are experienced by women as women, whatever the differences among them and whatever other injustices they also suffer from. (1989: 6)

Okin argues that the claim that gender cannot be understood as a distinct process is 'long on theory and very short on empirical evidence' (1994: 7), and that theoretically and empirically there is no justification for saying that wishing to understand the distinct operation of gender is to subscribe 'to the view that race or class oppression are insignificant' (1992: 327).

To advocate putting difference to one side implies two things:

1 That one can separate the operation of gender from other categories such as 'race' and ethnicity;
2 Difference is a problem; it is a difficulty to be overcome.

Feminists who prioritize difference argue that gender cannot be extracted from the other problems that women face or experience (Collins, 1989; King, 1995). hooks argues that gender does not exist as a category of oppression or influence on society separate from 'race' or class. 'Race' and gender interact to create the forms of oppression present in society; to ignore one is to misunderstand the influence of the other. People do not exist within clear-cut categories or groups – lesbians, Black women, working-class women – these sources of difference overlap; it is this overlapping that creates the interrelationship between them. Being working-class and lesbian is likely to be very different from being lesbian and middle-class. If feminism is to have an impact it must construct ways of thinking and acting that tackle the interaction of more than one category of oppression.

If it is a good thing to put aside difference, the implication is that it is a messy complication that undermines the purity of theoretical argument. Mariá C. Lugones notes that 'white women theorists seem to have worried more passionately about the harm the claim [for recognition of difference] does to theorizing than about the harm the theorizing did to women of color' (1991: 41). Can difference be thought of as an asset? If individuals are thought of as having identities formed through the intersection of differences, then difference becomes an intrinsic aspect of being human and something that enriches our sense both of self and of our possible communities.

One of the vital articulations of this possibility came from Lorde (1984a). Believing that everyone is essentially the same and in need of the same things is a mode of thinking that comes from dominant Western male thinking. If feminism repeats the fallacy of a universal human identity, it accepts the 'Master's tools' (Lorde, 1984b). If it only tolerates difference, as an inconvenience or a side issue to be discussed by those it matters to, then it continues to use the tools of segregation and exclusion. Tolerance is the 'total denial of the creative function of difference in our lives' (*ibid.*: 111). Through recognition of difference, an alternative political model can develop, based on something richer than the solitary individual; it can become about our interdependencies to each other and the different aspects of our selves. Difference can be thought of as 'that raw and powerful connection from which our personal power is forged ... it is learning how to take our differences and make them strengths' (*ibid.*: 112).

Differences are now central to feminist theorizing; the issue now distinguishing much of the work being produced is how difference is responded to. In part this is because, increasingly, feminists are wondering where the prioritization being given to difference is taking their agenda: political change.

Dilemmas in difference and recognition

The priority being given to cultural recognition and the critique of the Enlightenment has led to some feminist criticism. While few deny the importance of recognition and the validity of questioning universal frameworks, concern is appearing about the implications for the priorities of feminist theorizing and activism. Where does the prioritization of recognition leave the core objectives of feminism? The dispute is not so much about the need to incorporate questions of difference into feminist theorizing; the issue is *how* recognition is to be addressed. The different approaches to answering this question form the themes of this book. In what follows I will indicate the concerns being raised with difference and recognition and how this is producing the agendas for contemporary social and political thought, including feminism.

Securing identity

Acknowledging and recognizing difference produces 'attachment' (Brown, 1993) for the identities that are distinct from the norm. There is a concern that this 'attachment' is not wholly positive for those who articulate it and build a politics around it (Bell, 2000). Recognition implies certain levels of fixedness in the needs and identities of groups, which must be acknowledged for rights to be considered and equality obtained. In framing demands in this way, recognition can be an element in defining and securing difference, rather than something that provides testimony to what is already there. That is, in articulating the identity recognition produces it and does so in a way that can be thought of as problematic. The language of identity and recognition can become the 'language of unfreedom' (Brown, 1995: 66).

If recognition becomes the proposition that women and men are different, or racial and ethnic groups are different, or lesbians and gay men are different, it secures and threatens to essentialize the proposition in a way that some argue 'maintains inequalities of power' (Squires, 2001: 13). Sara Ahmed *et al.* argue that particular types of recognition place limits on 'the potential for transformation' (2000: 15). For Wendy Brown (1995) recognition does this by forming the identity in a sense of harm and hurt. The expression of identity and recognition revolves around a demand for acknowledgement of previous and present pain and wrongdoing, and as such the very expression of identity becomes 'invested in its own subjection' (1995: 70). Without continued exclusion and marginalization the identity loses meaning; it becomes invested in pain. For Lauren Berlant (2000) the politics of recognition is problematic because it implies that what all mainstream society owes the marginalized is an acknowledgement of previous harm. Recognition maintains no responsibility for dominant society to transform the current order of things. At its worse, recognition becomes a form of 'sentimentality', where the expression of felt pain defines politics and the boundaries between groups. In the process alternative versions of identity invested in positive and expansive possibilities are missed.

This critique has pushed the relationship between difference and identity ever further within social and political thought. Postmodern and queer perspectives have developed outside and within feminism, which argue against understanding what makes someone different as something that is intrinsic to them. Instead our identity is dependent on the social and relational production of differences. In debates about difference, notions of relational subjectivity have become increasingly important (Squires, 2001). What made 'Western Man' normal and everyone else 'different' is the comparison drawn between the two. The dominance of 'normal' subjectivity is based on rejecting and labelling as deviant, other forms of being. Society can only have a notion of good when it has a comparative notion of evil. The same can be said for notions of nature/culture, masculinity/femininity, homosexuality/heterosexuality and white/black. This has led to a concern with the politics of difference, which moves beyond exploring how more people and groups can be seen as subjects, to investigate the processes involved in producing subjectivity. These processes and feminist engagement with them are the focus of Chapters 4 (Postmodernism), 5 (Foucault), 6 (Queer Theory) and 7 (Social Studies of Technology).

Loss of the material

As recognition and deconstruction have taken centre-stage in feminist and wider social and political thought, questioning voices have developed over the subsequent marginalization of material issues, including material differences (Modleski, 1991; Stanley, 1990; Walby, 1992). Rosemary Hennessy and Chris Ingraham (1997) point out that while much – but not all – of feminism has taken what Michèle Barrett famously referred to as its 'cultural turn' (1992), material inequalities have increased and global capitalism has spread unchecked by any significant opposition. Few pretend that recognition does not matter; however, there is a desire to acknowledge the relationship between recognition and inequalities (Gibson-Graham, 1996; Hennessy, 1993). Is it culture or economic and social position that separates us? Both Marxists and a variety of feminists influenced by Marxism and materialism are asking this question.

Transnational feminism has developed as one strategy for bringing together questions of identity with material conditions (Kaplan, 1996). It aims to retain a global concern through capturing the role of transnational economic pressures and patterns and cultural movements in informing varied women's concerns and experiences. As well as thinking about local acts of identity formation and fluidity, feminism needs to connect with global patterns of colonization, exchange and hegemony (Alexander and Mohanty, 1997). Transnational feminism examines 'the (dis)array of localities and differences that have been produced through the material effects of discursive practices *and* the discursive effects of material practices' (Alarcón *et al.*, 1999: 3, original emphasis). For example, one important theme in transnational feminism is how women continue to be incorporated, often violently, into articulations of nationhood in ways that limit women's rights and ability to assert their own identities and sense of self. Transnational feminism both adopts postmodernism's concerns with difference and location and criticizes its inability to link difference and location to 'the effects of mobile capital as well as multiple subjectivities' (Grewal and Kaplan, 1994: 7). Inderpal Grewal and Caren Kaplan stress that 'If feminist movements cannot understand the dynamics of these material conditions, they will be unable to construct an effective opposition to current economic and cultural hegemonies that are taking new global forms' (*ibid.*: 17).

In suggesting a return to material concerns, feminists such as Stevi Jackson (2001) stress that it is important not to assume that all feminists have taken the 'cultural turn'. Contemporary approaches are right to indicate that Marxism could not explain 'why it should be women who occupied particular niches in the capitalist order' (2001: 285). However, removing all concern with the material is not the answer. Material concerns are important to ensure that questions about gender are not just about culture, but also about 'a hierarchical division between women and men' (*ibid.*). It is dangerous for feminist theorizing and activism if postmodernism is given a monopoly 'on theorizing diversity and complexity' (*ibid.*). In the postmodern account of the construction of identity, it is culture that dominates over a materially and sociologically embedded concern with social construction. Without this kind of embedding 'the task of overall change, that of re-organizing social relations of inequality as a whole, becomes peripheral to the main project' (Bannerji, 1995: 71). Separating 'boring' old materialist analysis from cutting edge, 'fun', identity debates is problematic. To understand articulations of identity and difference, the analysis must occur within the context of the social institutions and structures that inform the production of subjectivity.

Contemporary approaches to material issues are looking for a way to bring together questions of culture and the material, in a way deconstructionist analyses often fail to do (Fraser, 1997b). One way of bringing the debates together is to consider the possible material underpinnings to the enactment and recognition of different cultural expressions. Beverley Skeggs (2001) argues that material differences lie behind forms of misrecognition in which the subject is fixed 'in exclusion, pathology, harm, and pain' (2001: 296). When different identities are played out in different social spaces, some identities are recognized more than others are; the source of varied recognition can be drawn back to questions of material power: who get to define legitimate identities are also those who have material power. Understanding how this comes about requires a wider historical and social investigation, which encapsulates capitalism, colonialism, imperialism and patriarchy. Chapter 2 examines how both Marxism and feminism continue to do this through a discussion of Standpoint Theory.

The costs

The final concern relates to the implications these new debates and issues have for feminism's assumed project: the removal of gender oppression (Clough, 1994; Jagose, 1997). For feminism the criticisms levelled at the Enlightenment and the key concepts of reason, rationality and individual rights are not necessarily easy debates to enter. Feminism is in some ways a direct product of Enlightenment thinking. Once political writers began to suggest that individuals had citizenship rights, the door was opened for groups to argue they too had the ability to act with reason and the right to be citizens. Along with the anti-slavery movement in Britain and the United States, women were amongst the first to demand that they should be seen as actors capable of reason and worthy of freedom and political rights. Both the first and second wave of feminism, in varied ways, for good reasons, and with notable successes, demanded rights for women in the public sphere. Some contemporary feminists argue that the battle for rights and an equal role in the public sphere is yet to be fully won; particularly once you look outside of the West. In this context a move away from individual rights can only damage the chances of battles still to be won. Writers such as Hartsock (1998) and Rosi Braidotti (1987) point out that questioning subjectivity is a query only someone with rights can make.

Feminists are concerned that the deconstructionist agenda of destabilizing the subject and any foundational claim or position denies the possibility of critical theory and political engagement (Benhabib, 1995). Without a shared subject, can feminism have a shared agenda? If we stress the differences amongst women, does this mean that feminism itself has little purpose? Iris Marion Young warns that if feminism becomes the collection of apparently unconnected individuals, then it 'evaporates' (1995: 193). She warns against an endless critique of women sharing some form of shared subjectivity, because the end result could be liberal individualism and the 'me' politics that this brings. What should be the priority, identifying difference or finding some kind of – even partially fictional – commonality? If all we talk of is difference do we ignore the issues women do share? This has led some feminists to stress recognition of commonality as well as difference.

Various feminists are looking to regain the certainty of some form of agreed framework for monitoring equality and progress. Radical feminists argue that women, regardless of other aspects of difference, all experience some form of oppression because they are female. For example, all women have to deal with different kinds of inadequacies in reproductive rights and choices. A desire to rid different societies of barriers to women's equality, such as the denial of reproductive choice, can be a universal value shared by women. In short, women share a common condition of oppression that can only be solved by a common political strategy aimed at the removal of the varied sources of that condition. Our experiences and identity may be different, but can we find commonality in our shared respect for each other and the right to be different? Is, after all, a commonly agreed framework the best way to protect the space to be different? Without agreed notions of freedom, rights, or the subject, politics appears to produce 'barely masked despair'

(Brown, 1995: 26). Kathy B. Jones has neatly outlined the problem:

> The dilemma, of course, is how to respond to the particular while remaining committed to some vision of a feminist future that subscribes to generalizable criteria for determining progress toward greater equality and dignity for women and men. (1996: 86)

Without some shared framework about what is important for the human condition we will be unable to distinguish between 'choices worthy of respect and those based on distorted preferences or societal myths' (Quillen, 2001: 95). Different approaches to generate such a framework within social and political thought and feminism are the focus of Chapter 1 (Equal Rights) and Chapter 3 (Ethics of Care).

These last concerns in the debates over difference have broadened out into a concern over whether feminist theorizing has lost its way. In what follows I discuss the current significant concern about the direction feminist thought is taking. I do this in part because I think these concerns have some validity, but also because the ideas discussed in the book help indicate that there is hope for the continued well-being and relevance of feminist ideas. In particular their connection to activism and the need to challenge varied patterns of gender oppression.

Current health of feminist theory

The new debates within feminism are leading to their own identity crises. Does feminism as a term still have meaning, while some propose that its referent – women – should be deconstructed? Can feminist theory adopt the ideas of multiple differences and the fluidity of identity and still retain a clear purpose? Do these new ideas simply add confusion, doubt and little else (Nye, 1988)? For some feminists the debate about difference and feminism's involvement in it has become removed from activism and the 'every day'. Instead it looks inwards to the nuance of philosophical argument and the fun of playing with text (Barrett, 1992; Brooks, 1997). In this light, there has been a call to return to the 'real' feminism and politics of the second wave (Coole, 1994; Gatens, 1992; Oakley, 1998). In feminist debates, as elsewhere, material celebrating the flux and confusion of contemporary ideas now shares space with more sceptical writings questioning the value and benefits of these new directions (Bell and Klein, 1996). It is hardly new that a stable and agreed identity for feminism does not exist. In 1919 Rebecca West commented: 'I myself have never been able to find out precisely what feminism is: I only know that people call me a feminist whenever I express sentiments that differentiate me from a doormat or a prostitute' (The History Net, 2002). However, in contemporary disquiet there is a feeling that the transformations taking place in theoretical ideas risk erasing the very possibility of a feminist agenda. Diana Coole warns that 'the political momentum of feminism is being quietly deconstructed away as writers become increasingly reluctant to use terms like "women" (or worse, Woman)' (1994: 130). How can feminism demand change, if its own ideas now question the ability of theory to capture the reality or 'truth' of what needs to be changed?

The pessimistic case

An important institutional context to fear is the current health of feminist theory and its sharp decline during the last five years, particularly in the UK, in the number of Women's Studies degrees and departments. Women's Studies has been an important site for the development of feminist ideas and their dissemination to women. Such departments began with a commit-ment to ensure that feminist theorizing remained connected to political processes taking place outside the academy. The decline of Women's Studies has been offset, to a degree, by their replacement with Gender Studies, a shift that has been replicated by publishing trends. However, the extent to which such programmes, departments and publishing activities have a notion of feminist theorizing, pedagogy and activism at their centre is open to debate (Robinson and Richardson, 1996).

The relative absence of specific spaces for exploring feminist ideas (including within Gender Studies) and the minimal inclusion of the per-spectives in how social and political thought is taught, has led to a gap between ongoing feminist debates and its presence in much of the academy. The Women's Studies programmes that have survived have done so by becoming successfully institutionalized within university structures and values. A significant component of feminist theory is produced by lone academics working in Philosophy, Politics, Literary Studies, Sociology and Cultural Studies departments. There is a suspicion that the priority within the work of such scholars and institutionalized Women's Studies depart-ments is success within academic criteria of excellence, rather than the importance of making connections with and being a tool of feminist activism outside the academy (Davis, 1997).

The main theoretical concern with the state of feminist theory is that the 'cultural turn' alongside, or perhaps due to, the academic processes discussed above has weakened its ability to make political connections. Can it survive endless introspection? Can 'it' exist when its relationship to its subject, its foundation in experience, and its goal of revolutionary change have been consistently challenged by questions of difference and identity?

The dominance of postmodernism and questions of cultural identity in the debates about difference has led to a concern in feminist writings about what the future holds. Mary Louise Adams notes that 'along the way, the focus on personal experience and personal identity has cut off portions of the women's movement from larger struggles for social change' (1994: 350). In the words of Joanne Conaghan (2000):

> The gist of such criticisms is that feminism no longer concerns itself with the reality of women's daily lives or the material inequality which accompanies it; preoccupied by 'personal' issues surrounding identity and subjectivity, feminism appears increasingly irrelevant to those struggling to advance women's interests and counteract their disadvantage. (2000: 354)

Hortense Spillers (Lurie *et al.*, 2001) warns of a vacuum being created by feminism's retreat from debates about material politics, which right wing reactionary groups are all too happy to fill. While feminist writing has become introspective, others are very happy to define feminism in the public realm. Perhaps feminism has been deconstructed into nothingness, without a point or a subject? Has feminism been left less possible by the current trends in academic theorizing? Lynne Segal wonders whether feminism has become 'little more than a blip in the march of economic neo-liberalism' (1999: 1).

This critique has been fed by a feeling that existing feminist work has been caricatured in order to present this new and exciting world of identity and recognition. Was second-wave feminism really that insensitive to the importance of identity and the transience of subjectivity? New ideas are helping to bring new focus to changing social dynamics (happening at least in Western capitalist societies), however it is important to resist presenting the past as irredeemably flawed and simply wrong. Robyn Rowland and Renate Klein (1996) and Denise Thompson (2001), in defending different aspects of the work of the 1970s, argue that contemporary feminists should have better memories. There is a tendency in new works to present a false and narrow reading of past writings in order to make their ideas appear more new and exciting. If we take the time to go back and look at the work, which took place in the 1970s, we will find discussion of difference and recognition of identity. Jackson (2001) argues against assuming that postmodern writers are the first to notice the social construction of identity and subjectivity; again a better memory would help retain the work of feminist sociologists and others who were amongst the first to discuss the social construction of gender and sexuality. Segal also argues that you will find something in previous work not present in new texts, a feminism able 'successfully to mobilize them [women] (and not just signifiers) onto the streets and into campaigns' (1997: 7).

An article written by Stanley and Sue Wise (2000) brings together the worries about the current priorities of feminist theorizing. They make a distinction between academic feminism, **feminist Theory** and feminism. Their argument is that academic feminism has produced feminist Theory as a separate elitist body of work disconnected from the issues of women's lives. They note that feminist theorizing has, over the last 20 years, led to significant reconsiderations of epistemology, methodology and ethics; however, they challenge feminist Theory to reconsider its own practice and purpose in the same way. Several processes have taken place, which have drawn feminist Theory further away from its supposed object.

It has become institutionalized via academic feminism, within privileged university settings. Its institutional position in academia leads it to closely resemble 'malestream' social theory, more concerned with its rules of engagement and argument. In the process, Theory has become 'the preserve of specialist groupings of academics' rather than of 'feminists in general' (*ibid.*: 266). For a body of ideas so concerned with deconstruction and interrogation, it seems odd that little reflection occurs over Theory's purpose or approach. Without this reflection the work has become increasingly abstract and opaque; its only relevance is to those wishing to pursue an academic career. It is an area where academic stars dominate, in a prestigious network of prizes, elite conferences and institutions and media attention. All of this produces a form of Theory disjointed from the real world, unable to engage with the matters that count. The kind of differences focused on in such work are not the kind that matter; differences relating to experiences of violence, poverty, genocide and economic restructuring are left to the side, while questions of culture and representation dominate.

The optimistic case

The alternative scenario is to approach uncertainty and introspection as enabling, necessary and appropriate to current contexts, inside and outside the academy. Might current 'crises' in what is thought possible from theory and from feminism be productive (Butler, 1992)? Can a focus on culture and multiplicity be positive for feminist theorizing? The fact that there is a debate about what feminism is for and a range of responses to it can be thought of as a sign of strength. If there is disagreement, instead of seeing this as crisis, it is possible to think of this as a sign of feminism's vitality and growth. Few would argue there is no cause for concern, or reject outright the type of concerns raised by feminists such as Stanley and Wise. Instead, what the less pessimistic feminists (including myself) look to is building a new agenda for feminist Theorizing, which acknowledges both new times and important continuities.

Optimistic feminists situate current work in altered social and political contexts. Certainties are not appropriate to uncertain times. Politics and identity have fragmented as new patterns of life and interaction develop. New forms of coalition and connection are made possible in new types of global and local activism. Cultural experimentation is part of the agenda of protest politics, exemplified in the anti-capitalist protests where humour and parody are central strategies. Questions of identity and experiences of fluidity and multiplicity are part of daily life; confusion and flux surrounds social values and expectations. These processes can be experienced as liberating; they can also be experienced as threatening and confusing. Anxiety and doubt are part of women's lives as they carve out a sense of self and future. Feminist theorizing has a responsibility to capture these dynamics in women's lives and provide ways of making sense of them:

> To take responsibility is to firmly situate ourselves within contingent and imperfect contexts, to acknowledge differential privileges of race, gender, geographic location, and sexual identities, and to resist the delusory and dangerous recurrent hope of redemption to a world not of our making. (Flax, 1992b: 460)

Ahmed *et al.* argue that feminism must find a language that can allow it to understand and respond to 'the multiply determined bodies, spaces and histories "women" assume and occupy' (2000: 11). Previous certainties cannot be regained, because the world within which feminism exists has changed. Feminism must 'refuse to (re)present itself as programmatic, *as having an object which can always be successfully translated into a final end or outcome*' (*ibid.*: 13, original emphasis). It can be beneficial for feminism to destabilise its purpose, because this may fit better with the world around it (McLaughlin, 1997). Feminism does need to reconsider how it sets agendas, but this can lie at the centre of its future. Its future lies 'in the contingency of this present moment'. That present moment 'is a space in which we can speak of our uncertainties about what are or should be feminist agendas, rather than assuming that such uncertainty necessarily involves a loss or failure of collectivity' (Ahmed *et al.*, 2000: 13). Susan Lurie (Lurie *et al.*, 2001) argues that 'flawed feminisms' may offer new possibilities of alignments with other groups and strategies of resistance. The founding subject of feminism may have turned out to be an exclusionary fiction, but the multiple subjects with transient identities who have taken her place can form new coalitions with a broader politics, which brings together questions about the material with issues of cultural recognition and experimentation.

Caroline Ramazanoglu and Janet Holland point out that 'Questioning the Authority of feminists to speak as subjects with specialist knowledge of gender relations is not the same as invalidating their knowledge' (2000: 208).

Feminists involved in deconstruction and challenges to core feminist terms are concerned with the implications of their work. Challenging what we mean by and include in the notion of the subject or woman does not mean there is no scope for its use or a concern with politics. The works explored in this book all look to 'explain the relations between the sexes in society, and the differences between women's and men's experiences' (Ramazanoglu, 1989: 8). There is still a desire in varied feminist work to posit that things can and should be different. A political desire for change remains an important and distinctive element of feminist theoretical engagement. Judith Butler (1992) argues that the deconstruction of key feminist terms is a strategy aimed at ensuring they can be effectively and strategically deployed in political discourse and action. Feminists are still involved in attempts to define 'better' knowledge, social and political relations and societal structures; it is the mode through which the claim to 'better' is made that has changed.

The Stanley and Wise piece (2000) led to a series of responses to their work that dispute their picture of elitism and lack of feminism in what they term feminist Theory. Most writers who responded agree there are problems in current feminist writings and engagement with the real world. Stacey (2001) notes that the new orthodoxy is beginning to shift away from feminist Theory, towards a fashionable mourning of the missing revolution of Stanley and Wise's piece. It is not surprising that academic feminism has become institutionalized; the context of Western capitalism and bureaucratization ensures that most counter-movements at some point become incorporated into the practices and operations of the system. However, 'nostalgia' for how things used to be is too easy. Things may not be all bad. The model of disengaged feminist Theory does little justice to the bodies of work 'flourishing [in] non-western "feminist" practice', which hold more promise as a source of re-engaged feminist theorizing than 'reflexive meta-theoretical ruminations on our own intellectual practice' (Stacey, 2001: 101). Instead of reading contemporary theory's lack of revolutionary goals as proof of disengagement and elitism, Jackie Stacey reads it as suspicion with the politics of revolutionary ideas. Feminism can do without the concept and belief in revolution because as a notion it 'now seems fundamentally ahistorical and flawed' (*ibid.*: 101).

The debate about the state of feminist theory indicates current anxieties; it also indicates the need to continuously reflect on the implications of particular trends in feminist theorizing. One way of doing this is to consider how particular trends engage with social issues and political concerns. How can ideas be politically useful? To explore this question each chapter in this book contains a section examining how the perspective may be used to investigate a particular social concern or frame political activism.

To conclude the Introduction, I will summarize the structure and themes of the book.

Structure of the book

The book looks at how feminist theories are engaging with explorations of difference and subjectivity. As the previous discussion has indicated, there is more than one way to think about and respond to recognition, identity and difference. Each chapter examines a current feminist perspective and lays out its framework for responding to difference. Earlier it was noted how second-wave feminism reconfigured existing ideas from social and political thought in order to use them to analyse women's lives. This practice continues today. Each chapter takes an area of social and political thought and considers how contemporary feminists are involved in both critiques and reinterpretations of these works. In doing so it provides testimony to the continued role that feminists play in providing a vital critique of the priorities and values in the theoretical debates they are part of. In addition this strategy is adopted because feminist reflections on and appropriations of these existing works (some old, some new) are important catalysts for the development of new frameworks and ideas.

Before detailing the perspectives that are discussed in the book, I should make a few comments about the selection. First, the perspectives that have been selected have been chosen to reflect the diversity, strength and priorities of current feminist debates. The choice is not intended to imply that Marxist/socialist, liberal or radical feminism are not part of contemporary thinking. To ensure against this inference, various chapters discuss these important areas of feminist activity. Second, any selection is imperfect; there are areas of feminist work that are missing. It is hard to deny that my own interests and preferences influence the selection, but in exploring the different perspectives the intent has been to remain to some degree sceptical about their validity. The discussion focuses on capturing the development and scope of each. However, in the conclusion of each chapter I do reflect on my own position on the ideas discussed. Finally, by making the selection and dividing the work of various writers into the categories found below there is a process of simplification involved. Most writers are unhappy being placed in particular camps or given any apparent allegiance. Therefore, discussing various writers in the contexts of different perspectives is not to say they are postmodern, or Foucauldian, or so forth.

Each chapter follows the same structure. It begins by summarizing a key perspective within social and political thought, it then moves on to highlight the main feminist critiques of the perspective. The next section examines the strategies feminists have used to appropriate and adapt the perspective. In the fourth section the perspective under discussion is used to examine a particular social or political issue, and after a brief conclusion I end with some recommendations for further reading. The chapters are in the following order:

- *Equal Rights.* In debates about equal rights, contemporary liberal theorists deal with difference by promoting political and moral frameworks that transcend it. Feminists fear that such a strategy is exclusionary. To respond to this risk equal-rights feminists seek to incorporate more fully a concern with recognition within a desire to retain the language and benefits of rights. The political uses of this strategy are examined by discussing the 1995 Fourth World Conference on Women in Beijing.
- *Standpoint Theories.* Karl Marx's notion of historical materialism asserted that the distinct experiences of the proletariat could be the basis of revolutionary knowledge. Feminists have been concerned with the narrow range of different experiences deemed significant in this framework. Feminist standpoint theorists aim to identify ways in which women's different experiences and material position can produce a form of 'objective' knowledge about current harm and possible revolutionary futures. The political uses of this strategy are examined by discussing standpoint approaches for incorporating 'race' into feminist theoretical agendas and activism.
- *The Ethics of Care.* Psychology has presented a model of women and men's moral differences which continues to influence notions of justice and morality. Feminists have challenged the celebration of universality and impartiality in this work. Ethics of care writers propose that women's experiences of nurturing and relationship make them more able to identify and appreciate emotion and difference within their moral outlook and judgements. The political uses of this strategy are examined by using it to challenge the place and role of care in modern welfare systems.
- *Postmodernism.* Postmodernists approach differences as the product of language and look to deconstruct fixed notions of subjectivity and identity. Feminists are suspicious of the politics and priorities of this work. In acquiring some of the ideas of postmodernism feminists have adapted it to develop feminist subjectivities as alternatives to the fictional subject of modernity. The political uses of this strategy are examined by considering feminist postmodern approaches to the political subject and by summarizing two forms of activism that are considered postmodern in approach.
- *Moving On from Foucault.* Michel Foucault pursued a social constructionist argument to understand the production of power, knowledge,

truth, discipline and subjectivity. He did so, feminists point out, with virtually no concern with gender as an influential presence in processes of social construction. Feminists have brought gender and Foucault together to explore the social production of masculinities and femininities in local power relations. The chapter will indicate how feminist reinterpretations of Foucault's work on discourse, subjectivity and power have taken the ideas into important areas the original articulation did not allow for. The political uses of this strategy are examined by considering the role of discourses in the construction of welfare identities.

- *Queer Theory*. Queer perspectives use postmodern and Foucauldian ideas to identify the regulatory role of fixed notions of sexual orientation and identity. Feminists have again raised concern over the politics of this agenda and the separation advocated between analyses of sexuality and gender. Feminists incorporating queer ideas do so in order to retain the link between sexuality and gender; in particular to think about how heterosexuality and gender secure regulatory notions of identity and self. The political uses of this strategy are examined by exploring the different ways radical and materialist feminists and queer feminists approach the politics of butch/femme lesbian relationships and identities.
- *Social Studies of Technology*. Social studies of technology (SST) is a new area for feminist theorizing. SST uses social constructionist arguments to explore the mutual shaping of technology and society. Feminists point out that its has done so with little concern with how gender may be involved. Feminists have adapted SST to explore the gendering of technology and users as an element of power relations. The uses of this strategy are examined by exploring feminist SST accounts of reproductive technology. SST may appear an odd inclusion in this list, but the perspective is present because it is an example of the new kinds of theoretical application being developed in the context of social constructionism.

Equal rights

CONTENTS

Feminists are important critics and participants in rearticulations of liberal thought; in part this is because liberalism and its values of individual rights have a long heritage within feminist thought and activism. First-wave feminism was heavily influenced by liberal ideas developed by writers such as John Stuart Mill and Mary Wollstonecraft. The demand for women to be treated in the public sphere as equals to and the same as men remained prominent in US mainstream feminist political activism during the 1970s through the work of feminists such as Betty Friedan (1965). However, during the second wave, feminists began to highlight inadequacies in liberal arguments and political strategies. Feminists from various perspectives argued that liberal feminism privileged masculine ways of being. For many it appeared that to have the rights of men, liberal theories demanded that women be like them. Since then feminists have continued to engage with contemporary liberal arguments and search for different frameworks within which to situate equal rights.

The chapter begins by outlining how contemporary liberalism responds to arguments about difference. It then moves on to highlight the exclusions feminists still find in these proposals and the alternatives they have produced to incorporate difference more fully into rights claims. The benefits and limits of using an altered equal-rights framework are explored via a summary of the debates about the value and limitations of the 1995 UN Fourth World Conference on Women in Beijing.

Outline of the key perspective

Contemporary liberal writers have responded to the heightened recognition that has been given to difference by acknowledging it and asserting that the just and fair system is still one that protects the rights and wants of all individuals indiscriminately. We may all be different, but the best guarantee of equality is to treat us *as if* we were all the same. To go beyond this is problematic and leads the state into taking a role it cannot fulfil. The problem for such liberal accounts is to indicate how a just and fair society can exist when different constituencies, with competing definitions of what such a society should be, are present. One of most significant attempts to solve this problem is the work of John Rawls (1972, 1993).

Rawls retains liberalism's roots in a Kantian defence of the rights of the individual and Social Contract models for a just society (outlined in the Introduction). He responds to critiques of attempts to define universal human nature by arguing that he does not give individuality or the individual subject a metaphysical status. Instead, his defence for placing the individual at the centre of rights arguments is political. Treating us as if we are individuals makes for a better and more just political system, which is capable of providing greater opportunity for equality than any other alternative. His first key work – *Theories of Justice* – first published in 1971, remains influential in contemporary liberal thinking.

Rawls aims to define the conditions – which he terms the '**the original position**' – within which a society with divergent views of 'the good life' can come to agreement. His objective is to define a notion of 'pure procedural justice' (1972: 136). This is done through sketching a space within which fair and just principles of justice can be generated that treat all persons as equals. This space is achieved via the **veil of ignorance**. Behind the veil of ignorance those involved in defining the principles of justice would be shielded from knowledge about themselves in terms of status, skills and attributes. They would also have no knowledge of the society in which they live. In such a context 'the effects of specific contingencies' (*ibid.*: 136) are nullified. This 'blindness' creates a moral space within which representatives can define notions of justice not influenced by particular factors; instead 'they are obliged to evaluate principles solely on the basis of general considerations' (*ibid.*: 137). Such representatives would be conscious as rational actors that unless everyone benefits from the judgements they make, they themselves could be the ones who suffer. Since people would not rationally make decisions that could harm themselves, they look to benefiting every individual as much as possible.

The space behind the veil of ignorance is not real or possible. However, Rawls uses it as a template to consider what kinds of just practice and principles would exist in such a space. The kinds of principles of justice he thinks would appear behind the veil of ignorance include:

- First, each person is to have rights equal to the most extensive basic liberty compatible with a similar liberty for others.

- Second, social and economic inequalities are to be arranged so that they are both (a) reasonably expected to be to everyone's advantage, and (b) attached to positions and offices open to all. (*Ibid.*: 60)

In *Political Liberalism*, Rawls moves on to develop the mechanisms needed for consensus on what a fair society should look like when 'there are many conflicting reasonable comprehensive doctrines with their conceptions of the good' (1993: 135). He reasserts the classic liberal argument that the political system cannot be used to enforce one conception of the good. Instead, what he seeks to define is a **procedural model** for dealing with difference disputes. The resolution is to argue that each constituency has the right to its belief – its **comprehensive view** – but does not have the right to enforce it on others. The political system represents the moral value of equality and freedom for all citizens and cannot represent the values of one constituency. Each constituency supports this ideal, because it allows them the space in which to articulate their own view of the good life and the mechanisms through which justice and equality are achieved. A stable system is one where competing conceptions are allowed reasonable and rational expression: the **overlapping consensus**.

Rawls's articulation of political liberalism is echoed by one of the other key theorists of contemporary liberalism: Ronald Dworkin (1985). Dworkin argues that the political experiences and events of Western countries in the twentieth century have left the core values and political principles of liberalism unclear. His objective is thus to rearticulate those core values. Like Rawls, Dworkin begins by arguing that liberalism is concerned with ensuring that citizens are treated as equals. While this is a goal widely accepted in modern democracy, what this means and how it is achieved are less universally acknowledged. There are two opposing answers to how a government does this:

> The first supposes that government must be neutral on what might be called the question of the good life. The second supposes that government cannot be neutral in that question, because it cannot treat its citizens as equal human beings without a theory of what human beings ought to be. (Dworkin, 1985: 191)

This is the crucial question for liberalism: does giving people the right to live the good life require a definition of what that good life could be? We have seen that the answer for Rawls is no, the consensus lies in recognizing the right, not the method. Dworkin views this separation as constitutive of contemporary liberalism and calls it the **discontinuity thesis** (1990). Difference is responded to via the right of individuals or groups to have their own definitions of the good life as long as they recognize the right of others to have their alternative. This implies that liberal ethics are neutral, except to argue that 'no one can improve another's life by forcing him to behave differently, against his will and his conviction' (1985: 117).

In recent debates about the scope and nature of democracy, the work of Rawls and Dworkin has been used to help define the scope and operation of the **public sphere** (Ferree *et al.*, 2002). The public sphere is a concept that has become central to debates about the procedures required to connect the state and its citizens and to allow for justice and democracy. In these debates the public sphere does not refer (directly) to the distinction made between the public and private sphere. Here the public sphere is a communicative space where citizens are able to discuss problems and issues, which are then channelled to state actors to act upon. In a liberal version of the public sphere its role is to generate, through the veil of ignorance, rational discussion of social and political problems in order to protect the key values of liberal society.

One of the most important articulations of a communicative public sphere is by Jürgen Habermas (1996), who argues that a democratic state must have a public space of communication for 'the public' to come together to discuss 'public issues'. The role of the state is to then build the values and views of the public into its actions, in order that some link is maintained between universal values all agree with (individuality, free speech, justice) and the running of the state. In order for the public space to generate such values, differences amongst the public must be **bracketed off** to ensure that communication is comprehensive and not influenced by differences in status and background (Habermas, 1989, 1991). The issue for feminists is whether the operationalization of a veil of ignorance in *a* public sphere is enough to generate justice and equality for the entire public?

Feminist critiques

Feminist critiques of contemporary liberalism concentrate around the following themes:

- The status and identity of the individual.
- The split between the private and public sphere.
- The form of equality on offer.
- The exclusion of context and difference.

I will take each in turn.

The status of the individual

Feminists (and others, for example communitarian writers such as Alasdair MacIntyre (Knight, 1998) and Charles Taylor, 1991) have debunked the approach to individuality in liberal thought as based on a fictional and exclusionary notion of the human condition. The individual has been critiqued as a political construct that historically has only been open to particular groups in society. Drucilla Cornell notes that 'what is called human is only too often in patriarchal culture the genre of the male' (1992: 281). Susan Moller Okin (1991) highlights the gendered assumptions built into Rawls's analysis. Rawls argues that those in the original position can be thought of as 'heads of families' (1972: 128), and then uses the male pronoun to discuss how they would behave. He argues that individuals – fathers – are happy to participate in the original position because they have a desire to ensure that their offspring will live in a just society and have an equal opportunity to succeed. The male head of household becomes the representative of previous generations and the guarantor for future ones. Frances Woolley (2000) and Okin point out that many families are made up of two parents, and where one is represented as the head 'wives (or whichever adult member[s] of a family are *not* its "head") go completely unrepresented in the original position' (Okin, 1989: 94, original emphasis).

Carol Pateman (1988) has produced one of the most influential challenges to liberal ideas of both the classical and contemporary period. Classic liberalism is based on a definition of the individual as male: 'The meaning of the individual remains intact only so long as the dichotomies (internal to civil society) between natural/civil, private/public, woman/individual – and sex/gender – remain intact' (*ibid.*: 225). Liberal perspectives demand acceptance of the status quo of gender inequality for women to be included: in these terms women can never be equal (Cavarero, 1992).

The split between the private and public sphere

Writers such as Pateman and Margaret Moore (1999) argue that liberalism's celebration of impartiality and reason in the public sphere is based on the gendered separation of particularity and emotion into the feminized private sphere. The private sphere has been the site where all the things that make the individual not autonomous – dependency, need, emotion, connection – are dumped and dealt with by women (Kittay, 1995). Wendy Brown (1992) argues that this separation is based in classic liberalism's roots in an assumption of male patriarchal right that contemporary liberalism is yet to relinquish. Zillah R. Eisenstein's (1981) often-quoted thesis is that this separation could be the basis to liberalism's downfall. As it becomes clear that liberalism is incompatible with equal rights for women, feminism will look to alternative grounds to build its agenda. Feminists argue that due to the gendered separation of spheres, liberalism has had a lack of concern with the forms of oppression that take place in the private sphere.

Moore argues that even though 'liberal theory was invested in protecting every citizen's right to privacy, it was wholly unconcerned with the content of the decisions, judgements, and preferences exercised in that realm' (1999: 37).

The form of equality on offer

There are three main critiques of the definitions of equality used within liberal theory, which each point to the limitations of advocating **formal** or **procedural** equality. The first is that the abstract individualism of contemporary liberal democracy is a 'powerful impediment' (Phillips, 1993: 115) to genuine gender equality. Anne Phillips expands this critique by arguing that the limited promise of liberalism is based on a negative definition of individuality that offers 'an impoverished version of human existence, in which individuals are always and inevitably opposed' (*ibid.*: 39). A second significant problem is the stress on equality of **opportunity** over other criteria concerned with **outcome**. Brown notes that it 'is as gratuitous to dwell upon an impoverished single mother's freedom to pursue her own individual interests in society as it is to carry on about the private property rights of the homeless' (1992: 19). Finally, many feminists are unhappy with the focus on political rights over economic or social rights. Ruth Lister (1997) points out that political rights can sit alongside massive economic and social inequalities. Due to these three weaknesses feminists such as Lister call for more **substantial** definitions of equality that can encompass what is needed to ensure equality of outcome as well as opportunity. In particular, what are called for are definitions that do not divorce issues of economic equality from questions of political equality.

The exclusion of context and difference

Feminists worry that the abstracted conditions, which Rawls proposes can construct the environment in which individuals will be treated as equals, are insufficient for equality to be achieved. If lives are 'inescapably part of particular communities and contexts, and the values embedded there help us to set goals for ourselves' (Rudy, 1999: 48), why build a framework to abstract judgement and decisions from those communities? Brown argues that recent history proves that it is not feasible to obtain universal rights within the liberal state. The liberal state has lost its 'guise of universality as it becomes ever more transparently invested in particular economic interests, political ends, and social formations' (1993: 392). If particularity is inevitable then liberalism is a poor structure to protect the rights of groups different from those whose interests are at the centre of the state.

The dilemmas of 'bracketing off' difference are seen in versions of the public sphere that assume that one such sphere can encompass all citizens and allow for difference to be inconsequential. If you remember the earlier discussion of Habermas's public sphere, he defines it as a communicative space where private actors come together to talk about public issues with a reasoned and universal orientation. Nancy Fraser (1997b) disputes the notion that bracketing status and difference can occur. A liberal universal public sphere assumes 'a space of zero-degree culture, so utterly bereft of any specific ethos as to accommodate with perfect neutrality and equal ease interventions expressive of any and every cultural ethos' (1997b: 79). For Joan B. Landes (1995) the allocation of certain issues into the private sphere, beyond the concerns of the public sphere, is no accident. Only by placing particular concerns with no scope for becoming universal outside the concerns of the public sphere could the liberal model present a vision of a universal orientation within a singular public sphere. The possibility of a culturally-neutral and all-encompassing public sphere is only possible where 'public issues' are defined in such a way as to allow for the complete exclusion of all issues associated with the private sphere of family life (Cohen, 1995). The liberal and Habermasian model of a public sphere is 'structured by a logic of inclusion and exclusion' (Fleming, 1995: 117).

The liberal desire to separate out context is driven by a belief that its recognition can only contaminate good judgements. For a wide range of feminists this is rejected in favour of asserting that there 'is no presocial component because the self is always situated within a concrete set of circumstances, beliefs, and constructions' (Rudy, 1999: 48). Nira Yuval-Davis (1997a) faults liberalism for excluding community relationships in order to define the only consequential relationship as that between the individual and the state. Phillips (1999) argues that liberal demands for a focus on the abstract individual – so as to ensure that particularity and difference do not contaminate conceptions of the good life – means that the individual is abstracted from the very conditions that make her unequal.

In summary, a series of exclusions take place within liberal definitions of equal rights:

- Equality of opportunity is favoured over equality of outcome.
- Neutral contexts are favoured over recognition of the conditions within which individuals strive for equality.
- The abstract individual is favoured over incorporation of individual and collective differences.
- Political equality is favoured over economic and material equality.

These criticisms produce a feminist agenda concentrated on bringing differences into discussions about rights.

Feminist incorporations

The strategy of feminists working with liberalism and the rights agenda is to develop a format for incorporating recognition of culture and inequality into its template. There are a variety of feminist strategies for rescuing liberalism, and the four key ones outlined in this section are:

- Individual rights
- Gendered rights
- Concrete rights
- Group rights.

Individual rights

The first strategy focuses on defending the centrality given to impartiality and the abstract individual in rights discourse. Impartiality can be thought of as a demand to respect and care for others regardless of who they are. If this is rejected, the alternative is to care only for those who are like us. If we must know the person in order to protect their rights, then it is easier to accord rights to those we are familiar with. An aspiration to impartiality requires that we include in our politics and outlook on life 'some notion of stretching outside of ourselves, some capacity for self-reflection and self-distance, some imaginative – and, more importantly, some practical – movement towards linking up with those who have seemed different' (Phillips, 1993: 71). The emotional independence advocated by liberalism allows for a response that looks beyond individual preference (James, 1992). Differences do not negate the politics of justice and rights, instead the need to retain them as 'anticipatory concepts' is even more important: 'the more divergent forms of life become, the more salient justice is' (Flax, 1992a: 198).

Martha C. Nussbaum (1999b) is one of the most eloquent advocates of the need to hold on to some version of individual rights in the context of difference. She cautions against losing the clarity and values that come with acknowledging the equal worth of individuals. Women in many countries are still campaigning for this basic right; that is, to be thought of as human. Steering feminist campaigns away from this focus leaves women in such positions open to threat and persecution for the good of some other individual (husband, father, child), or group (family), or community. Individualism is a suitable counterpoint to the traditional position of women where they 'have too rarely been treated as ends in themselves, and too frequently treated as means to the ends of others' (1992: 63). The individualism that feminism can campaign for does not need to be the egotistical version they have found in some classical liberal texts; it can be one founded in dignity and compassion, in respecting the rights of others, in emotional connection, as well as rational detachment. The role of the state should be to protect and enable the space in which the individual obtains the capability to express their wants and live fully as a complete human being.

Cornell, in *At the Heart of Freedom* (1998), focuses on the space required for the individual to become and live as a full human being. In the book she lays out a feminist vision of political liberalism, which draws heavily on classic conceptions of individual rights and freedom from Kant through to contemporary articulations of political liberalism from Rawls. Cornell agrees with those feminists who argue that formal equality has come to mean equality for men. However, she rejects the solution of making rights and citizenship 'gendered' proposed by feminists such as Patemen and Okin. Such proposals run the danger of constructing a template of what a woman should be; in particular they appear to make heterosexuality and motherhood the cultural and essential centre of women's lives.

Cornell's analysis begins in a claim that patriarchy generates a template of what the good life should be. Women lack equality because they are judged against this norm and lack the right to construct their own vision of what their life should be. Cornell does not want to define an alternative conception of womanhood or non-patriarchal society, what she wants is for women to have a space in which to define their own articulations of the 'good life'. Her goal is thus to build a more feasible model of equality – without constructing a model of how women and men should live their lives. She holds constant with Dworkin and Rawls the belief that the state cannot become involved in defining the good life. The right we have is to express and live out our version of the good life, we do not have the right to coerce others to live that version, all we can do is argue and attempt to persuade.

The space within which individuals can define their version of the good life is the **imaginary domain**. Rather than protect the individual's privacy, the liberal state should protect the individual's imaginary domain. Cornell founds her model on the right to a conceptual space because of two key factors. First, the right to privacy is something in liberal theory that has been owned by the individual and is their 'property'. In contrast, the imaginary domain is developed relationally and is one we share with others. This allows the model to move away from the individualism of liberal writers such as Dworkin. Second, the physical space that has been defined in Western society as the private sphere is the site where women and others are systematically denied rights. To deny a person the right to marry or to live out their intimate choices because they are gay is to harm their imaginary domain. If the state protects the imaginary domain – which has no clear physical boundary – this gives the state the right to enter the private sphere to protect it.

The cornerstone of Cornell's articulation of a feminist liberal position is the claim that as individuals we have the 'right to be legally and politically recognized as the legitimate source of meaning and representation of our existence as corporal, sexuate beings' (1998: 8). Women, straight and lesbian, and gay men are denied the space to imagine what our life could be:

> When we ask gays and lesbians to closet their sexuality in the name of the welfare of others who are disturbed by a sexuality not their own, we are compelling people to confine and restrain their freedom in the name of the good of others. (*Ibid.*: 18)

A significant component of our sexuate being is our self-definition of our sexual orientation; it is such a fundamental aspect of our well-being that we cannot consider it a choice or lifestyle issue, which is not the state's business to legitimate.

It is here that we see what distinguishes Cornell from the liberal ideas she adapts. The individual of liberal thought is the rational reasoned actor, whose emotional and sexual life happens in the private sphere separate from the concerns of the state. The individual of Cornell's fair and just system is a sexuate being who has the right to define their private and public life in a way that demands the state gives them the space to do so. In current systems where gay men and lesbians are not allowed the same rights to marry and parent the 'state clearly is taking a space that should be left to the person' (*ibid.*: 41).

Cornell's articulation of political liberalism incorporates Rawls's notion of overlapping consensus and Dworkin's discontinuity thesis through her assertion of **equivalence** (1992). Previously we have seen that Cornell and others argue that notions of equality and equal treatment have become synonymous with the right to be the same. To remove this danger Cornell asserts that the state should legitimate and recognize our equivalent value as different kinds of individuals with different conceptions of the good life and our position within it. To be treated equally – equivalently – the reality of being differently positioned in society should be recognized.

Equivalence and individual rights resist specifying the forms of life to be encouraged or offered protection within society. For other feminists this is not enough to repair historical inequalities and denials. Other frameworks go further in incorporating specific differences into rights arguments.

Gendered rights

Rights have been formulated through placing the private sphere outside its remit; the role of women in providing care in this sphere has been central in the exclusion. The importance of the exclusion to shaping the terms and scope of rights suggests that 'an "add women and stir" liberal-feminist reworking' (Woolley, 2000: 3) is insufficient. Okin (1989) advocates – counter to Cornell – that theories of justice do need to incorporate an awareness of and response to gender inequalities – particularly within the family. She argues this for three reasons:

1 Inequalities suffered by women – because they are women – are significant factors in limiting women's lives;
2 Women do not have fair access to the opportunity to be equal while theories of justice do not respond to gender inequality; and
3 Families are important places where we learn to be gendered individuals and experience gender inequality.

This agenda explicitly seeks to place women's role in reproduction and childcare at the centre of rights. Pateman argues that asking 'whether sexual difference is politically significant is to ask the wrong question; the question is always how the difference is to be expressed' (1988: 226). Similarly, both Sylvia Walby (1997) and Cheryl McEwan (2000) assert that rights have to encompass the domestic realm to be of any use to women. In practical terms such arguments lead to calls for acknowledging women's caring role in the private sphere (Fraser, 1994). Those who advocate gendered rights propose that women's role in reproduction should be acknowledged both in the language of rights and the development of government policies. Other feminists are wary of making explicit reference to 'women's *special needs*' (Guerrina, 2001: 35, original emphasis) in these terms. There is a concern that identifying the distinctive requirements that women have, traps feminism into defining and essentializing women's identity.

Concrete rights

Phillips (1993) and Seyla Benhabib (1992) both call for alliances of difference within a framework of universal aspiration; that is, bringing together the subject of liberalism – **the generalized other** – with the subject of difference – **the concrete other**. Benhabib questions whether an individual can be protected and provided with rights while knowing nothing about them – remaining behind the veil of ignorance. Supplementing the principle of valuing the generalized other with knowledge of the concrete other is compatible with liberalism because impartial justice requires knowledge of the particularity of the individual – if outcome is favoured over opportunity. Universal and fair outcome requires particular knowledge and response. Awareness of the concrete other when making judgements would not lead to relativism, because the knowledge it provides is knowledge that allows one to make the right and just decision. Benhabib stresses that awareness of the concrete other is not a replacement for the generalizable other; rather its inclusion into political judgement is a reminder of the limits to abstract univeralism. While this suggests a significant move away from Rawls's veil of ignorance, it also has echoes with his overlapping consensus and Dworkin's discontinuity thesis. Phillips, in support of Benhabib, argues that we may not share a similar definition of what the common human condition is or should be, but we can share a belief that believing in it – looking beyond oneself – is a valuable ideal. This equates to Rawls and Dworkin's assertion that we cannot all share the same definition of the good life but can share a belief that we should have the space to articulate a definition of what it is.

Moore shares the belief that taking context into account is not intrinsically separate from liberal models of justice. She argues that a desire to be moral to those around us, through our experiences of attachment, underpins Rawls's call for a political system aimed at providing equality and rights. Moore asserts that liberalism 'must *presuppose* care' (1999: 10, original emphasis). Why, after being the motivation behind norms of justice and equality, should principles of care, emotion and particularity remain outside of the practice of such norms in the public sphere? Rawls appears happy for the autonomous individual of the public sphere to be supported and made possible by individuals who respond via care and attachment. Moore points out that women have been 'doing the caring necessary to the acquisition of the sense of justice' (1999: 12) while having limited access to the principles of justice themselves. Like Benhabib and Phillips, Moore argues for breaking down the 'dichotomy presented by liberal theory between self-interest and morality, particularity and the impartial standpoint' (*ibid.*: 12).

The perspective represented by Moore, Phillips and Benhabib is based on an often-repeated challenge to the assumptions made in classic and contemporary liberal theory about human nature. Theories grounded in enlightenment theory argue that 'man' is an individualistic, self-interested actor whose main preoccupation is the preservation of his own life and property. Such 'men' enter society and support individual rights for others because such support is the best guarantee of their own well-being – and that of their offspring. Rationality and reason are seen as the human qualities that allow us to make this calculation; they allow us to appreciate that to look beyond ourselves will allow our own individual prosperity to be achieved. Feminists therefore include in their critique of liberalism a rejection of this version of the human condition. Being self-interested is not a universal human condition, but the pattern of Western masculinity that has been fostered by, and privileged within, capitalism.

Group rights

Iris Marion Young articulates one of the most influential calls for group rights and participation. Rights for women, straight and lesbian, gay men, different ethnic and racial groups, and for the disabled are all representative of a politics that demands that special attention is paid to specific groups. Young argues that certain individuals do not benefit from universal rights because it is their membership of and association with groups that are systematically discriminated against in Western society, which leads to their rights being denied. To fix systematic discrimination requires that such groups have privileged treatment in the political sphere. This argument is linked to a belief, supported by other feminists such as Yuval-Davis (1997b), that pluralism – or the overlapping consensus – is not enough to ensure historical inequalities are rectified.

In *Justice and the Politics of Difference* (1990), Young argues that universal rights have offered only limited and unequal rights to certain groups. Denying the differences that exist in society has – in reality – led to the implicit and sometimes explicit demand that previously excluded groups assimilate in order to be granted equal rights in civil society. Participation involves acceptance of rules and codes of behaviour in the public sphere, which were set before such groups were allowed access. For example, contemporary lesbian and gay groups protest that gay men and lesbians are 'allowed' rights only if we do not push it too far, do not look too different or act 'too gay'. The problem with the current rules is that since they emerged in a period when it was believed that only certain people had a role in making them, it is likely that those rules will best serve those present at their formulation.

The alternative Young produces is '*differentiated* citizenship' (1989: 251, original emphasis) based on group historical differences. What does this mean for politics? Young advocates a political process that is held accountable for the specific harm it has committed against groups. In practical terms the right of previously excluded groups should be given privileged status in decision-making in areas of particular interest to them. One example she gives is that Native American groups should have the right to have a particular say on questions of environmental damage found on their land.

Phillips (1999) supports Young by arguing that at times it is valid to acknowledge group rights as more important than the protection of the unlimited rights of the individual. However, she also warns of possible dangers of group closure and narrowness if civil society and political structures do not retain a liberal ideal of abstract universalism. The debates that have been fuelled by Young's proposals highlight the tension between collective and individual rights within feminism and beyond (Deveaux, 2000). Liberal writers caution that individual rights are a better protection against discrimination and abuse than any form of collective rights, which hold within them the space in which to deny rights to the individual for the good of the 'collective'. Yuval-Davis (1997a) suggests that group rights can be legitimate when discussion is of material disadvantage and restitution. The problem is when the issue shifts to that of cultural rights.

Okin (1994) and Nussbaum (1999b) are important critics of incorporating culturally-based norms into definitions of equal rights. Both assert that our examination of cultural practices and customs should focus on generating better formulations of the general good and be motivated by a desire to find out 'that the other is one of us' (Nussbaum, 1992: 241). For women who are denied the right to work, or full participation in the public sphere, because of culturally-based community customs, the right as an individual of equal worth to equality of opportunity is a vital and just principle. This is an important right because women are often members of such cultures through birth rather than choice. Groups, who demand that their cultural values be given privileged representation within the civil sphere, also often maintain views and practices harmful to women. Traditional cultural practices, such as female genital mutilation (FGM), are valued by particular cultures but result in the subordination of women.

For Nussbaum, FGM is not compatible with treating women as human beings of equal worth. Refusing to critique the practice because of cultural differences is 'withholding critical judgement where real evil and oppression are surely present' (1999b: 30). Okin suggests better judgements will come through taking 'into account as many voices as possible' (1994: 18), rather than listening to particular cultural and different voices. Such voices may have internalized the oppressions they face – for example supporting cultural practices such as FGM. Such women would benefit from distanced – yet engaged – outsiders who articulate arguments of justice and fairness. Behind a veil of ignorance supporters of FGM would have 'second thoughts' (*ibid.*: 19) because they would not want the practice to happen to them. Individual-rights feminist campaigners are looking to retain a notion of what makes us all human and worthy of respect that can 'enable, rather than obstruct, the contemporary feminist quest for global justice and cross-cultural political work' (Quillen, 2001: 89).

Those in favour of cultural recognition and collective rights counter that individual rights are a Western concept, which do not necessarily offer greater protection for either the group or the individual (Rai and Lievesley, 1996; Yuval-Davis, 1997a). The use of perspectives and discourses developed by Western feminists to analyse problems women face in other contexts is more likely to serve the interests of the feminists who advocate their use, rather than the women in need of help (Doezema, 2001). For feminists working in non-Western countries there is a concern that liberal rights and citizenship will not resolve the problems women face in that context (McEwan, 2000). Transnational feminism supports the importance liberal feminism gives rights talk and global engagement. However, it identifies Western cultural imperialism in some of its responses. The dominance of Western approaches to rights tends to lead to the dominance of rights based in property and wealth and attached to the individual (Alarcón *et al.*, 1999), whilst broader notions of democracy and freedom are squeezed out by the imperialist dominance of free-market versions of both (Alexander and Mohanty, 1997).

Crucially, such writers reject that there is a choice to be made between demands for equality and cultural recognition (Block and James, 1992a; Lister, 1997). This rejection is based on a fixed reading of both rights and culture. Monique Deveaux warns against reading cultural and collective visions of commonly held rights as intrinsically opposed to the rights of women. Instead we should ask why they may be articulated in this way, and link that query to wider political and economic relations. Nationalist and cultural groups emerging from periods of colonial and Western domination do not have to articulate their identity in terms of the subordination of women. That they do can be linked to a habit of subordination picked up from periods of Western rule.

Feminism should not shy away from criticizing cultural fundamentalism, however, when the debate is presented as the importance of maintaining the superiority of modernist notions of the individual subject against the return of premodern religious fundamentalism, the contemporary reasons for its emergence are ignored. First is the relationship between fundamentalist positions and contemporary relations; contemporary fundamentalists are products and users of global movements and exchanges (Moallem, 1999). Second, fundamentalism is not just practised by Islamic organizations. Western attacks on Islamic fundamentalism too easily ignore fundamentalist Christian groups, powerful in the United States, who use their Western power-base to impinge on the work of international organizations such as the United Nations in areas such as birth control and recognition of lesbian and gay rights. Third, it is too easy to see religious groups as the only fundamentalist actors; the movements of free trade and the demands placed on developing countries by the IMF through Structural Adjustment Policies are fundamentalist in their allegiance to unconfined and unregulated capitalism (Vuola, 2002).

If cultural values are understood as the product of particular economic, political and social contexts, then they are open to negotiation and challenge. It is therefore important to engage in cultural production, rather than fall into the isolation and narrowness of individual rights as the only legitimate value. Placing rights and cultural recognition as complementary allows them to enrich each other. It is here that individual rights can play a role in three ways:

- First, Phillips (1999) argues it sustains an important distinction between cultural groups and their rights, and the rights of individuals who are members and participants in that group.
- Second, individual rights can be used to protect women against 'specifically *contemporary* forms of inequality and oppression' (Deveaux, 2000: 525, original emphasis), which have emerged in particular political and economic contexts. It is reasonable to demand that culturally-based articulations of values and autonomy retain an assertion of 'formal respect for the individual rights of their members' (*ibid.*: 536). McEwan argues that this is the solution that has emerged in the new South Africa, where the constitution ensures that 'culture/tradition and customary law apply only insofar as they are consistent with the provision of the Bill of Rights and the constitution more generally' (2000: 641).
- Third, women can claim the right to be participants in shaping their cultures' values and beliefs. Women and others are negotiating rights and cultural values in order to envisage their own articulations of 'religious traditions and cultural practices' (Cornell, 1998: 165). What is being sought is the 'political, moral and psychic space' in which to contest dominant practices and articulate their own perception of the good life. Yuval-Davis advocates 'transversal politics of coalition building, in which the specific positioning of political actors is recognized and considered' (1997b: 19) as a format for bringing rights and cultural recognition together. Group differences are recognized and valued, but also seen as contingent, negotiable and changeable. The focus is on the production of 'transversal dialogue', which is able to appreciate equivalence and ultimately solidarity 'based on a common knowledge sustained by a compatible value system' (*ibid.*). This form of politics breaks down and moves beyond the dichotomy between equality and difference by calling for substantive and historically specific definitions of both (Block and James, 1992b; Scott, 1988a).

Various feminists seek strategies to incorporate differences into political liberalism. While the strategies are varied, they share a desire to retain a belief that the individual, although situated rather than abstract, can be foundational to political life. They are also committed to the state having a role in encouraging conceptions of the good life to develop and flourish. This includes a belief that differences are important and foundational not just to our political and material life, but also to our spiritual life. Those wishing to retain the values of liberalism as a vehicle for achieving equal rights ask for a politics that can both incorporate our differences and look beyond them.

Political uses

Feminists continue to look for ways to retain and adapt liberal and equal rights arguments because they are seen as necessary and enabling to political activism; particularly in international politics. On a practical level the language of equal rights remains a central element of political discourse. Using the language of rights ensures that at least some of the audience will understand and approve of the demands being made. Phillips warns against throwing out all hope of abstract ideals and universality because in 'the last three hundred years, every oppressed group has found a lifeline in the abstractions of the individual and has appealed to these in making its claim to equality' (1993: 49). The demand for a space to define oneself as an individual remains an important value appealing to many.

1995 UN Fourth World Conference on Women in Beijing

The most recent global articulation and representation of equal rights for women was the 1995 UN Fourth World Conference on Women in Beijing and its follow-up Beijing+5. The Conference brought together 40,000 women from all over the world to discuss women's access to human rights. The key outcomes of the Conference were a *Platform for Action* and the *Beijing Declaration*, which individual states who are signed up to the CEDAW (Convention on the Elimination of All Forms of Discrimination against Women) are expected to enact. UN agencies such as UNICEF are expected to develop policies consistent with the principles of both CEDAW and the Beijing Platform (UNICEF, 1999). A key aim of Beijing+5 was to evaluate the implementation of these commitments and the *Platform*.

Alongside the Conference a separate NGO (non-governmental organization) conference was organized, which focused on women, development issues and strategies for change; the NGO conference itself had 30,000 participants. The 1995 Conference received a huge amount of publicity across the globe. In the West much of the publicity focused on Hillary Clinton's opening address; the irony of a World Conference on women's human rights being held in China; and the last-minute decision of the Chinese authorities to move the NGO conference 30 kilometres outside Beijing.

The *Beijing Declaration* and the *Platform for Action* maintain a strong liberal concern with the rights of individual women regardless of background or position. Point 9 of the *Declaration* asks for the 'full implementation of the human rights of women and of the girl child as an inalienable, integral and indivisible part of all human rights and fundamental freedoms' (UN, 1995a). It goes on to demand:

> The empowerment and advancement of women, including the right to freedom of thought, conscience, religion and belief, thus contributing to the moral, ethical, spiritual and intellectual needs of women and men, individually or in community with others and thereby guaranteeing them the possibility of realizing their full potential in society and shaping their lives in accordance with their own aspirations. (*Ibid.*)

The universality of these rights is, in the words of the *Platform for Action*, 'beyond question' (UN, 1995b).

At various points the documents do incorporate the context and cultural identity of the individual into the discussion of rights. In particular, arguments about the importance of gendering the language and operation of rights and citizenship are embedded in the commitments and proposals. For example, the *Declaration* stresses the need for greater sharing of family responsibilities if women are to have access to the full range of human rights. Throughout the principles laid down in Beijing there is a clear sense that human rights go beyond political rights to encompass rights in the economic, cultural, reproductive and private spheres. The Mission Statement of the *Platform for Action* notes that:

> the principle of shared power and responsibility should be established between women and men at home, in the workplace and in the wider national and international communities. Equality between women and men is a matter of human rights and a condition for social justice and is also a necessary and fundamental prerequisite for equality, development and peace. (*Ibid.*)

The debate about the implications of the Beijing Conference and the part it can play in improving the lives of women – particularly in non-Western countries – is still underway. In the varied benefits and limitations that different writers have highlighted we can identify some of the issues that emerge for feminist activism when it uses liberal frameworks.

Benefits

Various benefits have been identified from the Conference and its focus on human rights; some are practical, others look to long-term shifts in political activism, in particular around the needs and interests of women living in developing countries. The first practical benefit is that the considerable build-up to the Conference and the publicity it generated heightened the importance given to women's rights in China and beyond (Jinngwei, 1996). Women's groups in China found the government more willing and ready, with the glare of the world's press aimed at it, to provide material resources and to consider changes in law. These successes, and the experiences involved in preparing for and running the NGO conference, spurred women's groups in China to create a more independent structure and identity apart from the state (Howell, 1997).

The Conference itself generated considerable resources in the immediate and longer term for groups who attended (Jiaxiang, 1996; Perry, 1998). A considerable variety of networks were developed out of the conference, which allowed for coalitions to form across a variety of different groups sharing experiences and identifying commonalties, which have been maintained long after the end of the conference (Espinosa, 1997). The connections and networks have gone further and lasted longer than the Conference itself. One outlet of the activity was the creation of electronic communities and coalitions which continue to link groups and individuals from very different backgrounds, to share expertise and experiences. In addition, it highlighted the work of feminist activism in non-Western countries, which helped Western feminists realize that they had something to learn from feminists outside the West (Dutt, 1996). Mallika Dutt argues that holding the Beijing Conference was valuable because it made feminists from very different backgrounds and experiences look beyond (but not forget) their local identities to construct commonalties.

A wider benefit of the Conference has been the substantive notion of rights maintained in much of the agreements reached at the Conference. The *Declaration* and *Platform for Action* were strongly contested at the Conference and at preliminary meetings by various cultural and religious groups. For example, pro-life groups argued that the documents implied that abortion is an inalienable right. The hostile response suggests that the principles put forward at Beijing do have a radical intent and possibility. The *Declaration* and the Conference itself legitimated the feminist argument that programmes and rights require gendering, and that 'women may not always have the same concerns and interests as men with respect to major international issues such as the environment, human rights, and social development' (Charlesworth, 1996: 541).

Another wider benefit of the approach of the Conference was the way in which the articulation of rights sat alongside recognition of difference and community or collective identities. In this way the Conference and its aftermath attempt to reflect individual rights in coalition with cultural recognition. The Beijing Conference could be presented as the operationalization of the transversal politics called for by Yuval-Davis and others. The rights being demanded go further than formal equality and include recognition of gender and cultural differences in the articulation of rights. Eisenstein (1997) celebrated the importance of women articulating the politics of equality in a context where states wish to deny the possibility of egalitarian agendas; in this light Beijing offers promise because it 'stands as a fantasmatic of what women across the globe can begin to imagine' (1997: 163).

Limitations

Without disputing some of the benefits of the Beijing Conference, feminists have identified limits to its usefulness. The limitations are often linked to the dominance of particular types of rights discourses at the Conference and in the subsequent processes, and in practical terms feminists have questioned whether the event had greater symbolic significance than real impact on women. In the words of Jude Howell (who argues the Conference did have a positive effect), 'the ostentatious posturing of feminist elites makes little difference to government policy, let alone the day-to-day lives of poor women' (1997: 235). For some feminists, both at and outside the conference, it was a very expensive way in which to produce Declarations and Platforms that would have little immediate benefit (Charlesworth, 1996).

In order for consensus to be achieved and a united *Platform* to be launched, contentious areas were excluded from the document and discussion. For example, the efforts of the Vatican and various Islamic countries saw the removal of sexual orientation from discussion of discrimination and abuse. Some authors have therefore questioned the cost of gaining consensus across such different cultural and religious groups because it could only be achieved by removing any substance from the agreed Platform. In the *Declaration* and other documents, rights are often justified on two grounds which work to undercut women's individuality. First, part of the argument for rights for women is that if they have rights they will be better placed to protect their children. For example, the CEDAW is often articulated alongside the Convention on the Rights of the Child (CRC), and documents often talk of 'women and children'. Second, the documents stress that rights are good for women because the benefits will be felt by all of humanity. In both these cases it does not appear enough to advocate that rights for women are important for the benefit it brings them; instead, someone else has to benefit for it to be legitimate.

A concern raised by transnational feminists is the version of rights and democracy celebrated and called for in the *Declaration*. The imperialist dominance of Western values in global venues and institutions such as this leads to their neoliberal dominant approach to democracy and freedom taking centre-stage (Alexander and Mohanty, 1997). In the *Declaration*, the realization of rights is linked to free trade and access to the marketplace. Alternative conceptions of rights and democracy that link both to socialist or other collective economic and state/community practices are excluded through the hegemonic position of advanced Western capitalism as the framer of rights and democracy. That the debates in Beijing were unable to move outside or challenge this framework narrows its value as a venue to consider the impact global movements of trade and culture are having on the material lives and rights of women in varied vulnerable positions around the globe.

The final concern feminists have raised is that the liberal framework limited the ways in which gender, culture and identity were understood and incorporated into the language of rights. For example, Sally Baden and Ann Marie Goetz (1997: 7) argue that the form of 'gender mainstreaming' that Beijing represents, depoliticises gender's meaning to an 'interesting statistical variable'. The form given to gender in such processes underspecifies 'the power relations maintaining gender inequalities, and in the process de-links the investigation of gender issues from a feminist transformatory project' (*ibid.*). Some feminists felt that the *Declaration* and the focus of Beijing left little space in which to celebrate culture and difference as valuable; instead, universalism and a Western model of individuality dominated. Baden and Goetz warn of the 'cultural brutality of universalism' (*ibid.*: 20); and Ngai-Ling Sum (2000) argues that the liberal rights agenda at the Conference 'freezes women's identity and subjectivity ... it disembeds Western and Eastern women from historically contingent power relations and it ignores and silences the multiple and resistant voices of women located at diverse points in the complex social matrix' (2000: 135).

Those positive about the political usefulness of the liberal-rights framework adopted at the Beijing Conference stress the value of providing templates of what we all should demand and expect from the state we live in. Those who are unhappy question whether the templates exclude so much from what makes us who we are that they are meaningless.

Conclusion

For feminists who maintain the equal-rights agenda it is valuable because it makes a basic, but fundamental, point that as human beings women deserve a better deal. The contemporary liberal argument that it is dangerous to want the state to take on a role wider than the protection of everyone's right to define what they want from life, remains important to feminist explorations of what it is that women have a right to demand. Contemporary articulations of rights within feminism are conscious of the need to incorporate arguments about difference and culture. This includes broadening the remit for what women have a right to. It also generates alternatives to the individual as the actor for whom rights are there to protect. The strategies for incorporating difference are varied, and each attempt brings with it new uncertainties and dilemmas. Feminists who are working to bring rights and difference together remain an important part of feminist theorizing and activism. They are also at the forefront of the rights and difference debate in wider social and political thought.

My own thinking on the values of rights arguments and the desire to retain a language of universalism within their articulation has shifted while writing this book. In a theoretical context where cultural questions and recognition of difference are at the forefront, while economic and political inequalities continue to plague many women's lives in and outside the West, there is something inescapably useful and valuable about retaining a notion that women are of equal worth as individuals. Feminists working with equal-rights arguments are correct in their support for this principle; it reminds us of the importance of equality and the need to treat others with full respect. Where I feel some equal-rights feminists do get into difficulty is when they treat culture only as a source of limitation and as a barrier for women. Cultural values can do this, but they can also be a source of meaning and value for the women who participate in their articulation and development. For this reason, I believe that debates about rights are benefiting from their entanglement with claims about group and cultural recognition. What is important is that feminists continue to work to ensure that individual rights and cultural recognition are not seen or conceptualized as opposing values.

In the following chapter the focus turns to another area of established social and political thought which feminism has in the past used to consider gender inequality: Marxism. The chapter will examine how feminist stand-point theories have emerged out of engagement with Marxism and how these theories have been reformulated in the light of concerns about their treatment of difference and identity.

FURTHER READING

Anne Phillips (1999) *Which Equalities Matter?* (Cambridge: Polity Press). Phillips produces a concise and empirically grounded account of the tensions between equal rights and cultural recognition; chapters 3 and 4 are particularly valuable.

Nira Yuval-Davis and Pnina Werbner (eds) (1999) *Women, Citizenship and Difference* (London: Zed Books). A variety of writers explore the connections between gender and citizenship; crucially it has a strong international focus.

Martha C. Nussbaum (1999) *Sex and Justice* (New York: Oxford University Press). Nussbaum puts forward the case for maintaining a liberal equal-rights agenda within feminist activism on the international stage; chapter 1 encapsulates the foundations to her position.

Standpoint theories

CONTENTS

Equal-rights arguments maintain a neutral position on whether there are differences between women and men. Standpoint theory emerges as a framework for exploring the importance of such differences, in particular differences in material position and experience. A variety of standpoint theories focus on how women's experiences can be the source of knowledge about both oppressive processes and modes of resistance. Some of this work – although not all – has its roots in second-wave feminist engagement with Marxism, whilst other important sources include the women's movement itself and feminist critiques of science. The dilemma that has been raised by this framework is whether it requires the exclusion of differences amongst women to present its ideas.

The chapter begins with a summary of some classic and contemporary Marxist ideas, focusing on historical materialism. The next section indicates feminists' concerns with these ideas, in particular the treatment of gender and agency. The chapter moves to explore feminist standpoint theory as an alternative articulation of historical materialism, but one which has had to respond further to issues of identity and difference. In this section a particular focus is given to issues of experience and objectivity. The Political Uses section will explore how some Black feminists use a standpoint perspective to validate the collective knowledge Black women have of their experiences of exploitation and discrimination.

Outline of the key perspective

The link between Marxism and feminist standpoint theories is a methodological and epistemological one. Feminists have looked to **historical materialism** and the link it makes between material existence and consciousness to conceptualize the oppression of women. In particular, they are interested in adapting the role given to the proletariat in generating revolutionary change.

The key text that feminists have drawn from in the development of standpoint ideas is *The German Ideology Part 1* (Marx and Engels, 1976), written between 1845 and 1846 but not published till 1932. Karl Marx and Frederick Engels advocate a philosophical and political framework embedded in the material conditions for the reproduction of life. They criticize the key German theorists of their time for having 'never left the realm of philosophy' (*ibid.*: 28). Marx and Engels argue that human beings develop their sense of consciousness through their relationship with the real world, and the labour involved in producing the material necessities of life:

> This mode of production must not be considered simply as being the reproduction of the physical existence of the individuals. Rather it is a definite form of activity of these individuals, a definite form of expressing their life, a definite *mode of life* on their part. As individuals express their life, so they are ... Hence what individuals are depends on the material conditions of their production. (*Ibid.*: 32, original emphasis)

In essence, this represents a rejection of a universal consciousness: 'It is not consciousness that determines life, but life that determines consciousness' (*ibid.*: 37); a point that has led many to argue that, far from being opposed to poststructuralism, Marxism represents one of its first accounts (Bannerji, 1995). The problem is that in capitalist society, the consciousness that is held to be 'man's', is that of the ruling class, pretending to be universal. German philosophy is emblematic of the ruling 'perverse' consciousness or ideology, which looks to heaven rather than earth to define the characteristics of humankind. The ruling class and their supporters – the intelligentsia – cannot capture the human condition and its bond to the material world, because they are not part of it. Any attempt they make to theorize society and human relations within it cannot help but be partial and 'perverse', they lack an actual engagement with the world and humans within it. The problem is to explain why those who do labour collectively to produce material goods have lost sight of the consciousness that should develop from that activity, and have instead taken on the perverse ideology of those who rule. Why does man's labour, instead of being the root of his shared consciousness, become 'an alien power opposed to him, which enslaves him instead of being controlled by him' (Marx and Engels, 1976: 47)?

Marx and Engels propose that it is the methods of production developed by the ruling class within capitalism, in particular the **division of labour**, which 'alienates' men from the products of their labour. First, the division of labour involves a 'division of material and mental labour' (*ibid.*: 45).

Second, men become specialized into specific areas of labour and lose the chance 'to hunt in the morning, fish in the afternoon, rear cattle in the evening, criticise after dinner ... without ever becoming hunter, fisherman, shepherd or critic' (*ibid.*: 470). Third, selling the products of men's labour for the monetary profits of others – commodification – halts the development of a shared consciousness of the structures that lie behind current modes of production. The consciousness of the ruling class, while perverse and in some sense false, is able through the power it holds in society to shape relationships within it and thus become 'true'.

In the long term, through the cycle of history, a form of human consciousness that is able to offer challenge to the ruling class will emerge from key actors and processes. This is because:

1 The proletariat has the potential to have consciousness of 'the necessity of a fundamental revolution' (*ibid.*: 52).
2 If brought together collectively the proletariat will be able to identify the structures that lie behind the current human condition.
3 Their revolutionary consciousness will be able to recognize contradictions, which will begin to appear 'between the productive forces [the proletariat] and the form of intercourse [capitalism and commodification of labour]' (*ibid.*: 74) maintained in the division of labour in capitalist production.

Marxist ideas have suffered from both historical and theoretical critique, people point to the fall of the Soviet Union and the reemergence of democracy and capitalism in Eastern Europe as evidence of its inadequacy. Theoretically, its model of historical change and social relations has been labelled deterministic and/or functionalist. However, various writers argue that Marxist arguments still have something to offer the analysis of our times.

Two strategies have developed for continuing to work with Marxism. The first is, through close readings of original texts by Marx and Engels, to argue that critiques are based on superficial readings. Erik O.Wright *et al.* (1994) reject the notion that Marx positions the class division as the only source of revolutionary change. Henry Veltmeyer (2000) argues that the critics who argue that Marxism has no theory of the subject, or any notion of human agency, forget that it sees social transformation as emerging out of both objective and subjective processes. Ellen M. Wood argues that accusations of social and technological determinism neglect to acknowledge that 'the kernel of historical materialism was an insistence on the historicity and specificity of capitalism, and a denial that its laws were the universal laws of history' (1995: 5).

The second strategy is to revise Marxism to match contemporary times. One area of Marxist thought, which is the focus of revision, is historical materialism. Wal Suchting (1993) reinterprets materialism as an exploration of the interaction of abstract theoretical terms, rather than an analysis of the interaction of actual material processes. Wright *et al.* (1992) advocate what they call 'weak historical materialism' to suggest that it is possible – but not inevitable – that particular material conditions will lead particular groups to generate a collective consciousness of their position and trigger revolutionary change. Alan Carling reinterprets historical materialism to argue that just because particular groups of historical actors may attempt to rationally direct the nature of change does not mean they can.

Much of the work aiming to reinterpret or renew Marxism does so by linking that attempt to contemporary history and thinking (McLellan, 1999). One key intellectual context to continued engagement with Marxism has been the poststructuralist turn to deconstruction of subjectivity and experience. Ernest Laclau and Chantal Mouffe (1985, 1987) are prominent in attempts to update Marxism through a poststructuralist gaze (others include David Harvey, 1989 and Fredric Jameson, 1991); a move that is not without its critics (Veltmeyer, 2000; Wood, 1995). Laclau and Mouffe argue that their reinterpretation of Marx, stays 'within Marxism' (1987). The aim is to draw into the analysis of history, an awareness of subjectivity, heterogeneity and context they believe missing from original Marxist analysis. In part this is done by reinterpreting the major concepts of Marxist thought as discursive constructs with a theoretical relationship to reality (Laclau and Mouffe, 1985). We can only define the relationship of the wage labourer to the capitalist as oppressive in the context of a discursive framework of equality and human rights; the relationship itself is not inherently oppressive, it requires a theoretical framework within which it is judged.

Marxism remains a part of political debates about the structures and processes of oppression and division in the social world and the activities needed to change the order of things. In much the same way, the presence of Marxism in feminism continues into contemporary debates about the sources of women's oppression and strategies for change. However, for some feminists it is impossible to retain both a Marxist framework and fully acknowledge the issues of difference and identity.

Feminist critiques

Marxist ideas made an important contribution to the development of feminist ideas in the second wave. A continuum of feminist Marxist articulations emerged, from those who looked to its ideas to provide a comprehensive explanation for the position of women, to others who saw capitalism as a component alongside other structures of women's oppression. Of particular importance was Engels's *The Origin of the Family, Private Property and the State* (1985), originally published in 1884. Marxist ideas were used to look at various areas of women's lives. This included the public sphere of paid labour; however, it also considered domestic labour and women's role in reproduction and household activity as central in continued oppression (see Vogel, 2000, for a useful summary of this work). Christine Delphy (1977), for example, argues that housework is a form of oppression based in the mode of production constructed by capitalism, producing women and men as opposing classes and with it patriarchy.

Socialist feminism developed out of the assertion that it was a mistake to completely relate patriarchy and women's oppression to the workings of capitalism. This led to the development of **dual systems theory**, which argues that both capitalism and patriarchy operate as separate, related, and at times opposed systems of oppression (Barrett, 1980; Hartmann, 1979). Iris Marion Young (1981) produced a variation on dual systems called **unified systems theory**. Here she argues that patriarchy predates capitalism, but its present shape is determined by its position within capitalism. This means that 'the marginalization of women and thereby our functioning as a secondary labour force is an essential and fundamental characteristic of capitalism' (1981: 58).

It would be wrong to suggest that Marxist and socialist feminism are a thing of the past, a relic of the late 1970s. Marxist and materialist feminists continue to advocate a place for an analysis of structures of oppression, in the context of contemporary shifts away from 'global' theories in favour of deconstruction and heterogeneity. Materialist feminists argue that their work acknowledges the structures first identified by Marx and, also, the importance of gendered processes in the operation of class (Pollert, 1996), domestic labour (Vogel, 1995), the workplace (Edwards, 1986), sexuality and the body (Moi and Redway, 1994) and cultural relations (Landry and MacLean, 1993; Walby, 1990).

Anna Pollert advocates the continued validity of a materialist approach because its use can analyse 'the continual interplay of action and structures, ideologies and practices within a wider frame of political economy' (1996: 647). Contemporary feminist materialist approaches incorporate, to a degree, postmodernism and its deconstruction of subjectivity and experience (Hennessy, 1993; Kuhn and Wolpe, 1978). Himani Bannerji (1995) advocates a materialist feminism able to generate a dialectical understanding of the production of identity, difference and subjectivity in the context in which they are produced – in particular, colonialism, imperialism and capitalism. Marxist feminists have responded to the challenge of difference by advocating the political need for a framework capable of recognizing wider structures and processes of inequality, operating regardless of cultural and situated differences. It is worth acknowledging that not all Marxist feminists believe that Marxist arguments *must* draw upon deconstructionism. Martha E. Gimenez (2000: 25) argues that in the context of 'the objectively worsening conditions of working people, particularly women, it has become increasingly untenable to hold on to the notion that everything is socially or discursively constructed, or a localized, contingent story'.

Those working to retain Marxist or material concerns in feminism are faced with a considerable body of feminist criticisms, which doubt the value of adapting any form of Marxist framework to the analysis of women. The major concern is with the strategy of reducing social relations and divisions to a two-class category model. Two areas excluded by this model are particularly important: gender and agency.

Dominance of class over gender

Diane Reay (1997), whose overall aim is to retain a class analysis within feminist theory, argues that class in Marxism is narrowed to a singular position revolving around the labour market. Through focusing on the labour market, other oppressive relationships which constitute class oppositions are ignored. Feminists – and others – argue that a narrow class analysis is problematic for various reasons. First, it generalizes processes of inequality and identity formation. Second, it thinks it is describing real classes and real people as belonging to those classes. Finally, it no longer has validity due to significant changes in the economy and social relations.

The main difficulty that feminists have identified is that definitions of class that privilege labour-market relations inevitably construct gender as less important. Nancy Hartsock (1998: 33–5), in an article originally published in 1975, argues that this hierarchy produces itself in various ways in Marxist arguments:

- questions of gender are interpreted as 'cultural' and thus as less important than 'economic' questions;
- tokenism is developed where gender (alongside the other usual suspects of 'race' and sexuality) is listed as something to deal with later;
- class is seen as the universal category capable of being the foundation of revolutionary change;
- the 'male left' get to 'define what is political' (1998: 33);
- issues associated with the private sphere are not seen as important; and
- women's labour in both the private and the public sphere is ignored.

These priorities lead to a refusal to recognize that 'revolution begins in our own lives first and that it concerns our own identities as human beings' (*ibid.*: 34). These priorities have been maintained in Marxist feminism; in this work it is still class that is held as more important and which really 'determines the character of social relations and human history' (Flax, 1976: 47). Bannerji (1995) argues that Marxist feminist analysis has maintained a narrow, economistic and positivist reading of Marx in its account of the sexual division of labour. This narrow reading has ensured that 'lived social relations and forms of consciousness that constitute personal, cultural, home life' (1995: 76) are excluded. Adding gender to the structure of the analysis may help, but feminists have queried whether Marxism can 'address directly the gender of the exploiters and those whose labour is appropriated' (Barrett, 1980: 8). Many feminists have remained unhappy with the notion that one can identify and separate the systems of oppression into categories of class and gender without assuming (a) that one is more important (class) than the other, and (b) that they operate as separate processes (Acker, 1989).

Structure/agency tension

The dominance of *a* structure (capitalism) and *a* particular material relationship (paid labour) in Marxist accounts leads to several problems for feminists, summed up usefully by Pollert (1996: 641):

> The emphasis on material structures in this debate ran into the danger of reducing women's oppression or exploitation to the 'needs of capital'. Men and women pursuing a range of interests, sometimes together and sometimes in opposition were absent from this scenario. Further, capitalism itself appeared in the functionalist light of a self-regulating system pulling in its 'needs', without the conflict and contradictions which beset it.

Attempts to resolve the problem of gender by adding patriarchy to the discussion retain the problem of an overly structural/system analysis unable to respond to the activities – agency – of individuals in shaping their identities and relations. For example, adding patriarchy to Marxism fails because, 'this loses the tension between agency and structure necessary to understand social process, and ends in a static form of systems theory' (*ibid.*: 640). Excluding such issues and processes results in Marxism and Marxist feminism having 'little to say about political subjectivity' (Bannerji, 1995: 80).

For various writers this has meant that attempting to use a Marxist perspective to analyse the position of women is futile because it 'tacitly endorses the traditional Marxian position that "the woman question" is auxiliary to the central questions of a Marxian theory of society' (Young, 1997: 102). The structural force of the Marxist account leaves little space for recognizing the agency and everyday resistance of subjects: 'subjects have been seen as totally subdued to the driving historical dynamic of capitalist forces and relations' (Smith, 1987: 142).

The feminists who have developed standpoint theory recognize the issues of gender and agency discussed above. However, they still believe that there is a place for Marxism in feminism, if its foundations in experiences and collective subjectivity are the areas adopted. As such, their aim is to produce a framework able to make use of the relationship between material experience and of collective knowledge about current conditions and future possibilities.

Feminist incorporations

Various feminist writers have developed a standpoint perspective, drawing on the women's movement, Marxism and critiques of science. While the foundations of standpoint theories vary, what they share is these two central claims:

1 Different groups in society will maintain different knowledge about the world.
2 Some forms of knowledge are better than others.

This section will look at the different ways feminists argue that particular groups (not always equated to women) maintain 'better' knowledge.

Hartsock is one of the key standpoint writers, her ideas find their roots in feminist engagement with Marx. In a series of papers produced in the 1970s and reproduced in a collection published in 1998, Hartsock builds a positive relationship between Marxism and feminism. Her focus is to reinterpret historical materialism via women's experiences and forms of knowledge. The work begins in a claim that Marxism and feminism share similar methodological strategies for the production of knowledge and making epistemological claims. Feminist epistemology is – or should be – about finding ways to draw knowledge out from experience. Theory is 'appropriated experience' (*ibid.*: 38). The tenets of consciousness-raising within the women's movement maintain the ability to connect 'personal experience to the structures that define our lives' (*ibid.*: 35). By basing knowledge on experience, difference and agency are acknowledged and become parts of a process of theorizing structures of oppression across different relationships in society. Hartsock asserts that Marxism loses its potential via the narrowing of what generates knowledge to the relations that male workers have to production and the economy. Thus she aims to broaden the focus on human activity to a wider range of processes and relationships, which exist between us and the material world.

Hartsock's exploration of the similarities and differences between Marxism and feminism led up to her key text 'The Feminist Standpoint: Developing the Ground for a Specifically Feminist Historical Materialism', finalized in 1981 and first published in 1983. The article sets up two crucial equivalencies: the first is that patriarchy as a structure operates equivalently to capitalism; the second is that women are in an equivalent position to the proletariat. Hartsock argues that 'good-enough' knowledge – knowledge that is capable of generating social change – emerges from particular relationships to material relations and collective engagement. Explicitly, her defence of a standpoint links political objectives to epistemological claims. Knowledge generated through different kinds of means generates alternative understandings of the world, which can either emancipate or support existing – exploitative – relations. A standpoint is a method for understanding social relations that is capable of generating knowledge that can produce political change. Hartsock makes five distinct epistemological and political claims as outlined in Box 2.1.

The feminist standpoint is the opposing understanding of the world that offers a challenge to the dominance of patriarchy as a process and structure. The standpoint is feminist rather than female, because it is not something women have because of their essential or physiological condition. Instead, a feminist standpoint emerges from a collective engagement with the experiences of women and the structures within which those experiences exist.

Women's experiences and their relationship with the world have the potential to generate different and better knowledge about the human condition. Abstract masculinity is a dichotomous way of thinking about the world, which constructs a series of hierarchical oppositions – nature/culture, reason/emotion, and female/male – that legitimate patterns of oppression and domination. In contrast, a feminist standpoint will envisage a relation between humans and between humans and the material world which offers the potential to transform societal processes and relations. To describe the vision of the world which could emerge from women's experiences within the sexual division of labour, Hartsock draws from the psychoanalytic ideas associated with object relations theory and Nancy Chodorow in particular.

Chodorow (1978) reinterprets Freud's oedipal drama to argue that the relationship that infants and young boys have with their mother – within patriarchy – shapes them into rational, independent actors, forced to deny interdependencies and connections in the world. Women, in contrast as children bonded to their mothers, and as adults bonded to their children, remain aware and part of emotional connections with the world and others. Therefore, for Hartsock, the result of the role bequeathed to women in the

---

Box 2.1 Epistemological and political claims

Marxist Claim

1 Material life structures and limits the understandings people can have of the social relations that they are part of.
2 In contemporary society, material life is structured via opposing viewpoints.
3 The ruling group structures patterns of life and relations from its perspective, so its viewpoint is not simply false.
4 The oppressed group struggles to articulate a view of the world that is distinct from the dominant viewpoint.
5 The oppressed group's viewpoint can expose the 'real' relations that lie beneath the surface and 'carries a historically liberatory role'.
(Hartsock, 1998: 108)

Feminist Standpoint Claim

1 The sexual division of labour means that women and men have different experiences and understandings of the social world.
2 Women and men have opposing views of the world, men relate to the world through abstract masculinity, women – potentially – through the feminist standpoint.
3 Abstract masculinity produces a distorted pattern of life, damaging to nature and human beings.
4 Feminist consciousness-raising can be the vehicle for women to recognise their position in society and the structures that lie behind their oppression.
5 The feminist standpoint can expose 'the world men have constructed ... it embodies a distress which requires a solution'. (*Ibid.*: 125)

---

reproduction and rearing of children is 'the construction of female existence as centred with a complex relational nexus' (1998: 116). This form of existence is the direct opposite to abstract masculinity in that it leads to a construction of the self that opposes dualisms, values concrete everyday life, and is able to sense connection and continuities 'both with other persons and with the natural world' (*ibid.*: 120).

Within the same time period that Hartsock was laying the groundwork for her account, other writers were also beginning to explore the potential of standpoint perspectives. The ongoing debate about the suitability of and foundations to standpoint theory has developed into different themes focused on experience and objectivity.

Experience

Dorothy E. Smith, in writings first published in the late 1970s, has developed one of the most influential – and critiqued – accounts of standpoint's roots in women's experiences and the 'everyday world as problematic' (1987: 88). Smith argues that academic methods of theorizing the social world and approaching objectivity have developed from a male point of view, echoing the ideology of those in power. Academic methods of understanding the world have made the lives and experiences of women invisible and have denied the legitimacy of looking directly at everyday life. Smith's **women's standpoint** begins in direct experience, and grounds theorizing in the fundamental relationship people have with the material world.

Women's experiences cannot be understood within the consciousness of those who rule; instead, feminism needs to develop a social form of expression and intelligibility that is separate from the male standpoint. Similarly to Hartsock, Smith moves towards defining the experiences that women have, and share and which require an alternative framework to comprehend. For Smith, 'women's lives tend to show a loose, episodic structure' (*ibid.*: 66) made of up relationships and bonds to others, rather than definitions of self and instrumental interest. Women are capable of generating alternative frameworks for exploring the significance of their experience in analysing patriarchy, because they lie outside the dominant discourses that provide partial and perverse explanations. This conceptualization can be the core of women's agency; suggesting they maintain the knowledge needed to generate a better society. Smith argues that she is not treating women's everyday lives, on their own, as a source of revolutionary change; everyday experiences are the starting point for an inquiry that will develop an empirically-rooted and evaluated theoretical framework for explaining oppression and the relations that lie behind the sexual division of labour. Listening to women requires theoretical engagement to develop its full significance and meaning. The test of validity for the theories, which develop from the standpoint of women, would be to check 'back to how it actually is' (*ibid.*: 122).

Experience is one of the most contested aspects of standpoint theories. Critics focus on the danger of such a stance creating a false homogeneity about women's experiences, in particular the focus given to child-rearing by both Hartsock and Smith (Crary, 2001). While feminism 'cannot avoid the challenge of theorizing experience' (Mohanty, 1995: 71), there is little agreement on how that should occur. Hartsock and Smith's representation of the relational world of women, opposed to the dichotomous world of men, gives women an identity that is easily read as authentic. Once experience becomes the basis of theorizing and activism, the obvious question is which experiences are the core experiences that women are supposed to share?

Writers influenced by postmodern ideas have questioned the privileging of certain kinds of direct experience as the basis of political activity and the assertion that a direct relationship between actual experiences and political 'truths' is possible (Scott, 1992). If 'experience is *so* diverse, identity *so* fragmented, it is not possible to extract from the particular configuration of subjective characteristics informing individual outlook' (Conaghan, 2000: 367, original emphasis). Mary Hawkesworth rejects standpoint claims about the superiority of particular positions and experiences because:

> In relying upon experience as the ground of truth, feminist standpoint theory ... fails to do justice to the fallibility of human knowers, the multiplicity and diversity of women's experiences, and the theoretical constitution of experience. (1999: 135)

Nancy A. Naples (1999), while arguing that experiences are important trigger points to people's political perspectives and activism, suggests they can be problematic when they become the basis of a 'privileged stance' – I have been there/you have not. While a particular set of experiences may allow certain structures of oppression to become visible, they cannot make all processes visible.

Susan J. Hekman (1997) summarizes some of the difficulties present in standpoint arguments, in particular those of Hartsock, Smith and Sandra Harding (discussed below). She highlights three major problems:

1 Marxist foundations are no longer appropriate for exploring experience and knowledge.
2 Standpoint theories are ill-equipped to deal with difference.
3 Postmodern recognition of multiplicity and deconstruction of experience and knowledge make standpoint arguments appear old fashioned and naïve.

Hekman acknowledges that standpoint theories ask an important question for feminism: 'How do we justify the truth of the feminist claims that women have been and are oppressed' (*ibid.*: 342)? But their solution – the privileging of a particular group of experiences shared by women – is mistaken. While standpoint perspectives share the postmodern suspicion of the unified subject and the universality of knowledge, their desire to retain a belief that some forms of knowledge are better than others does not follow through the postmodern claim that sees all forms of knowledge claims as relative.

The key response made by standpoint theorists is to argue that they do not treat experience as innocently as their critics suggest. Hartsock (1997) and Smith (1997) reject that women – as mothers – automatically have better knowledge; experience must be interpreted and analysed before having meaning for political activism. Hartsock has acknowledged that there were some problems with her articulation of a feminist standpoint. By attempting to stay true to the Marxist framework her analysis wrongly retained the belief that societal relations are structured into two opposing groups (in her case sexes). Her presentation of two opposing modes of thought – abstract masculinity versus the feminist standpoint – denied other forms of human experience and relations, which can generate situated and heterogeneous knowledge of the world. However, what she wants to retain is the possibility that multiple subjectivities still share 'social and collective points of view' that operate 'as standpoints' (1998: 244).

While most feminists agree there are difficulties with working with experience, those working with standpoint perspectives argue that feminism cannot do without it. For example, Joanne Conaghan (2000) warns against assuming that no relationship between experience and theory is possible and suggests that discursive analysis is not an alternative to claims that some experiences are important for some women and therefore for feminism. Rather than deny the possibility of making some forms of general statements based on women's experiences, what needs to be thought through is the scope of and contexts where some forms of generalization are possible. This requires a consideration of the basis from which standpoint theorists justify the legitimacy of their arguments. In particular, how they attempt to retain a claim about objectivity.

Objectivity

Privileging particular experiences implies some objective criteria for selecting the ones that count. However, standpoint theorists challenge claims to objective neutrality and universalism. They also reject the view that their arguments are relativistic. The question is what kind of objective validity do they give the experiences that they identify and the claims they make? In standpoint accounts the focus is on giving objectivity a political dimension, while also believing that the framework can express some 'truth' and reality about women's lives.

In a direct response to Hekman's critique, Hartsock (1997), Harding (1997) and Patricia Hill Collins (1997) all argue for a politicized notion of objectivity. They assert that their concern is not with obtaining a theory of epistemology defendable only on philosophical grounds. Instead, they aim to develop theories that generate arguments about the reality of oppression, which are politically useful to women and feminism. This leaves objectivity as both contingent and real – from the politicized and embodied perspective of those who experience the results of oppression. What makes some ways of obtaining and forming knowledge better is what the knowledge produced can do. Knowledge obtained via standpoint strategies leads to awareness of harm and agendas for change, and on these grounds it is better knowledge.

Standpoint theorists reject universal objectivity, because they argue that claims to knowledge always come from somewhere. Epistemologically, the 'god-trick' is not possible; to know something of how the world works you have to be somewhere in that world. For standpoint writers universal objectivity is an ideology based in the abstract instrumentality of male modes of ruling. Because rulers are not involved in the reproduction of the material and social world, the irony is that they can only capture a perverse and narrow understanding of how relations between people and the material world exist. The objectivity associated with traditional social science and Smith's male mode of ruling is disembodied and thus unable to incorporate an awareness of the processes involved in the reproduction and continued existence of the human body.

Feminist engagements with scientific narratives of objectivity are an important foundation to objectivity debates in feminist standpoint theories. Feminist critiques of scientific activity echo the claims made by Smith and Hartsock and search for alternative epistemologies to justify a different approach to understanding how the world works. While there are a range of feminist critiques of science, most share a disquiet with dominant scientific approaches developed in the Enlightenment, which present science as a neutral activity capable of generating universal and true knowledge about the human condition (Merchant, 1980). Feminists have worked to shatter the illusion of neutrality and universality in science by reinterpreting it as inherently political and subjective (Hughes, 1995). Various feminists argue that science has become 'male', aimed at control and domination and unable to value emotion and connection. It is important to note that some feminists have disputed the vision of science such critics present. Ismay Barwell (1994) argues that standpoint perspectives – and other rejections of objectivity – rest on questionable interpretations that fail to recognize the contingency and situatedness already present in Enlightenment models of scientific endeavour.

Harding (1993a,b), an important critic of mainstream scientific methodology, has produced one of the most detailed accounts of the standpoint approach to objectivity. Her initial intent is to offer an alternative to scientific empiricist epistemologies, arguing that feminism cannot improve science by removing the sources of bias. A different way of knowing the world is required to challenge and provide alternatives to such filters.

Harding supports Hartsock and Smith's assertion that women have been excluded from the structures that have produced knowledge of the world, therefore their lives and experiences could 'decrease the partialities and distortions in the picture of nature and social life provided by the natural and social sciences' (1991: 121). However, this does not mean that women's experiences, of whatever type, can generate objective knowledge. They can generate interesting claims to knowledge, but something else is needed to produce a standpoint. As with other standpoint theorists, the experiences articulated by women must then be conceptualized through theoretical engagement within feminist politics and observation of social relations.

Harding retains a belief in objectivity by arguing that the 'scientifically better' location to generate knowledge of the world is the location marginal to those who rule and produce dominant knowledge. Feminist researchers are 'outsiders within' (*ibid.*: 131–2), living and conceptualizing 'the gap between the lives of "outsiders" and the lives of "insiders" and their favored conceptual schemes' (*ibid.*: 132). This position increases the level of objectivity generated by feminist standpoint research. Harding uses the term **strong objectivity** to define her position (1995). Strong objectivity is situated within scientific method; it asserts that claims generated from particular locations will be 'less false' than others. The argument moves through the following stages:

1 society is stratified by various divisions, including, 'race'/ethnicity, sexuality, class and gender;
2 people in privileged positions cannot see some of the processes that place them in that position and have a vested interest in not seeing; and
3 the problems of the marginalized can be the starting point of politics and science, because resolving their problems can create a better society for everyone.

The standpoint of the marginalized is more 'objective' because they are more conscious of the difficulties produced by the current way of doing things. Once the questions which emerge from their lives are made central, the less valid the perspectives that dominate society's way of thinking about the world appear. Research cannot evoke neutrality in its methods and questions when 'a hierarchically organized society exists' (1991: 134).

Donna J. Haraway produces a similar and equally influential discussion of objectivity in her article 'Situated Knowledges: The Science Question in Feminism and the Privilege of Partial Perspective', first published in 1988 in *Feminist Studies* and reprinted in *Simians, Cyborgs and Women: The Reinvention of Nature* (1991). Haraway begins by warning against creating a false and simplistic dichotomy between bad male 'objective' science and good feminist 'relativistic' science. Feminist critiques of science have created a problem for themselves by concluding that no knowledge claim can be privileged over others. Science, in 'the radical social constructionist programme' (1991: 185), is reduced to a rhetorical exercise, contested and produced within wider power relations. This is problematic, *if* it does not allow claims – necessary for political action – about the real world. Are claims to oppression simply another subjective, equally valid and equally contestable knowledge claim? In lyrical language Haraway indicates the impasse feminist critiques of objectivity and science have led to:

> I, and others, started out wanting a strong tool for deconstructing the truth claims of hostile science by showing the radical historical specificity, and so contestability, of *every* layer of the onion of scientific and technological constructions, and we end up with a kind of epistemological electro-shock therapy, which far from ushering us into the high stakes tables of the game of contesting public truths, lays us out on the table with self-induced multiple personality disorder. (*Ibid.*: 186, original emphasis)

The desire to challenge the foundations of scientific objectivity ended with 'one more excuse for not learning any post-Newtonian physics' (*ibid.*: 186). By ruling that all forms of scientific knowledge are contestable, feminism disallows progressive as well as reactionary claims to knowledge.

As a political entity, feminism must do more than deconstruct; it, like Marxism, must work towards 'a better account of the world' (*ibid.*: 187), and achieving such an account involves:

> A no-nonsense commitment to faithful accounts of a 'real' world, one that can be partially shared and friendly to earth-wide projects of finite freedom, adequate material abundance, modest meaning in suffering, and limited happiness. (*Ibid.*: 187)

This agenda only appears inconsistent with objectivity if being objective is defined as being transcendent. Haraway proposes 'a doctrine of embodied objectivity that accommodates paradoxical and critical feminist science projects: feminist objectivity means quite simply *situated knowledges*' (*ibid.*: 188, original emphasis). The move away from the 'god-trick' – of believing disembodied and abstract objectivity is possible – produces useful objectivity based in the particularity of vision and place. Evaluating the knowledge claims of others requires knowledge of the position from which they make that claim. However, Haraway warns against romanticizing the position of the subjugated as – necessarily – the best position from which to generate knowledge about the real world. The subjugated standpoint is no more innocent than that of the powerful.

Harding and Haraway reject any notion that women share an essential set of experiences, and both are less willing than other standpoint writers to stipulate the types of world view that are generated by the standpoint of particular groups. What they do argue is that 'embodied' objectivity is collective or communal – not individual. Social and political relations, not the characteristics of the particular groups, shape experiences and understandings of the world. Experience of oppressive relations produces 'situated' knowledge of the problems that face human beings, but not their answers.

Both Harding and Haraway point to the contemporary ways that collective experience is understood in standpoint perspectives. Communities are understood in a dynamic sense, formed in the relations that they share and conceptualize. In the words of Naples 'community is constructed, sustained, and redefined by community members in different contexts' (1999: 48). This focus on collective experiences and articulations is based on the assumption that the self emerges collectively, therefore so does the interpretation of experience (Hallstein, 1999). For example, Naples proposes a dynamic sense of the collective expression of being an outsider, which is rooted in particular spaces and times; people move from being insiders to outsiders in different collective encounters and experiences. Lynn H. Nelson (1993) challenges arguments that suggest that individuals can generate knowledge, knowing agents are community agents. Arguing that knowledge is generated at the level of community is more than saying communities can produce agreed consensus; this understanding suggests that knowledge pre-exists the process of community negotiation. Instead, it is to say that 'your knowing or mine depends on our knowing' (1993: 124). When we produce and evaluate knowledge we do so through community-defined sets of standards and arguments.

The political and collective foundation to expressions of knowledge is fundamental to Haraway and Harding's defence against relativism. As with other standpoint articulations, they argue that collective knowledge claims about the real world can be defended on political as well as epistemological grounds: 'It follows that politics and ethics ground struggles for the contests over what may count as rational knowledge' (Haraway, 1991: 193). Critical knowledge, which emerges from both political and epistemological coalition endeavours, makes a particular and an objective claim about how the world actually is (Weeks, 1996).

In summary, standpoint perspectives have developed over time, moving on from an initial articulation that linked women's experiences of reproduction to alternative and resistant bodies of knowledge. Recent articulations focus on the situated nature of objectivity and any claim to knowledge, but retain the desire to link social position to the generation of 'better' knowledge.

Political uses

Some Black feminists have looked to a standpoint framework to articulate experiences of marginalization, subsequent collective consciousness and the grounds for political action. They have explored the similar knowledge (not always constituted as a standpoint) which can develop from the marginal locations experienced by being female and a member of a particular racial or ethnic group (hooks, 1984; Moya, 1997). In part, this work has emerged as a response to the exclusion of 'race' and ethnicity issues from mainstream feminism in the 1970s (Guy-Sheftall, 1995; Mirza, 1997; Ramazanoglu, 1986).

Black feminist standpoint

Collins (1991) has developed a Black feminist standpoint perspective to encompass the experiences of being both Black and female in the United States (one that has been challenged by other Black feminists (James, 1999)). Her analysis highlights many of the key arguments of standpoint theory and the way it can be used to direct both theoretical engagement and political action. For Collins, standpoints are rooted in the political activism of marginalized groups struggling collectively against 'the matrix of domination' (a term Collins borrows from hooks) (Collins, 1991: 234). African American history indicates a strong recognition – necessary for survival – of the collective basis on which both experience and change occur. Due to this history and the struggles that have ensued, 'Black women have a self-defined standpoint of their own oppression' (Collins, 1995: 339).

Marginalized groups achieve a better standpoint because of their position outside mainstream epistemologies and explanations of how the world operates. Challenges to oppressive ideas about the inferiority of Black people are unlikely to come from the dominant modes of thought which produced the ideas in the first place. When African American women move into areas of privilege, they become aware of their identity as 'outsiders-within' (*ibid.*: 350), and through this experience can 'trace the line of fault' that exists between the different worlds they now move between. For example, African American women scholars have the privilege of existing in an academic world and the problem of dealing with the racist frameworks and language that make up that world. The history that African American women share means they have 'a distinct set of experiences that offers a different view of material reality', which stimulates 'a distinctive Black feminist consciousness' (Collins, 1995: 339). However, the wider system makes it difficult for this consciousness to be articulated. What is needed is Black feminist thought to produce a framework in which this knowledge can be articulated and acted upon.

The content of a Black feminist standpoint is rooted in an 'Afrocentric feminist epistemology'. Significantly, the way in which this epistemology attempts to understand the world echoes the way of looking at the world associated with women. Based on this observation, Collins proposes that 'the material conditions of oppression can vary dramatically and yet generate some uniformity in the epistemologies of subordinate groups' (1991: 207). The key value and approach to the world, which Collins identifies as Afrocentric, is the role of wisdom drawn from experience. Experience, and drawing from the particularity of that experience, remains important to Black academics in a way that challenges the presumed superiority of 'white masculinist epistemologies' (Collins, 1995: 346). Remaining rooted in the concreteness of experience ensures that Black feminist standpoint perspectives articulate a politics of change which is embodied, empathetic and connected to others.

Collins argues that the knowledge and wisdom of African American women, which is the root of Afrocentric feminist epistemology, is consciously generated in collective experiences and explorations of both their history and present situation. Groups are brought together through 'common location within hierarchical power relations' (*ibid.*: 376), which for African American women are the 'long-standing patterns of racial segregation in the United States' (*ibid.*: 376). Again, it is not through individual choice that people become members of different groups; at the global level we are positioned within different group locations depending on the form of oppression we face at that particular time. While we may wish to be individuals and experience free agency, patterns of oppression still emerge from 'group-based experience' (*ibid.*: 377).

Collins argues that her notion of group location does not disallow recognition of multiple patterns of oppression, division and group membership. Groups marginalized in different ways develop their own standpoints, which can come together to develop a richer picture of patterns of oppression that have 'stronger' objectivity. The politics that this represents is consensus and coalition, rather than the segregation of different camps and 'fixed' standpoints (see Mann and Kelley, 1997, for a critique of her claim here).

In a number of debates within Black feminism we can see standpoint perspectives being used to ground both theoretical arguments and political activism. Some argue that Collins's Black feminist standpoint reflects the core links made by Black feminism between experience, theory and activism. Heidi Safia Mirza argues that it is important for Black feminism to recognize the relationship between local experiences and identities, and the wider structures that inform their production. She stresses that the 'theoretical framework of black feminism combines the reality of our personal experience within the context of a definite economic and political overview'

(1986: 103). Collins (2000) has used Black feminist standpoint epistemology to examine the 'black political economy' in the United States. Starting from the specific experiences of African American women's lives indicates the intersection of structures of gender, 'race' and class operating via issues relating to property, consumerism and marriage-rights to produce Black female poverty. The agenda for challenge that this produces is one that begins by advocating financial independence for Black women, includes an awareness of the role of family norms, rights and structures, and finally resists public and private distinctions which place questions of family and gender outside the scope of economic analysis.

Hawkesworth (1999) argues that African American perspectives on welfare policies (in comparison to liberal and socialist feminist approaches) emerge from a standpoint rooted in their experiences in the United States. This leads to an interpretation that focuses on policies as incorporating a 'racist code, grounded in white supremacy, that reasserts racial stratification' (1999: 146). The standpoint highlights the ways that a framework of white superiority lies behind the conservative critique of welfare policies, enabling a false representation of social problems, which 'provides a soothing balm to the egos of thoroughly mediocre whites' (*ibid.*: 147). This standpoint allows for an engagement with policy discourses rooted in the experience of those marginalized by welfare strategies and highlights the structures of oppression that lie behind the policies.

Bannerji discusses the academic, social and personal exclusion she experienced as an Indian woman studying in Canada. In these experiences 'my self and interests were rendered more silent than I would have thought possible' (1995: 57). Conceptualizing this personal experience as something she had in common with others marginalized and harmed by neo-colonialism and racist practice in academic method and wider society became the cornerstone to her theoretical writing and political activism. Bannerji uses the standpoint notion of 'outsider within' to outline how her – and others' – experiences of being non-white in the privileged arena of education can be the basis of challenge and critique:

> we non-white women, can begin to use our alienating experiences in classrooms as the point of departure or a set of references for a comprehensive social analysis. Any such experience of alienation holds in it the double awareness of being 'self' and the 'other', our personal and public modes of being. (*Ibid.*: 88)

Joy James (1996) makes a similar argument when she notes the constant questioning she receives to 'prove' her ability to be present and teach theory. She notes that for her, 'teaching theory courses on the praxis of African American women permits me to claim that I think. Connecting my teaching to community organizing allows me to say I theorize' (1996: 38).

Standpoint perspectives can and have been used by particular groups to:

- Explore the significance of their experiences for the ways in which they look at the world and desire it to be different.
- Conceptualize the link between collective experience, knowledge and action.
- Validate experiences and forms of knowledge denied legitimacy in mainstream ways of knowing.
- Form coalitions with other marginalized groups who have developed similar knowledge and agendas for political action.

The dilemmas to consider in their use are:

- Do some processes, connections and experiences need to be denied to allow the standpoint to come together?
- Do aspects of people's group identity and affiliation remain denied to forge a collective position?
- Does it allow varied group histories, positions and projects to come together or force them apart?

Conclusion

Standpoint perspectives developed out of two important sources. The first was a wish to use material experience to build collective theoretical understandings; this work maintains a Marxist interest in the division of labour, but broadens out that division to include the reproduction of life. The second source was the aim to rescue objectivity from universalism and instead define it as situated and political. The variations on standpoint theory that have developed all focus on the relationship between experience and theory. In particular, the stress is on collective or community-based understandings of experience. Hartsock has summarized what is fundamental to standpoint perspectives:

1 Marginalized people are not better, and certainly not lucky, but they are 'less likely to mistake themselves for the universal man' (1998: 241).
2 Knowledge is more than a story, but is not founded in absolute truth, what it needs to be is 'good enough' to generate political activism.
3 Practical daily activity can produce – through collective debate – understandings of the world.

4 Constituting alternative epistemologies is a difficult and collective enterprise.
5 Standpoints can be calls to political action.

Therefore, feminist standpoint theory can be thought of as a distinct way to think about the links between experience, knowledge and political change, which aims to incorporate the multiple experiences and the positions of various oppressed social groups in society.

Critics of standpoint theory warn of the dangers of going down the problematic road of identifying commonalties in how women feel and think. I feel that this criticism is valid, certainly in the initial accounts by Hartsock and Smith. However, the shift marked by Haraway and Harding is important. For them women and other marginalized groups share common problems, rather than a common outlook, and this is a more defendable position. This proposition has more scope for acknowledging that women will also experience different problems and different outlooks on life. From the life experiences of varied marginalized groups can emerge agendas for identifying the crucial political problems of our time, problems that are not visible from positions of power and prestige. What women and other marginalized groups share are collective experiences of being the outsider to methods of ruling and theorizing the world. Women and others do not experience outsider status as individuals, we become this by proxy, via our bond to particular communities and groups. Beginning processes of theorizing in such experiences ensures against exclusions that will limit the objectivity of the ideas produced. This shared experience of 'being there' may be traumatic, but it can generate an understanding of the costs of marginalization, which can be a foundation for collective and coalition politics.

Standpoint theory is significant for trying to theorize the different material position of women and link it to knowledge claims. The next chapter examines the 'ethics of care' debate, which centres on whether women and men exist within different moral worlds, leading to different approaches to making judgements. Here, too, questions of difference amongst women have problematized the claims made within the debate.

FURTHER READING

Nancy Hartsock (1998) *'The Feminist Standpoint Revisited' and Other Essays* (Boulder, Colorado: Westview). Various books contain Hartsock's essay, but the Introduction here and other texts provide invaluable context and reflection.

Rosemary Hennessy and Chrys Ingraham (1997) *Materialist Feminism: A Reader in Class, Difference, and Women's Lives* (London: Routledge).

This Reader brings together classic texts from Marxist and socialist feminism in the 1970s with current work. Some of this material is very difficult to get hold of elsewhere; an invaluable resource.

E.F. Keller and H.E. Longino (eds) (1996) *Feminism and Science* (Oxford: Oxford University Press). A useful introduction to feminist debates on science; the chapters by Keller and Harding are particularly relevant to the discussion here.

The ethics of care

CONTENTS

Theories for understanding morality within philosophy and psychology approach definitions of fair judgements and good moral actors in a universal discourse. However, the debates on difference destabilize the terms in which we approach what is moral and just. The ethics of care is one feminist response for exploring the contextual nature of moral judgement and action.

The ethics of care debate brings together psychology, philosophy and political theory. It began as a feminist challenge to the way in which psychology defines women as morally inadequate. It has sought to replace traditional moral theory appeals to universality and reason, with a concern with the particular and caring responsibilities. Its emergence has led to a debate, at some points fraught, within feminism about the nature and significance of care. To understand the development of the ethics of care it is important to outline the arguments it has wished to challenge, in particular the work of Jean Piaget and Lawrence Kohlberg. After detailing the feminist challenge the chapter summarizes the first major feminist alternative to develop: Carol Gilligan's *In a Different Voice* (1993a). It will move on to feminist criticisms of Gilligan, and new political articulations of an ethics of care that have emerged out of them. The Political Uses section discusses the ways in which an ethics of care framework can be used to interrogate the treatment of care in welfare debates and policies.

Outline of the key perspective

The gender difference framework within psychology can be traced back to Sigmund Freud (1961). His work concluded that men are more able to think with reason and rationality, while women are trapped in immediacy and emotion. The identification of a hierarchy of thought processes, with reason and rationality at the top and emotion and particularity at the bottom, has continued to influence psychology's approach to differences in moral outlook. Two key theorists – Piaget and Kohlberg – have produced models for understanding the development of moral thinking which remain influential today. Their ideas have been important frameworks for feminism to challenge in order to bring forward new explanations of the different moral lives of women.

Jean Piaget

In the 1920s, Piaget (1932) developed theories and models for understanding the acquisition of moral values and reasoning amongst children. His approach was influenced by a structuralist philosophy: thought processes can be split into different structures of interpretation and judgement within which new events or processes are conceptualized. Children move from one mental structure to the next when new experiences and processes cannot be explained within the existing structure. They move through different structures of understanding to become increasingly developed in their moral thinking. Morality can be thought of as a set of rules. The question is how children come to recognize the correct rules.

Children learn how to be moral and follow rules through playing games. Morality is not something that can be imposed on children; instead it develops through their interactions with their peer group, within which game play is of fundamental importance. Piaget observed children playing; in particular he studied boys of different ages playing marbles. Through watching their game he outlined the staged development of moral thinking through different structures of understanding and judgement:

- Stage 1: motor response – marbles are played without any concept of purpose or direction.
- Stage 2: egocentric response – rules begin to influence play, but the child is still primarily playing by himself.
- Stage 3: cooperation – players play to win within the rules, but the rules retain a level of ambiguity and vagueness.
- Stage 4: codification of rules – the procedures and rules of the game are shared and followed by all concerned.

As children move through stages 2 to 4, they are developing different approaches to rules. Movement through the stages can be thought of as 'a sort of law of evolution in the moral development of the child' (1932: 225). Once they reach stage 4, they no longer follow rules because they are supposed to or because of coercion; instead, stage 4 rules are the result of mutual consent achieved through cognitive and rational deliberation. Rules are no longer sacred and unquestionable; instead they can be renegotiated amongst those actors sharing the same structural framework. In adopting the rules as codified the child swaps personal fantasy for 'a common and obligatory imagery which will go hand in hand with the code of rules itself' (*ibid.*: 24–5).

Piaget argued, radically for the time, that it is better for the child to learn the processes involved in following moral rules, rather than simply being obligated to by others, particularly adults. In game play children are gaining the skills that will enable them to come to reasoned and consensual decisions. From his study of games, Piaget drew inferences about the operation of moral rules in society. Good judgements are those that are reached after careful discussion, and reason emerges in interaction and cooperation. The development of both autonomy and agreed rules of morality shared by all is an important aspect of the production of society. If society's rules are the product of cooperation and reason, then reciprocity and distributive justice take precedence over punishment and retributive justice. Notions of equity of treatment and judgement develop alongside the evolving development of rules and cooperation. At least some element of being equitable involves a reasoned ability to think of individuals in 'relation to the particular situation of each' (*ibid.*: 316).

Piaget studied boys playing marbles; he also wondered about girls, how do they approach rules and morality? He observed girls playing hide and seek, a simpler game than marbles, because he was 'questioning only girls' (*ibid.*: 66). The legal/rule-bound approach to game play was 'far less developed in little girls than in boys' (*ibid.*: 69). The index to the first English edition simply says 'girls, deficient in legal sense' (*ibid.*: 416). Hide and seek, as well as other games girls play, requires fewer rules and 'never presents the splendid codification and complicated jurisprudence of the game of marbles' (*ibid.*: 70). The girls do develop through increasing rule recognition, but they never reach the universal quality of rule cooperation obtained by the boys.

Lawrence Kohlberg

The major contributions Kohlberg (1981) made to ideas about moral development occurred in the 1960s and 1970s when he was based at Harvard's Center for Moral Education. His major research was a longitudinal study of a large group of American boys as they grew into adulthood. His approach concentrated on analysing people's responses to particular moral dilemmas. A key dilemma he used was the 'The Heinz Dilemma':

> In Europe, a woman was near death from a very bad disease, a special kind of cancer. There was one drug that the doctors thought might save

her. It was a form of radium that a druggist in the same town had recently discovered. The drug was expensive to make, but the druggist was charging ten times what the drug cost him to make. He paid $200 for the radium and charged $2,000 for a small dose of the drug. The sick woman's husband Heinz, went to everyone he knew to borrow the money, but he could get together only $1,000, which was half of what it cost. He told the druggist that his wife was dying and asked him to sell it cheaper or let him pay later. But the druggist said, 'No, I discovered the drug and I'm going to make money from it.' Heinz got desperate and broke into the man's store to steal the drug for his wife. (1981: 12)

It was not important whether the boys said Heinz was right to do what he did; instead it was the reasoning they employed to come to their judgement. Progressively, at different speeds, the boys moved up the moral hierarchy in order to make increasingly rational and cognitively-based judgements about the dilemma. From the changing responses of the boys as they grew up, Kohlberg generated a typological scheme which could represent the process of moral development. Like Piaget, he argued that as children grow they develop the cognitive skills, through social interaction, with which to make moral judgements. He produced a hierarchy of moral thinking; as an infant develops he moves from judging the world in simplistic ways, through six stages, until as an adult he is able to make good moral judgements. Not all individuals reach the sixth stage, or reach each stage at the same age, but all must go through the same path, and all if they reach the final stage of the hierarchy will share the same principles from which they make judgements. The six stages (*ibid.*: 17–18) can be summarized as:

- *Pre-conventional level*
    Stage 1: the punishment and obedience orientation
    Stage 2: the instrumental relativist orientation

- *Conventional level*
    Stage 3: the interpersonal concordance or 'Good boy – nice girl' orientation
    Stage 4: society maintaining orientation

- *Postconventional level*
    Stage 5: the social contract orientation
    Stage 6: the universal ethical principle orientation.

What is significant about the stages is that they represent the increasing reduction of particular and emotional response in favour of universal, abstract and rational judgements. If stage 6 is reached, what lies at the heart of judgement is 'principles of justice, of the reciprocity and equality of human rights, and of respect for the dignity of human beings as individuals' (*ibid.*: 19). As with Piaget, Kohlberg's model leads to a celebration of rationality and autonomy as the foundations to our ability to judge well.

Kohlberg stresses that the stages 'seem to represent an invariant developmental sequence' (*ibid.*: 20). To test this he undertook cross-cultural analysis of boys' responses to his dilemmas. Based on this study he asserted that 'I can propose a solution to the relativity problem that has plagued philosophers for three thousand years' (*ibid.*: 12). The individual results of moral thinking might vary because of the contexts in which those judgements would take place, but the principles behind those varied judgements will be the same. For boys, in any area of the globe, the highest form of moral reasoning involves questions of duty, the morally right and impersonal ideals. Kohlberg later undertook a study of women and scored their responses using the same six stages (Kohlberg and Kramer, 1969). He found that women could only reach stage 3, because they remained centred on irrational values of pleasing others and immediacy. He felt that this deficiency could be rectified, if women spent more time in the public sphere they would be able to develop further in their ability to correctly morally judge. Other researchers using his stages have come to the same conclusion (Broverman *et al.*, 1972).

Various social and political theorists build upon Kohlberg and Piaget's model of human cognitive development in their ideas. Of particular importance is Jürgen Habermas's adoption of their model in his articulation of a communicative public sphere discussed in Chapter 1. Habermas (1990) uses the notion that people gradually develop an ability to think rationally and universally to argue that a public sphere is possible, which has an 'orientation' towards universality and is based on values of reason and justice.

In summary Piaget and Kohlberg's main claims are that:

- The development of morality moves through various stages, the order of which is universal and hierarchical.
- The higher stages of moral judgement are premised in reason and rationality.
- Independent and autonomous actors are the most capable of moral judgement.
- Reason and rationality allow moral judgement to be based on universal rules, agreed to by all.
- Women have difficulty being able to follow and agree to rules.

Feminist critiques

There are arguments within Piaget and Kohlberg's work that are in keeping with feminist perspectives. In particular, there are two aspects of both their models which their reinterpreters and critics have maintained. First, the importance both give to social interaction in the development of moral thinking is retained. Second, most reconstructions maintain the assertion that a desire for equality and recognition of individual human worth are important moral values. However, feminists charge that structuring moral thought around a hierarchy and prioritizing impartiality is deeply flawed. It is worth noting that feminists are not the only writers to make such criticisms (Williams, 1985).

The first obvious problem with Piaget and Kohlberg's moral hierarchies is women's apparent inability to reach the higher stages. Are women simply lesser moral actors? Even if it were empirically true that women did not respond to moral problems in a way that reflects the later stages of their models, how can the models claim to present human development if only one half of the population has any chance of reaching the higher stages? There appears to be an unwritten assumption that human refers to men. A framework constructed from studies of one half of the population is used to define the other half as inadequate. Could the fault be with the framework, rather than with women? In Gilligan's words 'the failure of women to fit existing models of human growth may point to a problem in the representation, a limitation in the conception of the human condition, an omission of certain truths about life' (Gilligan, 1993a: 2). It is worth noting that in response to Gilligan and others, Kohlberg later defined stage 6 as a 'matter of theoretical and philosophic speculation' (Levine *et al.*, 1985: 97), rather than a stage that identified anyone's observed response to moral dilemmas.

The next concern is the approaches to judgement that are identified as the pinnacle of moral and cognitive development (Porter, 1999). Ethical decision-making appears to be a process geared at discovering 'the highest principle, in order to determine which claim should take precedence' (Sevenhuijsen, 1998: 12). As we saw in Chapter 1, the application of universal highest principles is only fair if all are similar in their position in society and in their needs and wants (Held, 1997; Opotow, 1990). Since we know that this is not the case, denying the significance of difference equates to 'privileged irresponsibility' (Tronto, 1993b). Requiring people to approach all problems in an abstract rational way inhibits the different styles that can be applicable (Turkle and Seymour, 1990). If we acknowledge that society includes people who want different things and think in different ways, then talk of the common good, the universal right, requires a lack of recognition of those varied wants and thoughts.

Recognition of difference helps indicate the role of particular interests in the formation of supposedly universal rules and frameworks. The right to autonomy and property has taken precedence in moral and political thought because it has suited the interests of a particular group in society. In this case it is the values associated with men and masculinity which are being presented as universal. The problem is not that this celebrates men's capabilities over those of women. The problem is that it is a fiction, a fiction 'of an individual who imagines himself free from particular relationships and living conditions as well as from his dependence on women and the existence of "feminine" characteristic within himself' (Sevenhuijsen, 1998: 48). There is no essential reason, either biological or cognitive, why men are capable of reason and incapable of emotion. Or that reason is a higher value than care. However, by constantly focusing on questions of autonomy and reason, moral theorists and others such as Habermas give the impression, by omission, that they believe these values are of a higher order than notions of care and interdependence.

The good citizen is presented as the actor capable of reason and rationality (Benhabib, 1992). This seems a narrow definition of what values and attitudes can make someone a good citizen. The citizen can be thought of in this way because there is an assumption that 'there will always be a group of women doing the caring necessary to the acquisition of the sense of justice' (Moore, 1999: 12). The invisibility of care in discussions of morality stems from the separation of the private and public sphere. This separation places care outside the consideration of public actors and public dilemmas, but to do so is to deny the possibility that the public can benefit from responses generated from empathy, intimacy and care. The dominant approach to citizenship and the public sphere helps create the notion that care is 'above and below' politics (Tronto, 1995, quoted in Sevenhuijsen, 1998). The removal of concerns about care confirms that the public sphere is a site of commerce, individuality and property. It is a site where contract, rather than trust or negotiation, is favoured as the mediator of morality (Baier, 1997: 617). Therefore, while Piaget and Kohlberg make explicit claims to universality, their frameworks are rooted in Western patterns of life, in particular the separation of the public sphere from the private.

To conclude, feminist criticisms of Piaget and Kohlberg argue that their vision of the moral world is inadequate; it remains blind to interconnected, situated and different kinds of people, needs and wants. An abstract model of reason and rationality can only leave morality as judgmental and intolerant; a different 'repertoire' of moral response is needed for feminism. What would happen if you started from women's lives to build a picture of moral thinking and judgement?

Feminist incorporations

The feminist challenge to existing models of moral and intellectual development has been the springboard to a vital element of current feminist thinking and debate: the ethics of care. What it reflects is a desire to find different moral approaches appropriate to different areas of human life (Held, 1984), and it began with Gilligan's *In a Different Voice*, first published in 1982. In Gilligan's text she refers to an 'ethic of care', whilst other feminists talk of the ethics of care. Ethic of care will be used to refer to Gilligan and where others use this form, elsewhere ethics of care will be used.

Carol Gilligan's ethic of care

Gilligan worked with Kohlberg as a graduate student and published with him (Kohlberg and Gilligan, 1971). She became a critic of his approach when, listening to women, she heard 'a contrapunctual theme, woven into the cycle of life and recurring in varying forms in people's judgement' (1993a: 1). Gilligan's contribution has been to construct a different approach to thinking about the development of moral thinking, which replaces a focus on the ability to achieve rational cognitive thinking, with the ability to care. To develop this understanding she undertook a series of interviews looking at abstract moral dilemmas with female and male college students and young girls and boys. In addition, she interviewed young women about their decisions to reject or go ahead with an abortion.

Gilligan begins by comparing how a young girl and boy respond to Kohlberg's Heinz dilemma. The girl appears less able to give a clear answer on what Heinz should do. However, this is not because of an inability to make judgements; instead it is due to a fuller understanding of the consequences of stealing the drug or deciding not to. The moment of theft cannot be separated from a 'narrative of relationships that extends over time' (Gilligan, 1993a: 28) and makes a clear judgement less feasible. The dilemma makes no sense to the girl, because she cannot understand why it would emerge if all the parties were in a relationship with each other that allowed them to recognize each other's pain and ongoing human condition. For the girl, the solution must be found within the immediate relations that exist in the conflict. For the boy, the law produces an abstract, impersonal sphere for resolving the conflict (he believes a judge would rule that Heinz was right as a moral actor to steal the drug). The problem is that the boy's strategy of looking to the law gives him a high score in Kohlberg's model, while the girl's response is seen as indicating a lack of moral ability.

In the interviews with adolescent girls, Gilligan noticed hesitance come into their response to moral concerns. During adolescence a girl goes through a silencing of moral voice, which is 'enforced by the wish not to hurt others but also by the fear that in speaking, her voice will not be heard' (*ibid.*: 51). In a later book written with Lyn M. Brown, she talks of adolescence as a 'time of disconnection, sometimes of dissociation or repression in women's lives' (Brown and Gilligan, 1992: 4). In interviews, fragments of a moral self come out, but the girls appeared conscious of being seen as selfish or wrong to voice their own opinion. The dominance of masculine values and judgements creates a problem for women developing their own moral voice and narrative. In a context where the rules of femininity and moral judgement do not appear to supply a framework for understanding the dilemmas girls/ women face, silence results. The different experiences which women have growing up and being in the world, produce a particular path towards a distinct mode of thought. Relationships, responsibility and connections remain important guiding factors; the difficulty is finding a moral framework in which to express them.

The moral attitude the girls have difficulty expressing is one based on an ideal of care, 'of seeing and responding to need, taking care of the world by sustaining the web of connection so that no one is left alone' (Gilligan, 1993a: 62). If it were fully developed it would be an **ethic of care**, revolved around the importance of relationships to the human condition. It would be concerned with questions of care and responsibility, rather than rights and rules. Gilligan's ethic of care retains the notion that moral thought develops through levels; however, she provides the following alternative to Kohlberg's:

- The pre-conventional level is a 'focus on caring for the self in order to ensure survival' (*ibid.*: 74).
- The conventional level is where 'good is equated with caring for others' (*ibid.*: 74).
- The postconventional level is where 'care becomes the self-chosen principle of a judgement that remains psychological in its concern with relationships and response, but becomes universal in its condemnation of exploitation and hurt' (*ibid.*: 74).

Without the development of the third level, it is difficult for women to encompass both a sense of moral response and a belief that it is not selfish to care for the self. At the third level care can become a moral principle, but one where it is 'freed from its conventional interpretation' (*ibid.*: 90). Here there is recognition that one is obligated not just to others, one has a duty of care to the self. This does not mean that dilemmas do not surface; conflicts do emerge in responding to others as well as oneself. Instead of looking to abstract principle to resolve conflict and minimize hurt, the ethic of care looks to the particular. Universality exists, but it is the universal imperative to care for others and the self and to be cared for. This universal standard does not allow the 'blind willingness to sacrifice people to truth', a practice encouraged by 'an ethics abstracted from life' (*ibid.*: 104).

The difficulty for women is that patriarchy traps them in level two of conventional response. Here sacrifice dominates and women are rewarded for their femininity and sense of duty and obligation. But there is potential for this to change; due to feminism and other shifts in the private and public sphere, women's entrapment in the conventional stage is weakening and the language of self is becoming more prevalent. Women are articulating more strongly their right to care for themselves and to be cared for, alongside their continued desire to care for others. This indicates that recognition of an ethic of care does not mean that notions of justice and rights have no place in moral judgement. Instead, an awareness of individual rights sustains an awareness of self-worth and responsibility; with rights comes recognition that 'the interests of the self can be considered legitimate' (*ibid.*: 149). This awareness ensures that care exists in a way that does not become confused with duty and self-sacrifice; rights therefore act as a catalyst for postconventional approaches to care and self.

Does all this imply that women and men have distinct moral frameworks? In Gilligan's text there is the impression that relationships and care have a stronger presence in women's moral outlook. In contrast, men appear to exist in a world of separation and individual achievement, framed in an **ethic of justice**. However, Gilligan proposes that given that rights are an important context to the operation of the ethic of care, the different moral frameworks of women and men can be thought of as complementary. Women and men go through different paths of development, but for each, if they reach the fullest stage, justice and care, responsibility and choice operate. What is important is that an ethic of care, which has been associated with women, should be valued as a form of moral thinking that the human community would be greatly diminished without, and one of equal value to an ethic of justice. The implication is that 'in the end, morality is a matter of care' (*ibid.*: 147).

To summarize the differences between Gilligan's approach to that of Piaget and Kohlberg, the key claims are compared in Box 3.1. Gilligan's book has spurred on a significant debate within feminism. One of the first developments was work exploring mothering as a possible model for moral thinking (Held, 1997; Ruddick, 1990). In this work mothering is presented as a creative enterprise, which is concentrated in values of nurturing and emotional growth and connection. Both Virginia Held and Sara Ruddick look at the practices and relations embedded in mothering as values that can enrich the public sphere. In supporting the possibilities of maternal ethics, neither author argues that it should become the only framework, instead its presence and validity in the public sphere challenges the notion that justice and impartiality are the only frameworks within which to make judgements. Both authors also acknowledge that mothering is not inherently moral, indeed some practices, in terms of the direct harm they cause to the child, can be thought of as immoral from a perspective grounded in care or justice.

Box 3.1   A comparison of Gilligan's, and Piaget and Kohlberg's, approaches

Piaget and Kohlberg

- The development of morality moves though various stages, the order of which is universal and hierarchical.
- The higher stages of moral judgement are premised in reason and rationality.
- Reason and rationality allow moral judgement to be based on universal rules, agreed to by all.
- Independent and autonomous actors are the most capable of moral judgement.
- Women have difficulty obtaining the ability to follow and agree to rules.

Gilligan

- The development of morality moves through various stages, the order of which is varied due to different life experiences and contexts.
- The higher stages of moral judgement are premised on relationships.
- Relationships allow moral judgement to be based on universal consideration of care and harm agreed to by the parties concerned.
- Interdependent actors with a sense of self-value are the most capable of moral judgement.
- Women and men can base judgements on an ethic of care or justice when notions of femininity or masculinity do not inhibit their psychological development.

It is unsurprising, perhaps, that Gilligan's ethic of care, and notions of mothering ethics have been met with criticism by many feminists. The criticisms listed below echo concerns seen elsewhere in the book on the dangers inherent in trying to stipulate values associated with women.

Feminist critiques of Gilligan

Gilligan's approach has been met with anxiety by feminists troubled with its perspective and conclusions (Davis, 1992). Critics ask the following questions:

- Is care a useful metaphor for talking about women's lives and the values that emerge from them?

- Is a psychological approach a valid framework for understanding women's values, when in the past it has been used to castigate women?
- Can the ethic of care be a vehicle for bringing rights and care together?
- Where does difference sit within the framework?

The criticisms begin by questioning the radical potential of the ethic of care when it still works with strict and hierarchical categories of moral response (Flanagan and Jackson, 1987; Sher, 1987). Roe Sybylla suggests that 'because humans are complex and amazing beings, such efforts to define them closely inevitably diminish and limit their possibilities' (2001: 72). Linda J. Nicholson wonders why we should be limited to two modes of thinking, one female and one male (1993)? Although the distinct role women and men play in the private and public spheres is an important element of Gilligan's account, there is not enough care taken to consider the particular practices within each sphere, over time and within different social groups and actors (Kerber, 1993). In working with the same gendered divisions present in existing psychological work, ethic of care ideals perpetuate notions that at some essential level women and men are different (Nails, 1983; Williams, 1989).

Few have been able to replicate findings that suggest that different frameworks can be attributed to gender (Brabeck, 1993; Walker, 1984) and this has led to questions about Gilligan's methodology and selection. There is no attempt in her selection of respondents to capture the kinds of variation in background, belief and hardship, which would lead to variation in women's responses to dilemmas and choices. If context plays such a significant part in shaping moral frameworks, suggesting that two frameworks are possible appears to shrink the world of difference. There is a remarkable silence in her first book about contexts such as 'race', class and sexuality (Moody-Adams, 1991), and real anger has been expressed by Black feminists (Narrayan, 1995):

> Gilligan's theory of women's moral development has taken root in native soil. It is a powerful and persuasive theory that derives a female model of moral development from the moral reasoning of primarily white, middle-class women in the United States. (Stack, 1993: 110)

Gilligan has taken significant steps to rearticulate her position and her research practice to encapsulate this concern (1987, 1993b). In her book with Brown (Brown and Gilligan, 1992) the research practice and findings give increased space to diversity in the paths taken by women towards moral development. While the respondents in the book are all from a private school, 'race' and ethnicity are given a much higher profile. Gilligan and Brown acknowledge that the experience of restraint, cultural norms, and the narration of this experience, will be different for women who are separated by class, 'race', ethnicity and sexuality.

The psychological foundation leaves the ethic of care inappropriate for many feminists. The focus on psychology and moral development can individualize experiences of a contextual and intersubjective nature (Flax, 1993), but the emotional and moral dimensions of care have to be seen in their material condition. For example, the significance of the caring relationship to women and its ability to make them feel fulfilled can be connected to material conditions which withhold hope of other forms of fulfilment (Puka, 1993). Representing women as morally responsive leaves them open to being the 'natural carers'; a role for which there will always be a demand. Feminism 'cannot assume that any attribute of women is automatically a virtue worthy of feminists embracing it' (Tronto, 1989: 172). The voice of care and connection, which Gilligan places at the core of women's outlook, is the same voice used by employers and others to argue that women do not have what it takes to succeed in the public sphere. Michele M. Moody-Adams argues that Gilligan is not far from arguing that 'a woman's biology is her destiny' (1997: 690).

There are several ways in which Gilligan's different voice has been identified as conservative. First, Claudia Card (1997) asks whether it is enough to adopt the values of women as a counterpoint to those associated with men, without considering where these different values come from. If moral frameworks emerge in 'forms of life' identifiable as oppressive, it could be argued that the continued existence of such frameworks helps maintain the 'forms' that gave birth to them. If women's values have developed within a patriarchal society, then their role in women's lives require interrogation not validation. For Card, it is systematic patterns of exploitation that 'lead us to identify with service, find our value in our utility or ability to please' (1997: 648). Marilyn Freidman suggests that Western society has 'a division of moral labor' which 'has had the dual function both of preparing us each for our respective socially defined domains and of rendering us incompetent to manage the affairs of the realm from which we have been excluded' (1997: 667). This division is a variation in expectations, it is what 'we *attribute* to women and men' (*ibid.*: 668, original emphasis). In a slightly different form, Bill Puka makes the same point when he proposes that Gilligan's different voice 'is a set of coping strategies for dealing with sexist oppression' (1993: 215). Her third level of care of the self as well as care of the other emerges from recognition that care of the other is a social demand imposed on women. At the third level, women accommodate to the demand, but through some level of emancipation (for example through the activities of feminism) they also claim some right to care for their individual self too.

The second area of conservatism is the way in which gender is identified as the factor creating variation in moral voices. The problem is that 'if feminists think of the ethic of care as categorized by gender difference, they are likely to become trapped trying to defend women's morality rather than looking critically at the philosophical promises and problems of an ethic of care' (Tronto, 1993a: 241). Discussion of the different moral outlooks of women and men drifts easily into discussion of their separate spheres: women as the private, emotionally empathetic actors, men as the public rational actors (Calhoun, 1988). The concentration on gender ensures that the ethic of care supports the validity of existing male ethics (Hoagland, 1991). Although in later articles (Gilligan and Wiggins, 1987) and in her new preface to the second edition of *In a Different Voice*, Gilligan stresses she is not making essentialist claims, not everyone has been convinced by her arguments.

The third area is the apparent focus on caring for those around one. If care occurs in the context of immediate relationships and empathy, it suggests that care has a narrow range of response. Since we are likely to know and be in relations with people who are similar to us, it becomes a recipe for having an obligation of care only to those we recognize. Card notes that 'resting all of ethics on caring threatens to exclude as ethically insignificant our relationships with most people in the world, because we do not know them individually and never will' (1990: 102). The ethic of care approach does not appear to resolve the problem of how we extend 'some form of sympathy further than our own group' (Tronto, 1993b: 59). The final concern about conservatism is, if care is embedded in ongoing relationships, from where do we draw 'critical reflection on whether those relationships are good, healthy, or worthy of preservation' (Tronto, 1993a: 250)? There appears little scope for changing the context within which relationships and patterns of care can be harmful; there is little 'analysis of the differences between good and morally problematic or even corrupt kinds of care' (Flanagan and Jackson, 1987: 627). Does the ethic of care 'enable us adequately to resist evil' (Card, 1990: 101)?

Even those who are critical of Gilligan's formulation see value in her work. Her contribution is seen in the recognition that relativistic judgement can be thought of as a product of the development of moral thought, rather than a symptom of regression (Brabeck, 1993). It stresses the need to know the other in order to respond well (Blum, 1993), and it values and recognizes ongoing connections and relations as the core of appropriate moral response. What Gilligan's critics have looked to do is provide a different context, in particular a political one, in order to situate these values.

Rearticulations of an ethic of care

Selma Sevenhuijsen links feminist reticence towards the ethic of care to second-wave approaches to care. In the 1970s care was identified as the 'labour' (Graham, 1983) that women were trapped into by myths of femininity. The primacy of care in women's lives was something feminism had to move away from and reject. For radical feminists, such as Shulamith Firestone (1972), the key was to free women, through technology and communal living, from the burden of pregnancy, childbirth and child-rearing. For liberal feminists, greater availability of childcare facilities would help women take a greater role in the public sphere and dispel notions that the private was their primary sphere. For socialist and Marxist feminists, care in the private sphere should be recognized as labour and paid accordingly (Delphy, 1984). Feminist psychologists such as Nancy Chodorow (1978) argued that shared parenting would challenge notions that only women are capable of care and produce children with less fixed gender roles. In this context the ethic of care, particularly the work associated with maternal ethics, appears a step back, placing women back in the private sphere and open to the exploitation that caring responsibilities bring with it.

Feminists who have taken the ethics of care forward argue that feminism cannot ignore questions of care or present it as someone else's problem. Joan Tronto (1993b) argues that the fierceness of some of the criticisms against Gilligan comes from a desire to contain the implications of taking care seriously. Sevenhuijsen (1998) argues that feminism must make care dilemmas central because of important current contexts. Leaving care to the state or to technology seems less tenable when the social and ethical costs of either solution have been so clearly identified. At the same time, most Western societies are currently having to think about how they care in response to pressures on and critiques of social and welfare service provision. Finally, changes in forms of relationship and life bring with them new patterns of caring, connected to commitment bonds outside traditional models of heterosexual family life (Aronson, 1998). These new patterns of care and commitment bring into stronger relief the confining nature of traditional gendered models.

To avoid romanticizing care, which occurs when it is founded on a celebrated subject (the good mother/woman/carer), Sevenhuijsen focuses on care as a **social practice**. Care is something one does in varied ways and for varied reasons, and therefore the responsibilities that come with it should be thought of as grounded and unromantic. Thinking of care practices helps distinguish between good and bad forms of care and between different types (Tronto, 1989). The activity of caring includes moral judgement in order that the response is appropriate, which requires sensitivity to the contextual world of the person; that is, to approach them as a concrete other rather than a generalized other (Benhabib, 1992). The importance of narrative and interpretation to the practice of care ensures that care is linked to actuality and cannot be guided by abstract criteria. Listening and responsiveness are a form of reason, 'attentive reasoning' (Sevenhuijsen, 1998: 62).

The care practices that can be at the core of an ethics of care cannot be based on a fixed model of the caregiver and the cared for. Such an account 'reproduces a one-sided image of human nature, enshrined in the idea that the self-sufficient individual should be the basis of moral existence' (*ibid.*: 27). A hierarchy reappears in the apparent normal state of the caregiver and the abnormal state of the person in need of care. Instead no one is in either category, we move between different moments where we give and receive care, in ways which overlap, and which refute notions that to be normal is to be the one who has no need of care. A model of autonomy as the ideal condition lies behind the celebration of the person who gives care. The ethics of care must be explored in a way that understands the human condition as one where 'all people are vulnerable, dependent and finite' (*ibid.*: 28). The social practice of care helps inform the moral world of the parties involved because the self is not a fixed property, fully formed forever once a series of stages have been moved through. Instead 'moral identity is continually being developed and revised' (*ibid.*: 56). We have a moral subjectivity that is always evolving and is formed and reformed through interactions and responsibilities. The vision of the moral subject that this produces is one 'who is aware of his or her own limitations, dependencies, vulnerability and finiteness, and who is prepared to accept responsibility for these things' (*ibid.*: 57).

Political uses

In recent ethics of care work, there is a desire to find a way forward out of the dilemma: *how to value ethical principles associated with caring, without romanticizing experiences of care, that justify the seclusion of women in the private sphere*. Various feminists advocate working with the ethics of care through a political, as opposed to psychological, discourse. The shift in framework avoids a drift into 'a nostalgic return to harmony and consensus' (Sevenhuijsen, 1998: 13). In discussions framed by political considerations, the focus is less on the models of care that appear in the private sphere and more with the lack of care in the public (Jagger, 1991). The priority in this work is to find a way for ethics to be involved in the 'diminishment of dominance and subordination' (Hoagland, 1991: 252).

The first step is to shift the focus of investigation away from being about caring relationships that exist between two people; particularly mother and child (Boling, 1991; Dietz, 1985). Ethics of care arguments which concentrate on relationships existing between individuals 'dismiss from the outset the ways in which care can function socially and politically' (Tronto, 1993b: 103). Next, the explanatory framework of psychology is replaced with a concentration on the impact of 'modern society by the condition of subordination'

(Tronto, 1993a: 241). This shift leads to the proposal that 'if moral difference is a function of social position rather than gender, then the morality Gilligan has identified with women might be better identified with subordinate or minority status' (*ibid.*: 243). Margaret Moore echoes this point suggesting that an approach based in care is better thought of as 'morality embodied in particular concrete relationships' (Moore, 1999), rather than some specific female voice (Hallstein, 1999).

If the ethics of care are interpreted as the coping strategies of people linked by experiences of subordination, then the skills that it celebrates can be understood as those practices that emerge from group action and resistance (Hoagland, 1988). If approaches to care, associated with the ethics of care, can be found amongst varied groups who experience oppression and marginalization, then it follows that it can be practised amongst strangers as well as intimates. In this way, 'caring cannot be insular and it cannot ignore the political reality, material conditions, and social structure of the world' (Hoagland, 1991: 260). In this way the care discourse can be understood 'as a table of values, those surrounding the activities of caring and connection, upon which a politics of democratic community can be built' (Ferguson, 1984: 165).

Investigating the ethics of care in the public sphere involves two stages. First, a consideration of how the public sphere operates in a way that excludes questions of care and second, development of the mechanisms or strategies through which care can be introduced into the public sphere. Some of the aspects of the first we have seen in the criticisms of traditional moral theory. We do not, in the West, have a language for thinking about 'dependency, responsibility, vulnerability and trust; the importance, but also the fragility of intimacy and connectedness; the ever-recurring problem of establishing boundaries between the self and others' (Sevenhuijsen, 1998: 3). Tronto argues that there are three boundaries that exclude care from political discourse. First, the distinction made between politics and morality; second, the central position of the disinterested individual moral actor; and third, the separation of private and public spheres.

The second stage involves breaking down the dichotomy of the public/private world by placing questions of care and responsibility within debates about the role of the state and the responsibilities of citizens:

> The qualities of attentiveness, of responsibility, of competence, or responsiveness, need not be restricted to the immediate objects of our care, but can also inform our practices as citizens. They direct us to a politics in which there is, at the center, a public discussion of needs. (Tronto, 1993b: 167/168)

Such ideas strengthen an important element of Gilligan's arguments often missed: care flourishes in a context where notions of individual rights exist.

Care, as well as justice, can be thought of as a component of citizenship in that it entails recognition of others who have a right to their own view of the world. In this context, good citizens are those who respect differences and maintain an active dialogue over the varied values and morals of a society. Responsive justice helps ensure that the 'enabling conditions' (Narrayan, 1995) of positive care exist. Democratic citizenship requires space to negotiate values and principles of both care and justice. Without this values and principles become obligations and duties that are abstracted from the lives of those meant to live by them. The values that are associated with the ethics of care – 'attentiveness, responsiveness and responsibility' – can enrich citizenship by encouraging it to encompass 'diversity and plurality' (Sevenhuijsen, 1998: 15). At the same time, retaining scope for questions of justice allows care to be evaluated and debated in socially-situated contexts of judgement.

Welfare systems

Explorations of care are central to contemporary welfare debates; can the ethics of care be part of this debate? Questions about care and welfare within feminism, particularly in Britain and Europe, have concentrated on women's role as the unpaid, informal carers of the welfare state (Finch, 1989; Ungerson, 1987). This work captures the ways in which the welfare state was built on an expectation that there was 'a private sphere of the family that would provide succour to those who could not compete in the market' (Daly and Lewis, 2000: 283).

Feminists working within disability studies were the first to point out that an exclusive focus on the carer is ethically, politically and theoretically problematic (Sheldon, 1999). Jenny Morris (1993) criticizes feminists who analyse the 'plight' of women as carers, but show much less concern for women and others who require material and social support. Such work has advocated residential care of people with significant care needs as the only way to free women from the 'burden' of care. For disability activists this suggestion is unacceptable; it fails to recognize the harm this form of provision can result in for disabled people (Barnes, 1992). The impingement on the rights of disabled women, particularly in a context of residential care, appears of little concern (Kallianes and Rubendeld, 1997). When no attempt is made to capture the dynamic of care and the subjectivities of all those involved it strips care of its full significance (Fawcett, 2000); it retains the notion that the problem with care is the impact it has on the 'normal' person – the person not in need. In doing so the full scope of the interdependencies between people, which mean that no one is this autonomous figure and instead all of us are in need of care, is ignored.

There are various ways in which the ethics of care debate has entered welfare discussions within and outside feminism (Lappalainen and Motevasel, 1997). The different directions taken indicate the variation in approach between those focused on individual practices of care and those concerned with the organization of care in society. The first inclusion considers the attributes associated with the ethics of care and proposes that this may improve the practice of individual professionals involved in welfare provision. This approach has become prominent in discussions about nursing (Bradshaw, 1996; Tong, 1998) and social work (Freedberg, 1993). The suggestion is that the types of power inequality between professional and client, which can lead to negative and oppressive care experiences, can be reduced or removed by care practices focused on principles of empathy, reciprocity and emotional connection. This body of work is criticized for the same reasons that some feminists have found fault with Gilligan's initial framework. It retains expectations that caring roles within welfare, paid and unpaid, are carried out by women (Kuhse, 1995); and it focuses on individual attributes of care without considering the wider contexts and structures of care (Gremmen, 1999). In doing so it fails to fully respond to disability studies' concerns about the processes encapsulated in professional and state care provision which contribute to the production of disability for those who have impairments.

A different strategy for including the ethics of care is to focus on the ways in which, as a political framework, it can interrogate the place of care within society (Daly and Lewis, 2000). Priorities within this include questioning the pattern of private and public responsibilities for care. Demands that caring for others should be placed more centrally in the public sphere are hindered by the assumption that care is the preserve of the private, and it is the identification of this role with women that maintains the separation. What an ethics of care, interpreted from a political stance, stresses is that care entails wider obligations on the part of society. Sevenhuijsen and Tronto advocate placing ethical questions about how we approach care at the centre of welfare debates. For example, the implications of welfare structures that produce a limiting model of care dependency and individual failure. Particular welfare models of care secure the division between the autonomous normal person and the dependent person in need of care. In this way we can think of welfare institutions and practices as significant in shaping expectations about what care encapsulates and who is the carer and cared for.

A politicized ethics of care model can help envisage alternative approaches to care in welfare and society. Such alternatives would include:

- recognition of interdependencies;
- the right to be part of and receive just forms of care;

- the benefits of recognizing the whole subjectivity of those involved in care processes;
- the value of both commonality and differences in practices of care and justice; and
- a notion of citizenship that encompasses the importance of empathy and care responsibilities.

Conclusion

Through exploring inadequacies in psychological approaches to moral and cognitive development feminists have developed new models for thinking about the place of care in society. These models respond to difference by considering the role of context in the development of moral thought and the appropriateness of response. Instead of seeing a hierarchy in different approaches to moral and intellectual problems, feminists find different styles of problem-approach and solution appropriate to different situations. Some articulations of the ethics of care link it to patterns of care women have developed in the private sphere, in particular within the care of children. However, for some feminists this is dangerous, as it appears to define and depoliticize the ways in which we can think of care and women's identities. Out of this critique has come the most valuable element of the ethics of care debate, a political debate about the approaches to care found in the public sphere.

A politicized ethics of care allows for links to questions of citizenship, state responsibility and interconnection; it generates alternative visions of human and social relationship which broaden notions of citizenship and justice. At the centre of these visions lies a rejection of the 'self-made', autonomous individual who can exist without care. The ethics of care framework concludes that if interdependence takes the place of independence, then it follows that engagement must take the place of disinterest in definitions of both citizenship and moral theory. I favour this approach since it moves away from categorizing morality according to gender, it ensures that rights talk remains prominent in the discussion and it places the state at the centre, demanding a caring approach from it.

Both standpoint theory and the ethics of care debate emerge out of a desire to link approaches to knowledge or care to the experiences of women. In the next four chapters I will explore frameworks that seek to destabilize such attempts by focusing on the socially constructed nature of any notion of knowledge, experience, identity or technology. I will begin with an examination of postmodernism and the stress that it places on the role of language and binary divisions.

FURTHER READING

Carol Gilligan (1993) *In a Different Voice* (London: Harvard University Press). The second edition includes an important reflection by Gilligan on how her ideas have continued to develop and how others have responded to them.

Selma Sevenhuijsen (1998) *Citizenship and the Ethics of Care* (London: Routledge). A vital text for working through the connections that can be made between moral questions about care and political questions about citizenship.

Joan C. Tronto (1993) *Moral Boundaries: A Political Argument for an Ethic of Care* (London: Routledge). Provides an important critique of psychological approaches to care issues and a powerful call for the state and politics to place care on the agenda.

Postmodernism

CONTENTS

Postmodernism is a major source of the greater uncertainty and scepticism now prevalent within social and political thought. Much of this work seeks to reposition claims to knowledge and truth as particular interpretations, and in this light postmodernism can be seen as having important parallels with feminist strategies (Fraser and Nicholson, 1990). Postmodernism and feminist theories, as we have seen in standpoint theories and the ethics of care, identify particularity where other theories identify universality. Despite these parallels, the inclusion of postmodern ideas into feminist debates has raised significant concern and animosity.

After outlining some of the key ideas of postmodernism, the chapter will highlight the reasons why some feminists have had a strong reaction against it. It will then move on to discuss how other feminists have responded to these concerns through the development of a postmodern perspective that they argue is of value to feminist politics. The Political Uses section details the postmodern claim that deconstructing the subject is politically valuable, and also looks at two examples of activism that have been identified as postmodern.

Outline of the key perspective

Summarizing postmodern debates is a difficult endeavour. First, the ideas themselves are complex and challenge many notions usually taken for granted. Second, postmodernism is an ambiguous term, often used interchangeably with poststructuralism and used to describe a variety of trends and ideas. Judith Butler distinguishes between postmodernism and poststructuralism by suggesting that poststructuralism claims that 'the subject *never* existed', while postmodernism claims that 'the subject once had integrity, but no longer does' (1992: 14, original emphasis). Postmodernism is variously described and analysed as a stage of capitalism, a particular historical movement, a rejection of the Enlightenment, and as a new form of aesthetics (Bordo, 1992). Rather than try to cover all these different possibilities, the focus here is on postmodern and poststructural concerns with subjectivity, language and difference. Before discussing these key concerns, I will highlight the background to their emergence.

Background

Postmodern writers question why, in modernity, a desire for truth, both in language and in knowledge of the self, has come to dominate philosophy and self-perception. This question has its roots in re-workings of Martin Heidegger (1962), Friedrich Nietzsche (1990) and Ferdinand D. Saussure (1959).

The structuralist writings of Saussure are particularly important as a backdrop to the analysis of language in postmodern and poststructuralist writings. In *Course in General Linguistics* first published in 1959, Saussure outlined a linguistic theory that proposed that the link between objects and the words that refer to them is **arbitrary**. Language operates through difference; words have meaning in relation to and in comparison with other terms. Networks of signs (the concept or **signified** – bushy thing for example – and the sound/image or **signifier** – tree) create a system of language which is secured by convention. While individual signs are arbitrary, the network of signs that constitutes our shared language is not. Without a system to fix meaning, the arbitrariness of the link between signified and signifier would disable language. The network of signs is thus ideological, composed through, as well as an important vehicle, in the reproduction of social structures and power relations. For Saussure language is structural, operating as a complete system of meanings that have a determining influence on how we experience the world; we cannot interpret what we see without language, therefore reality can never be experienced without a process of interpretation and translation. Equally, our sense of self emerges through a preexisting system and is therefore not of our own making.

In the 1960s, poststructuralism emerged in France from a desire to move away from Saussure's focus on the overall system of meaning (Grosz, 1999). Critics identified three main limitations to the approach:

1 Structuralism misses the contingency and fluidity of processes of signification and meaning.
2 It erases the role of human actors and relations in interpreting and shaping language.

3 The system is ahistorical, it is unable to identify when, how and why meanings change, and the relationship between the signifier and the signified may alter.

The setting of France in the 1960s is significant. The poststructuralist turn can be situated in the politics of the New Left of the period where, in various realms – the political, economic, psychoanalytic, literary and philosophical – writers and activists were concerned with finding modes of thought and action able to open up structuralist ideas to difference and subjectivity.

Deconstruction of language and the self

Jacques Derrida (1998) is one of the key poststructuralist writers. In *Of Grammatology*, originally published in France in 1967, Derrida is still interested in systems of language (although he prefers to talk of modes), but what changes is his focus on **deconstructing** them. Through deconstruction he aims to highlight the role of **binary oppositions** in constructing meaning in language. Systems of language are built from oppositions, one of the most important being **self** and **other**, and in each pair, one term (for example good, white, masculine, culture and heterosexual) is valued over the other subordinated term (evil, black, feminine, nature and homosexual). Philosophical humanist notions of the individual sovereign self hold dominance in Western thinking, not because they are intrinsically real, but because the system of language supports their dominance through the operation of binary oppositions. By indicating the relationship between the two terms (light can only be light when there is a notion of dark), the terms no longer appear in opposition; instead they depend on each other to have any kind of meaning. The implication is that reality and the individual are constructs of language with no inherent meaning outside of their relationship with other terms.

Deconstructionism does not aim to celebrate the subordinated term of the binary opposition – for example, femininity over masculinity. Instead deconstruction **plays** with the opposition, removing the slash between the two terms, in this case femininity/masculinity. The chief mode of inquiry is the critical analysis of texts to challenge the internal oppositions and differences through which they come to have meaning. The implication for notions of the subject is that she is a product, an embodiment, of a set of discourses or codes of signification that construct her actions, beliefs and her notion of self, within a social nexus of structures of knowledge, meaning and power.

One example of how the work on language and binary divisions has been used to analyse the production of meaning and identity can be found in

postcolonial writing. This body of work (more complex and wide-ranging than is discussed here; Goss, 1996; Schwarz, 2000) explores the role of colonial processes, institutions and relations in producing European modernity and the modern Western subject. The binary division between the savage other and the Western subject is at the centre of the perspective. The image of the 'savage' was/is the necessary other that secured/secures the rational, white subject (Said, 1993) in the West. Ato Quayson (2000) argues that postcolonial writings are concerned with the politics of identity formation in the context of 'the *reception* of otherness in the metropolitan West' (2000: 141, original emphasis). Postcolonial writings prioritize issues of racial and ethnic histories and politics within the production of otherness in language and subjectivity. This work, by indicating the role of a demonized 'other' in securing myths of racial superiority, challenges the universal concepts of modernity. Along with shaping national boundaries and contemporary economic and political processes, colonialism has helped secure proper notions of the subject.

Postcolonial writings examine how Western notions of the sovereign subject are built upon racialized structures of meaning. Postcolonialism resists looking to a precolonial past to counter the racial myths generated within colonialism; to do so is to retain modernist notions of authentic cultural origins and purity. Instead, much of the focus is on deconstructing and resisting the binary oppositions built into notions of the West and non-West, centre and periphery. Such work begins in history, but is very much positioned within contemporary racial politics and battles over identity. In contemporary interactions between different cultural perspectives, Western frameworks still play a role (although the patterns of dominance and signification change) in defining proper subjectivity and experiences of marginality (Spivak, 2000). Homi K. Bhabha summarizes postcolonial analysis by saying that it 'bears witness to the unequal and uneven forces of cultural representation involved in the contest for political and social authority within the modern world order' (2000: 105). Western dominance, secured in economic and political global institutions, problematizes identity formation for those defined as 'the other', both inside and outside the West. Attempts to retain fictional myths of national identity, to be protected from outside cultural invasion, can be seen in battles over Englishness in Britain, asylum-seekers in Australia and Europe, and conflicts over English becoming a second language in areas of the United States.

Grand narratives

Various postmodern writers have focused their deconstructionist energies on challenging the notion that it is possible for theories or ideas to capture and explain the full scope of social and human dynamics (Bauman, 1993). Two of the most significant are Jean-François Lyotard (1984) and Richard Rorty (1989).

Lyotard is distinct from Derrida and most poststructuralists because he asserts that, at least in the West, we are in a postmodern period qualitatively different from modernity. Lyotard's *The Postmodern Condition*, first published in French in 1979 and in English in 1984, uses Ludwig Wittgenstein's (Kenny, 1994) notion of **language games** to argue that language is made up of rules that determine how utterances can be used and what they mean. Such rules are open to negotiation by the players, but they cannot simply reinvent them. The social bond, the underlying assumptions about how society operates and interacts, is formed in the rules and narratives of the language game. Society cannot exist without language and the particular pattern of meanings and rules that form the language game. Lyotard argues that in postmodern society, existing 'grand narratives' of legitimization – in particular, notions of scientific or emancipatory progress – have lost their validity. However, the decline of such grand explanations is not inherently negative:

> Most people have lost the nostalgia for the lost narrative. It in no way follows that they are reduced to barbarity. What saves them from it is their knowledge that legitimation can only spring from their own linguistic practice and communicational interaction. (1984: 41)

Social, economic and technological changes mean that universal theories and consensus are no longer the vehicles to resist and challenge the way things are.

Rorty aims to dispute classical and modern philosophy's belief in a 'truth', out there, waiting for discovery and beyond human mediation. Since descriptions occur in language they cannot escape contingency and interpretation: 'where there are no sentences there is no truth' (1989: 5). In a move fans of the X-Files may query, Rorty states that 'Truth cannot be out there' (*ibid*.: 5). He argues that his rejection of universal claims to knowledge and understanding can allow for our knowledge of the world and each other to be based on 'contingent conversations' with each other. Our sense of the world and ourselves is no 'more than the habitual use of a certain repertoire of terms' (*ibid*.: 22). The human condition that is valued by philosophy is one that can transcend contingency 'into the world of enduring truth' (*ibid*.: 29). Like Nietzche before him, Rorty warns against the costs of searching for the unattainable. Instead, one should think of human life as 'always incomplete, yet sometimes heroic' (*ibid*.: 43). In contrast to the philosopher seeking truth, Rorty proposes the ironist as the most suitable knower in a postmodern world. The ironist has continual doubt as to the validity of her arguments; she remains aware of the possibility that other 'vocabularies' may offer the potential to respond to her doubts; and she does not assume her vocabulary has a greater correspondence to reality than another's (*ibid.*: 73).

To summarize, the key arguments of postmodernism are that:

- Meaning and identity are produced through the operation of language.
- Language produces meaning through binary oppositions.
- For some writers meaning and identity have become more contingent, for others contingency has always existed.
- Language is a factor in power relations, creating proper and improper subjects.

Feminist critiques

Feminist concerns with postmodernism are broadly that (Zalewski, 2000):

1 Its deconstruction of the subject leaves it difficult to make claims on the subject's behalf (equal rights for women).
2 Its denial of 'truths' leaves it difficult to make claims to truth (women do not have equal rights).
3 Its priorities do not produce an agenda for political activism or the possibility that political change can occur (women, through feminist activism, can obtain equal rights).

I will take each of these concerns in turn.

Subjectivity/identity important

Many of the different feminist perspectives discussed in this book, although acknowledging difficulties with 'the subject', continue to assert that *a* subject, however defined, is a necessary political category. Feminism has spent several centuries trying to obtain subject status for women. In the politics of both the first and second wave, and in contemporary feminist battles across the globe, arguments for the rights of women *as* individual subjects were and are dominant. For some feminists the authenticity of the individual subject is the line that theoretical exploration must not cross (Gagnier, 1990; Grimshaw, 1988). Humanism's celebration of the sovereign subject and its values of autonomy and individual rights may be troubling, but it is something feminism cannot do without. Equally, feminism requires a vision of women as its collective subject. Christine Di Stefano (1990) queries whether feminism can act on behalf of or with women if it is no longer able to articulate the identity or interests of that constituency.

Numerous feminists argue that rejecting the importance of subject status is only appealing to those in a position to voluntarily give it up: 'one cannot deconstruct a subjectivity one has never been fully granted ... In order to announce the death of the subject one must first have gained the right to speak as one' (Braidotti, 1994: 141). The uncertainty and fluidity, which postmodern writers see hidden by the confining illusion of coherency, matches the indeterminacy women suffer by being denied subjecthood. For this reason uncertainty is not necessarily a liberating experience for women. Lynn S. Chancer argues that the loss of a notion of the sovereign self will only leave women 'quite familiarly powerless, filled with self-doubt, unable to assert the ethical necessity and certainty of anything' (1998: 26). Denise Riley (1988) notes that 'ain't I a fluctuating identity' does not have the same resonance as Sojourner Truth's original plea.

Feminist disquiet with the loss of the subject is fuelled by postmodernism's use of feminine subjectivity as a 'powerful vehicle for conveying the critical attempts to redefine human subjectivity' (Braidotti, 1994: 140). Derrida, Lyotard, Michel Foucault and others use the metaphor of the 'feminine' to symbolize the other of male subjectivity. Derrida discusses the disfiguration of the 'living feminine' (1985: 21) in modern modes of language and subjectivity. Jacques Lacan (1968) proposes that the unconscious feminine is the other of the dominant symbol of meaning and presence in language – the phallus. Jean Baudrillard asserts 'I consider woman the absence of desire. It is of little import whether or not that corresponds to real women. It is my conception of femininity' (quoted in Moore, 1988: 180).

Rosi Braidotti views the postmodern rush to embrace the feminine as a 'male desire to carry on the hegemonic tradition that they inherited; it reveals their attachment to their traditional place of enunciation' (1994: 141–2). Postmodernism's fascination with and use of femininity is problematic because it draws on essentialist notions of it, subsumes important differences within the experiences and outlook of women, and has little to do with actual women (Gallop, 1987; Jeffreys, 1994). Suzanne Moore (1988) argues that such work is a form of 'gender tourism', where writers get to play with femininity as an interesting metaphorical tool, but do not have to live with its consequences in the real world. Talking of the symbolic feminine means that they do not have to come into contact with or reflect on actual women's lives as part of their travels. They also do not need to reflect on their complicity, as men, in the powerlessness that women daily experience.

A final query feminists have raised over postmodernism's approach to the subject is concerned with why it chooses to question its authenticity. Liz Bondi and Mona Domosh (1992) suspect that postmodernism is a reaction led by those in power – Western men – to deconstruct subjectivity in order to maintain their position. For Nancy Hartsock (1998) postmodernism is a rearguard action triggered by the demands of wider constituencies outside the West. Its hidden agenda is to maintain the privileged position of Western man in the face of the downfall of their Enlightenment:

> Why is it, exactly at the moment when so many of us who have been silenced begin to demand the right to name ourselves, to act as subjects rather than objects of history, that just then the concept of subjecthood becomes 'problematic'? Just when we are forming our own theories about the world, uncertainty emerges about whether the world can be adequately theorized. (1998: 210)

Kate Soper (1993a) argues that postmodernism could have only come from a position of privilege and power, a position as yet unavailable to many outside (and inside) the Western world. Those against postmodernism know:

> that revelling in the loss of progress is a Western metropolitan privilege which depends on living in a certain state of grace, a condition where no one is starving you, no one torturing you, no one even denying you the price of a cinema ticket or tube fare to the conference on postmodernism. (1993a: 21)

The implicit conclusion of Soper's argument is that to defend postmodernism is to defend this privileged position; while denying the tools of improvement to others. The postmodern approach to subjectivity is seen as traditional academic elitism, aimed at ridiculing everyone else for their foolish belief in their own identity and experiences.

Grand narratives are necessary

The second wave of feminism introduced or politicized terms such as patriarchy, gender oppression and the sexual division of labour, that have gradually won recognition as significant political and sociological terms in public arenas. By labelling such notions and frameworks as particular narratives rather than having a correspondence to reality and truth, postmodernism appears to cast doubt on their validity (Oakley, 1998). Marxist feminism, with its analysis of patriarchal structures, has a scope and agenda for action it wishes to protect from the playfulness of postmodernism. Sylvia Walby (1992), while acknowledging that patriarchy is complicated, and perhaps flexible, fears the political consequences of losing the term completely to a postmodern project. Postmodernism means 'losing the theoretical categories (gender, patriarchy, even women) through which we can understand and then challenge the world' (1992: 13).

Linked to the discomfort with postmodernism's approach to grand narratives is the argument that it operates as one, making the same mistakes of other grand narratives of the Enlightenment. Hartsock (1998: 207) and Susan Bordo (1992) argue that postmodernism presents itself in opposition to the Enlightenment in order to stress its superiority; an old trick borrowed from other Enlightenment modes of thought. Anna Pollert (1996) argues that postmodernism shares the same failures of the structural analysis it aims to offer an alternative to:

> Both deny that lived experience or material existence can be validated in any way, and both operate at the level of the autonomy of ideas (in post-modernism, language) and a type of theorisation which is self-enclosed in its own activity. (1996: 651)

Feminists have used the notion of narrative to explore the ways in which postmodernism produces its own claims. Stevi Jackson (1999) argues that the narrative of postmodernism generates a problematic interpretation of existing work, including feminism, in order to appear new and different. Tracing work within sociology she identifies a long tradition of social con-structionist analysis in areas such as social labelling (McIntosh, 1968) and symbolic interactionism (Gagnon and Simon, 1974); both of which predate poststructuralism. Ignoring this body of work produces a parody of feminist ideas in order to present the new as more exciting and hip (Matisons, 1998).

Political dangers

Feminists wishing to engage in practical politics have found post-modernism's focus on deconstruction and difference *dis*-abling. There is a suspicion that it is easier to break things down than attempt to build up forms of coalition across difference. Chandra T. Mohanty warns against losing processes of historical interconnection and responsibility through a fixation with 'questions of discrete and separate histories' (1995: 69). Such approaches can become an excuse for failing to acknowledge shared posi-tions and responsibilities for the conditions and lives of others (Bannerji, 1995). Postmodernism is a 'failure of imagination' (Hartsock, 1998: 211) over how to deal with increasing calls for recognition. As a response to dif-ference it has 'often denied women the possibility of constructing political identities from which to name their oppression' (Jackson, 1999: 5). Susan A. Mann argues that in all the analysis of difference, class has become an 'invisible ghost' (2000: 495).

Through this critique, feminists who are associated with postmodernism have become symbolic of academic feminism's removal from the everyday lives of 'ordinary' women (Connor, 1993; Waters, 1996). Robyn Rowland and

Renate Klein refer to feminist postmodern writing as 'disengagement theory' (1996: 13), and Judith Squires warns of a 'loss of hope, of utopian vision' (1993: 3) and 'political paralysis' (*ibid.*: 9). Martha C. Nussbaum describes Judith Butler (a leading figure associated with both postmodernism and queer theory) as a 'collaborator with evil' (1999a: 45), although this collaboration is by default rather than wilful intent. Butler's 'disdainful abstractness' (*ibid.*) leaves her less able to identify and challenge the material and violent forces damaging many women's lives, particularly outside the protected environment of liberal Western academia.

The strong language is an indication of what some feminists see as at stake in the priority being given to postmodern ideas in some circles. There is a genuine fear that any association of feminism with postmodernism will lead to its assimilation. Feminism's incorporation of postmodern ideas is considered a bad survival strategy, as working in the words of Audre Lorde with the 'Masters' tools' in order to be heard, accepted and approved (Brodribb, 1992). Postmodern language and perspectives reflect academic criteria, rather than a concern with 'a world that does definitely exist, and that remains obdurately structured by a dualistic, power-driven gender system' (Jackson, 1999: 143). The debates and concerns of postmodernism may be interesting for privileged subjects in academia, but are irrelevant to women – and other marginalized groups – struggling for rights and material issues, which privileged subjects take for granted (Scheman, 1993). Feminists wishing to retain a material focus argue that the 'cultural' turn of postmodernism requires that feminism abandons 'analyses of the material conditions of women's lives and the denial of any systematic inequalities – patriarchal, capitalist or racist' (Jackson, 1999: 5). This at a time when we 'inhabit a global context characterised by extremely stark and worsening material inequalities' (*ibid.*). This is a particular concern with postcolonial writings, where the politics of disadvantage are seen to take backstage to questions of cultural representation and identity formation. Himani Bannerji comments that in the past 'we saw colonization as destruction of economies and drains of wealth, now we see its crimes as being those of robberies of representation' (1995: 36).

Feminists who reject or query the role and value of postmodern ideas within feminism are concerned that its adoption requires the loss of important tools for feminist activity. In particular, those most resistant do so out of a desire to retain some sense of:

- the validity of the subject;
- the reality and importance of material relations;
- the need to recognize and go beyond difference in order to find commonality and connection; and
- the possibilities of genuine political change and liberation.

Feminist incorporations

It would be a mistake to imply that the incorporation of postmodern ideas into feminist writing has been the result of external forces enabling feminism to realise the error of its modernist ways. Simone de Beauvoir's famous declaration 'one is not born a woman, one becomes one' can be thought of as an important antecedent to postmodern ideas.

The investigation of subjectivity has taken a postmodern turn within feminism because of internal reflections on differences amongst women. The work of Black and lesbian feminists is an important starting point for feminist and wider social theory's interrogation of the production of subjectivity and the exclusions in grand theory (Fraser and Nicholson, 1990). Such criticism within feminism has resulted in the shift away from 'grand narratives' as explanatory resources. Marxist feminism and liberal feminism have both been scrutinized for their lack of sensitivity towards different histories and subject positions.

There are important variations between how different feminists approach postmodern questions. Some of these differences are associated with groupings within specific cultural and academic environments: Anglo-American feminists focus on deconstructing gender, while French and Italian feminists explore, and at times celebrate, sexual differences and femininity. However, this distinction has become less sustainable due to internal divisions and the emergence of important writers from Australia, The Netherlands and outside of the West. This section will identify key areas shared by different feminists working with postmodern ideas; however, where specific variations are important they will be indicated. A final point is that many writers for good reasons are hesitant to talk in terms of 'postmodern feminism'; bringing the terms together suggests a unity of perspective and outlook that is not necessarily present (Singer, 1992). For simplicity's sake the next section does talk of postmodern feminism, but this does not deny the importance of recognizing the differences – both political and theoretical – between the two bodies of work. In what follows I will explore the distinctive approach feminists take to postmodern concerns with subjectivity and theoretical frameworks.

Subjectivity

Different understandings of subjectivity are important elements that unite postmodernism and feminists considered to be postmodern (indeed Butler, 1992, argues it is *the* common strand). Marysia Zalewski summarizes postmodern feminism's approach to the subject by noting that 'it is not a question of *choosing* between retaining the subject or not, rather it is a question of revisiting our understanding of what the subject is' (2000: 39, original emphasis).

Braidotti is an important figure in feminist encounters with postmodernism. In *Nomadic Subjects* (1994), which brings together new writings with papers produced during the late 1980s and early 1990s, her concern is with the forms of subjectivity possible in postmodern society. For Braidotti, postmodernism denotes a particular moment in time where 'in-depth transformations of the system of economic production are also altering traditional social and symbolic structures' (*ibid.*: 2). The economic restructuring such processes trigger and the crisis in meaning and identity that have come with it cause pain and suffering. However, at the same time new possibilities open up for envisioning forms of subjectivity in opposition to the sovereign individual of modernity. Braidotti shares the postmodern concern with contingency and multiplicity, but is hesitant to completely adopt the arguments of the people discussed above. While 'grand narratives' may be in decline, she rejects that this implies 'that there is no system, no interpretation or understanding, and no reality' (*ibid.*: 141).

Key aspects of Braidotti's analysis indicate a distinct feminist approach to postmodernism:

- Autobiography is used to develop her ideas. Experience may be multiple, fictional and contingent, but it is also lived and something that can generate political change.
- Materiality is retained through an awareness of embodiment and sexual difference.
- Alongside deconstruction, she constructs and identifies forms of connection, solidarity and interrelationship between social actors.
- She uses 'political fictions' about subjectivity, identity and agency to allow for political action.
- Her desire is to find a form of 'legitimate political agency' in a context where fixed and universal identities and subjectivities are no longer feasible or legitimate. That is, she is not willing to fully let go of the political subject, however contingent and constructed.

In a number of ways Braidotti's approach to subjectivity is symbolic of feminist approaches to postmodernism. First, embodiment is supported by a 'radically anti-essentialist position' (*ibid.*: 4) on womanhood. Feminists should speak of and as women, but without assuming some monolithic essence to the category. In part this is important because differences amongst women mean that 'the signifier *woman* is no longer sufficient as the foundational stone of the feminist project' (*ibid.*: 105). This echoes the argument of Butler, who in her key text *Gender Trouble*, published in 1990 (discussed in more depth in the next chapter), argues that treating 'woman' as a universal subject is not beneficial to feminism because it does not allow for an analysis of the differing social and economic roles women participate in.

Second, Braidotti explores subjectivity, again with a nod to Butler, as 'performative' (1994: 6). Subjectivity is something one acts out, rather than is. Two aspects of the performative quality of subjectivity are important to Braidotti. First, she is concerned with the power relations and ideological apparatuses, the material relations, which help shape enactment. Second, she is concerned with the role of gender in shaping the possibilities and limits to subjectivity. Butler explores this relationship through her treatment of gender as a **verb**; through the regular enactment of behaviour and attitudes read as gendered, gender takes on the appearance of stability and fixity. Therefore, gender is 'constituting the identity it is purported to be. In this sense, gender is always a doing' (Butler, 1990: 25). This is not to say that gender acts are freely chosen; performativity is regulatory. The repetition of actions and meanings as gender creates regulation, by appearing to suggest that such meanings are natural and unchangeable.

The third aspect of Braidotti's work, which makes it symptomatic of a feminist postmodern account, is a concern with the symbolic and the use of psychoanalysis to analyse the production of gender and subjectivity. Braidotti uses reinterpretations of Sigmund Freud and Lacan to examine the relationship between the formation of the self and society. Both Freud and Lacan brought to the fore – in ways feminism has long found problematic – the processes through which the self is formed in relation to others and societal norms and values. In Lacan the importance of language and the distinction between self and other indicates the relational quality of subjectivity.

In feminist postmodern interpretations of psychoanalytic arguments, the social processes involved in the production of the coherent subject are felt both at the unconscious and conscious level (Flax, 1993). Elizabeth Grosz stresses that, whatever the failings of Freud and Lacan, terms such as 'the unconscious, desire, drive, identification, etc., seem necessary for explaining the transmission of sexual roles, and moreover, for attempting to challenge or subvert their transmission and reproduction' (1999: 106). Teresa de Lauretis argues that the unconscious is resistant aspects of femininity that are excessive to 'phallic definition' (1990: 126) in language and the social symbolic. Beyond postmodern adaptation of psychoanalytic ideas, other feminists such as Dorothy Dinnerstein (1987) and Janet Sayers (1986) explore the non-social aspects of self and identity, and Teresa Brennan (1989) has produced an excellent collection that details the variety of feminist incorporations and criticisms of psychoanalysis.

Braidotti (1994) uses psychoanalytic arguments to consider the role of the symbolic in the maintenance of gendered subjectivity. The gendered self is a product of negotiations between culture, language and the self. The subject **Woman** is 'constituted, as psychoanalysis convincingly argues, through a process of identification with culturally available positions organized in the dichotomy' (*ibid.*: 162). The implication of this kind of argument is that gender is something that cannot be deconstructed away at the conscious level. Focusing on the unconscious or psychic aspects of the self highlights the difficulty involved in changing these structures, making identity something that although transient cannot be changed by will alone. A psychoanalytic approach may help us understand how femininity 'actually gets into our heads (and hearts) so that we often seem to be colluding in our own subordination' (Moore, 1988: 171).

A fourth aspect of Braidotti's approach is symptomatic of some feminist postmodern accounts. Like French feminists such as Luce Irigaray (1985) and Julia Kristeva (1984), she rejects other feminist endeavours to develop a gender-free position. Braidotti advocates retaining some form of sexual difference as 'the positive affirmation of women's desire to affirm and enact different forms of subjectivity' (1994: 158). The universal subject is a 'male-identified' figure whose celebration of the mind, reason and transcendence of the body and time is a masculine creation, made meaningful through its identification of all things feminine as less than, as negative. Within a mode of thinking which retains binary divisions, a form of femininity as anything more than the lesser opposite of masculinity cannot be imagined. The way out of the binary division is to represent difference, including differences between women and men, as positive.

Due to the types of social and economic change, which Braidotti associates with postmodernity, the symbolic processes that produce feminine identity are more visible and open to deconstruction and challenge (Bordo, 1992). The replacement of grand narratives with contingency, ambiguity and reflexivity provides the opportunity to 'intervene upon *Woman* in this historical context, so as to create new conditions for the becoming-subject of women here and now' (Bordo, 1992: 168, original emphasis). Before moving to a gender-free position, the forms of subjectivity that could be open to women amidst the deconstruction of Woman require exploration. The aim is to find a way of investigating what women bring to the operation of subjectivity, without assuming that it derives from their biology. Braidotti argues that searching for feminine subjectivity does not deny other forms of difference. Women share the condition of being defined as 'Woman' by the networks of material and symbolic interaction discussed, but this does not mean they are the same because, as women, they experience other aspects of difference too.

Braidotti develops the metaphor of the **nomad** to express a positive and political form of feminist subjectivity. The nomad is a form of subjectivity both able to express its multiplicity and be open to forms of connection and solidarity that can occur through a yearning for empathy, a term she adopts from hooks (1990). The nomad does not wish to be homeless, but to recognize each home as a transient connection, 'a fluid boundary' to somewhere else. The nomadic figure is at ease with the fluidity of place and identity, is engaged in the intellectual exercise of exploring the experience of belonging in different places, is aware of the relations and crossovers between different forms of knowledge, and is involved in exercises of resistance. The nomad is at ease 'in a lifestyle based on the permanence of temporary arrangements and the comfort of contingent foundations' (Braidotti, 1994: 11).

It is worth mentioning that other feminists have queried using the nomad as a metaphor. In much the same way that male postmodernists have been questioned for using the feminine as their metaphor for the other, Braidotti's use of the nomad appears to be based on a set of privileges that make the metaphor available to the Western thinker. Sara Ahmed, as part of a critique of postcolonial 'fetishism' with the stranger, argues that Braidotti's metaphorical use of the nomadic figure 'erases' actual nomadic people (2000: 82). This erasure allows the Western self to develop 'critical consciousness' through the appropriation of 'all that is threatening under the sign of the nomadic' (*ibid.*: 83). The Western subject travels into different cultures, but only to reinforce the marginality of others and the centrality of the Western norm (McClintock, 1992). When Western lives are explored via metaphors derived from 'marginal lives', the West retains the role of determining itself as the centre and others as the 'marginalised' nomad or stranger. Braidotti's nomad, as opposed to actual nomads, can choose to become homeless *'because the world is already constituted as its home'* (Ahmed, 2000: 83, original emphasis). Irene Gedalof argues that Braidotti's use of the nomad 'strikes a discordant note in a contemporary context of forced displacements, which, we have seen, have disastrous consequences for women' (2000: 342).

Braidotti's nomad joins a variety of feminist subject figures that deconstruct and challenge the Western male subject:

- The eccentric subject (de Lauretis, 1990).
- The cyborg (Haraway, 1991).
- The postcolonial subject (Minh-ha, 1989; Spivak, 1990).

Each of these ways of conceptualizing subjectivity includes some sense of positive subjectivity as being without a home, without a centre of meaning. In de Lauretis's account, the eccentric subject embraces homelessness because home was never available due to the exclusionary nature of dominant notions of subjectivity. The space for the development of an eccentric consciousness and subjectivity is possible because the individual retains a role in engaging with 'the practices, discourses and institutions that lend significance (value, meaning, affect) to the events of the world' (de Lauretis, 1984: 80). The subject may emerge in language, but the individual plays a creative role making her enactment of it. Donna J. Haraway's (1991) cyborg is an attempt to move feminism away from binary divisions between technology/nature and mind/body. The cyborg is a metaphor for a form of subjectivity that questions the boundaries between human bodies and the technological artefacts they come in contact with. The cyborg is an embodied subject, but it is embodied through its discursive and material relations with other things.

For Gayatri Chakravorty Spivak and Trinh T. Minh-ha the postcolonial subject is homeless due to the legacy of colonialism in shaping modernity and global politics (Kapur, 2001). Of particular importance in feminist postcolonial work is the analysis of boundaries. Connections are made between experiences of being caught in the shifting, bloody boundaries of global politics and the boundaries between and within bodies and discourses. Gloria Anzaldúa describes borders as:

> the places that are safe and unsafe, to distinguish *us* from *them*. A border is a dividing line, a narrow strip along a steep edge. A borderland is a vague and undetermined place created by the emotional residue of an unnatural boundary. It is in a constant state of transition. The prohibited and forbidden are its inhabitants. (1999: 25)

Growing up and living in the border between Mexico and the United States as a lesbian Chicano woman, Anzaldúa is aware of the cultural and social relations which emerge from being positioned within different boundaries. The alien becomes so culturally, economically and politically on each side of the boundary. Experiences of boundaries cannot be solved by a search for home, and at the same time as Anzaldúa questions the dominance and exclusivity of American culture, as a lesbian feminist, the Chicano culture presents its own forms of denial and limitation. Aspects of her identity, which do not fit within dominant articulations of Chicano culture, cannot be revealed if she stays at home. Other postcolonial feminists have echoed this point. Gedalof (2000) argues that home is a dangerous metaphor for women because both their identity and bodies are often violently appropriated in national and ethnic battles over boundaries and territory. Staying within one home does not reflect the multiplicity of boundaries most of us travel through, particularly those whose identities do not fit dominant norms. This feeling of homelessness can be a harsh experience: 'Alienated from her mother culture, "alien" in the dominant culture, the woman of color does not feel safe within the inner life of her Self' (Anzaldúa, 1999: 42).

Home must then become something one invents, which emerges from the entanglement of border relations to present something distinct. Postcolonial feminists envision forms of collective or communal subjectivity that escape the myths of home and nationalism, which have led to the brutalization of women and others. The consciousness or subjectivity that represents this transient and fluid experience of boundary-living is the 'alien' culture of the **mestiza**, the 'consciousness of the Borderlands' (Anzaldúa, 1999: 99). Like the nomad, a mestiza consciousness moves between different cultures and languages and is based on a 'tolerance for ambiguity' (*ibid.*: 101). Anzaldúa believes that social and political change will mean that cultural multiplicity will increase; the mestiza is the one who will be psychologically, politically and socially able to cope with what this will mean.

The role of global patterns of economic and cultural change in the production of varied subjectivities and harm is also taken up by transnational feminism. It considers the multiple boundaries Anzaldúa highlights as creating new patterns of 'scattered hegemony' and hybridity that modernist notions of the West and non-West, centre and periphery, and postmodern notions of postcolonialism do not fully capture (Grewal and Kaplan, 1994). Transnational feminism adopts a distant connection to the term postcolonial, fearful that the notion of 'post' traps the framework into an assumption that colonialism belongs to the past, making it less able to consider processes of recolonization. New hybrid and hegemonic forms of subjectivity are connected to 'cultural production in the fields of transnational economic relations and diasporic identity constructions' (Grewal and Kaplan, 1994: 15).

Feminists use postmodern arguments about the constructed nature of subjectivity to explore the role of the opposition between femininity and masculinity in producing the myth of the universal, rational subject. The gender opposition is also linked to myths of nation and community and within this global and local politics. As well as deconstructing the male universal subject, postmodern feminists present visions of feminist subjectivities, which are relational, fluid and multiple as alternative and challenge (Lorber, 2000; Nicholson, 1994). Braidotti and Anzaldúa argue that deconstruction and social change are opening up a space in which alternative visions of subjectivity, which challenge the dominance of the male, Western, (neo)colonial subject, can be explored in language and enactment.

Interpretative theoretical frameworks

Postmodern feminists are uneasy with attempts to explain the world and make universal claims to Truth. This includes claims to truth within feminism.

Spivak (1990) does not deny that feminism should attempt to explain the world, her concern is that it recognizes the narrative element – and thus limits – of such explanations. In her words 'we cannot but narrate' (*ibid.*: 19). Allowing for the narrative quality of theoretical frameworks brings into vision the role of the narrator and questions the privileges of that position. It high-lights that any explanation, as a narrative, to give the appearance of coher-ence, will 'exclude the possibility of the radically heterogeneous' (1987: 105). For Spivak, exploring the narrative quality of theoretical frameworks allows for an examination of 'the itinerary of the silencing' (1990: 35).

Perhaps one of the most important grand narratives of feminism is experience and its role in validating knowledge and commonality. As I out-lined in both feminist standpoint theory and the ethics of care, particular sets of experience are taken as the foundations for both theoretical argument and political activism. Feminists working with postmodern ideas reject the following traditional assertions about experience within feminism:

- Women form similar identities through the reality of the experiences that they share (Elam, 1994).
- Theory can emerge from collective processes of building theoretical structures from shared experience.
- Experiences of victimhood are the centre of feminist activity and legitimization.
- Particular experiences are a requirement for, or guarantee of, authenticity for particular claims to identity or theory.

If we accept that gender ideologies and meanings help shape interpre-tations, then surely they help shape experience. Rather than rely on experi-ence, postmodern feminists are interested in exploring its production. Experience is resituated as something to be deconstructed. How does a grand narrative form around a particular experience? Experience is viewed as something not immediately transparent or available; experiences are understood and interpreted through **social and cultural discourses** that produce our frames of reference. Joan W. Scott argues against any 'appeal to experience as uncontestable evidence and as an originary point of expla-nation' (1992: 24). Feminism should not see its task as making women's experiences 'visible'; such efforts are a form of naïve empiricism which, in the words of Linda M. Alcoff, 'renders invisible the historicity of experience and reproduces the very terms and conditions on which that experience is, in fact, founded' (1997: 13).

Most postmodern feminists do not wish to suggest that experience should be denied any role in feminism. Theorists such as Alcoff argue that decon-structing experience does not mean it is not available in some form as a resource for the production of knowledge, which emerges from the valid interpretations of situated subjects. Making the lived experience of marginal subjects visible can be useful in generating new kinds of knowledge and challenging existing grand narratives about how the world works and people live. Such experiences 'challenge existing epistemic hierarchies concerning what kinds of embodied speakers have credibility and authority' (Alcoff, 1997: 16). Acknowledging the role of language and social processes in the production of meaning should not 'blind us to the continuing truth of the political and cognitive salience of life experience' (*ibid.*: 18).

How to maintain and benefit activism is as important a criterion for evaluating postmodernism in feminism as elsewhere.

Political uses

The feminist argument against decentring the subject focused on the link between political agency and the subject. If the subject is dead and all that is left are social forces and networks of language games and significations, frankly why bother? In response, postmodern feminists have defended the political usefulness of losing the subject in two main ways:

1 Identifying the exclusions maintained by the fiction of the sovereign individual is politically important; and
2 Rejecting the individual subject opens new opportunities for forms of political activity and coalition.

Diana Fuss (1989) argues that securing the importance of one kind of identity, or even a collection of identities requires the 'exclusion of the Other, the repression or repudiation of non-identity' (*ibid.*: 102–3). For postmodern feminists, identifying 'systems of violent exclusion' (Alcoff, 1997: 7) in the production of proper subjectivity – even feminist proper subjectivity – is a valid form of social and political criticism. Challenges to the centrality of identity become political in a context where definitions of woman (the good daughter/mother/wife) are understood as oppressive, bringing with them sanctions for those deemed 'out of place'.

Butler suggests that feminism has little to lose by challenging 'prized premises' (1992: 4); politics does not need to be focused on the individual subject as the foundational point. This is a form of political grammar that removes the conditions within which the individual and her claim to rights is produced. The unitary subject does not preexist the political structures that have been designed to protect and enable the exercise of individual rights. Articulating the claim that 'I have certain rights', creates the notion that I, as a legitimate political actor, exist. In making the subject the foundation, and presenting that position as universal and natural, the production of the subject through the denial of other forms of collective or transient subject positions is erased. Deconstructing this subject allows for the identification of forms of political subject position (I am an authentic English person, I am a taxpayer) that are 'politically insidious' (*ibid.*: 13).

Letting go of the unitary subject opens up new possibilities for political agency and connection: 'The insistence in advance on coalitional "unity" as a goal assumes solidarity, whatever its price, is a prerequisite for political action. But what sort of politics demands that kind of advance purchase on unity' (Butler, 1992: 14)? Chantal Mouffe (1992) argues that discarding the rational and individual subject of traditional politics opens up a space 'to theorize the multiplicity of relations of subordination' (*ibid.*: 371). The particularity of subjectivity is something one engages with to produce identity and politics, rather than something one transcends to find what we share above and beyond our local interests and connections. A shift away from an assumed foundational subject and common identity/cause can allow feminism to explore the self-conscious processes involved in producing the politics and identities of feminism:

> For me the unity of women is best understood not as a *given*, on the basis of a natural/psychological commonality; it is something that has to be worked for, struggled toward – *in history*. (Mohanty, 1995: 77, original emphasis)

From this understanding, a project is possible that is historically and culturally specific and focused on the variable multiple categories of oppression.

Ahmed (1996) explores the legitimacy of postmodern politics within feminism by questioning whether the division implied by some feminist critics – you cannot bring together postmodern theory and feminist politics – is legitimate. Given that both feminist humanist politics and feminist postmodernism centre their concern on gender, they can coexist and resolve each other's inadequacies. While humanism may be unavoidable, this does not mean that it cannot be problematized, challenged and rearticulated. What is needed is a form of 'pragmatic historicism' (a term she associates with Fraser, 1990) focused on 'interrogating the ways in which gender inequality is produced within linguistic practices and institutional norms ...' (Ahmed, 1996: 79). This pragmatic approach points to a postmodern agenda. However, like humanism, postmodernism has limitations. A feminist agenda requires a move beyond the deconstructive moment in order to find spaces where commonality and continuity occur within institutionalized power differences. Difference is delimited by 'structural relations of power and constraint' (*ibid.*: 90), which a rearticulated form of humanist, rights-based politics can intervene in.

It is for the reasons detailed by Ahmed that most of the feminists discussed here are unwilling to fully give up existing forms of feminist activism and intervention. Identity politics cannot be ignored – it is useful, and it can be theoretically grounded (Hekman, 2000). Spivak rejects 'theoretical purity' (1990: 12) in favour of acknowledging the strategic benefits of universal terms – if used carefully. Political engagement requires more than deconstruction, because deconstruction means that you 'say yes to that which interrupts your project' and ends in a project that resembles 'pluralism' (*ibid.*: 47). 'People' may be a fictional category, but 'those of us who agree that *people* includes some things that do better when they are fed and protected from climatic trauma than when they starve, burn, freeze, or drown' (Gagnier, 1990: 30, original emphasis) can use it to engage in global political demands. The dominance of humanist notions of the sovereignty and centrality of the subject make it an inescapable vehicle for feminist politics. However, what postmodern feminists stress is that when such groups and categories are spoken of, a consciousness must remain of the interpretative element and historical specificity involved in the articulation. Butler argues that feminism may make a claim to *a* foundation, but such a claim will always be a site of 'contest and resignification' (1992: 7).

To give a sense of the variety of feminist postmodern politics taking place I will briefly detail two very different examples. The first comes from Sasha Roseneil's account of the Greenham Common women's peace camp, the second from a protest against barbie dolls.

Peace camps and Barbie dolls

Roseneil argues that what radical feminists see as the problem with postmodern politics – a focus on fluidity, aesthetics and culture – is one response to the question 'what might feminist politics look like in an era in which beliefs in transcendental reason, rationality and "Truth" have lost their grip, and when grand systematic theories of oppression no longer inspire allegiance' (1999: 163–4)? Roseneil uses the camp (set up in 1981 and continued until 1994, and usually associated with radical or socialist feminism) to detail a form of politics that rejects modern feminism and has emerged out of postmodernity.

The peace camp represents the politics of postmodernity because, over time, it rejected grand narratives as its legitimization and instead became based on varied and situated individual consciences. This rejection 'expressed a postmodern disillusion in science and technology and a reflexivity about the dangers consequent on modernity's trust that science and technology carry with them progress' (1999: 171). Dichotomies within modern feminism, difference/equality, essentialism/social constructionism, were challenged and rejected. The camp's politics 'were primarily cultural and symbolic', through the use of 'dancing on the missile silos, picnicking on the runway, cutting down the fence, and living a rather chaotic domesticity in front of a Cruise missile base' (*ibid.*: 168–9). Attitude, dress and forms of living and relationship transgressed notions of womanhood. The organization of the camp itself stressed networks over structures; fun and parody were recognized as important political strategies; ethics were situated and differences constantly acknowledged and supported. What the camp indicates is that without 'grand plans or systematic theories, and never claiming to express the "Truth", a postmodern feminist politics plays with existing possibilities and opens up new ones' (*ibid.*: 177).

The second example of postmodern politics is a protest in New York in 1992 against Teen Talk Barbie. As the name suggests, the doll was able to talk, when pressed it would exclaim, 'I love shopping', 'Meet me at the mall', and 'Math class is tough'. Feminists reacted strongly against the message the doll promoted particularly girls' inability to do maths. To protest, a group calling itself the Barbie Liberation Organization (made up of feminists, anti-war advocates and 'culture jammers') got hold of some dolls before they entered stores in New York and hacked the voice box by swapping sound chips with Talking Duke G.I. Joes. Instead of detailing her problems with maths, Teen Barbie announced 'Eat lead, Cobra' and 'Vengeance is mine'! This left GI Joe to bemoan 'Will we ever have enough clothes?' After the publicity and further protests against Teen Barbie's inability with maths, Mattel (the company responsible for the doll) removed the troublesome phrase. Barbie remains a focus of postmodern-type campaigners (for example, the Barbie Disinformation Organization) who use new communication networks to play with barbie and challenge gender cultural codes. The protest, in its choice of cultural subject, its collaboration amongst different activists, its playful displacement of correct gender identities, stressed the performativity of politics. Web sites still celebrate the event and other Guerilla Girl activities focused on cultural production and challenging gender identity. A certain cyberspace mythology has developed around the protest, with different versions circulating and copied, often with only a tangential link to what 'actually' happened.

Postmodern feminists consider these forms of political activism appropriate to current times because of the strategies they employ. In particular:

- The use of new communication technologies to both disseminate information and satirize mainstream culture.
- The generation of coalition links with other opposition groups.

- The stress on cultural expression and play as an aspect of political engagement.
- The localized, yet global, nature of their activities and significance.

The two examples also raise questions about the scope and possibilities of postmodern politics:

1 Are there some issues/concerns that postmodern strategies fit better more than others?
2 When does feminism need to intervene via claims based on the rights of the individual?
3 What are the limits and possibilities of cultural and aesthetic politics?
4 Are their strategies any different from forms of satire within political activism that can be dated back to the French and American Revolutions and before?

Conclusion

Feminist postmodernism aims to move beyond the narrow agenda of post-modernism to ask important questions about the everyday politics of identity and resistance. The feminists discussed here argue that the cost of assuming that it is possible to transcend difference to find universal subjectivity, is to leave hidden the regulatory and oppressive exclusions based on categories such as 'race', class and sexuality involved in the production of the universal. Feminism's critiques of the universal subject go beyond the deconstructive moment to produce visions of subjectivity that acknowledge and flourish within contingency, fluidity and transience. For some, but not all, of the key postmodern feminist writers, such visions of subjectivity appear now because of changes in social, political and economic formations. The visions produced also try to maintain a sense of political agency and engagement. For those feminists less enthusiastic about postmodernism, the concern is that the agency envisioned cannot be sustained.

Advocating postmodern ideas within a feminist agenda is contentious for good reason, I believe. For postmodernism to be valid as a feminist strategy it must be evaluated in terms of the politics it allows and disallows. If material concerns are completely displaced by postmodern debates, then feminism does lose. The anxiety amongst feminists about the fashionable-ness of postmodern language and priorities is valid; fashion should not be an excuse for forgetting that inequality and injustice are shared and experienced by many differently positioned subjects. Where postmodernism helps identify inequalities and injustice is where it remembers to pay attention to the material, economic and political processes embedded in subjectivities and identities.

The next chapter focuses on one particular social constructionist whose work has been adopted, critiqued and adapted by feminists interested in the role of gender in the production of discourses, subjectivities and knowledge. The writer is Michel Foucault and the approach feminists have taken to his work has radically taken that work forward into new directions and issues.

FURTHER READING

Sara Ahmed (2000) *Strange Encounters* (London: Routledge). This text is useful for bringing together debates in postcolonialism and postmodern feminism; Part 1 provides a new perspective on how the 'stranger' should be conceptualized.

Judith Butler and Joan W. Scott (eds) (1992) *Feminists Theorize the Political* (London: Routledge). A collection which brings together some of the key writers in feminist postmodern debates; the chapter by Butler is particularly clear and thought-provoking.

http://www.guerrillagirls.com/ is a web site detailing the activities of Guerrilla Girls. Guerrilla Girls are explicitly postmodern in their outlook on activism, and this site details their activities and art work.

Moving on from Foucault

CONTENTS

Michel Foucault's work encapsulates a variety of theoretical interest and empirical focus (Dreyfus and Rabinow, 1982; McNay, 1994). His main contribution within social constructionist analysis is to link subjectivity and knowledge to the production of meaning within discourses. Discourses for Foucault are a source both of regulating and enabling notions of subjectivity and identity.

Initially it was his work on discipline and surveillance that was the first to find its way into feminist analysis. However, increasingly it has been his ideas about resistance, subjectivity and sexuality that have taken centre-stage. As Foucault's ideas have become increasingly popular, feminists have continued to debate their value. In particular, the focus of attention has been whether the ideas of someone so uninterested in gender can or should be used. After detailing the different feminist strategies for working with Foucault, the Political Uses section will outline how discourse analysis can be applied to welfare polices; in particular the US Welfare-to-Work Program. What the chapter will indicate is that feminists have taken from Foucault's work some important ideas relating to power and subjectivity, but in doing so have significantly moved on from important limitations in his work. His work is therefore useful to look at here, because in considering what feminists have done with it we can see how their adaptation does more than passively adopt the ideas – it changes them; it improves the gaps and inadequacies in their formation. This model of engagement is a template for much of feminist engagement with existing social and theoretical ideas.

Outline of the key perspective

In the discussion below I focus on the key ideas Foucault raised about the role of discourse, the operation of power and the social production of knowledge and subjectivity.

Discursive analysis

In Foucauldian terms, a discourse is made up of rules that authorize what is the correct form of speech, action or word, within its boundaries. Foucault (1971) was interested in discourses because he believed that they play an important role in producing meaning, subjectivity and knowledge. He distinguished discourse from ideology by claiming that discourses do not hide from sight something real. In a direct challenge to Marxism, Foucault (1972) argued that things emerge through their interpretation in discourse.

Foucault's approach to discourse goes beyond the text itself to consider the conditions of its articulation as a contributor to the meanings it produces (1984a, 1991c). The shape and meaning of discourses are linked to the historical and material conditions in which they are articulated, and this relationship is explored through a **genealogical** focus on moments of change, both within discourses and in the conditions of their articulation.

Power

Foucault's approach to power was influenced by the political unrest he witnessed in the 1960s, a period which generated new challenges and struggles previously unarticulated in the political arena, and which raised new questions and problems about social and political relations. The new struggles required a new analysis of power:

> From all these different experiences, including my own, there emerged only one word, like a message written in invisible ink, ready to appear on the page when the right chemical is added; and the word is *power*. (1991d: 145–6)

In these problems the concern with power could not be reduced to questions of the state and material economic relations. In this context, Foucault wanted to explore the varied dynamics of power at different levels of society and between different types of actor. In his work these dynamics are explored in two related approaches to the operation of power.

Discipline and the panopticon

In *Discipline and Punish* (1991a), Foucault argues that there was a dramatic change in the organization of state power in Western Europe during the eighteenth century with the shift from sovereign authoritarian power to that of the modern democracy. The sovereign ruled by force, whilst in the modern state power has developed over the last two hundred years to be both more local and more encompassing. The main tactic is **discipline**, the main method is **surveillance**, and the main agent is the **individual actor**. Through an analysis of changes in penal systems, approaches to crime and methods of punishment, Foucault maps the emergence of **micro**-techniques of power that turn man (his term), in particular his body, into an object of knowledge and that knowledge into a mode of control and regulation. Techniques have developed that are concerned with the minute operation of 'movements and gestures'. As such, 'discipline is a political anatomy of detail' (1991a: 139). In the nineteenth century the new institutions of medicine, law and psychiatry began to classify and monitor the body in order that its functions and failures could be calculated and regulated. At the same time, prisons, hospitals and asylums were built to house those bodies categorized as bad, mad or sick. The threat of being categorized in this way created the self-monitoring that is now at the core of discipline; for what was and is demanded in this mode of power is that the individual disciplines 'himself' to produce the **productive** and **docile** body.

In the nineteenth century, techniques of surveillance of individual action, which are still with us, were integrated into everyday life. In factories, schools and hospitals the design of space was structured around ensuring that individuals were visible, and aware of their visibility. Individualizing the techniques of power generated the individual it monitored; this is what ensured its success, for it produced an individual who is both the object and instrument of the exercise of power. Surveillance reached its ultimate point when it was possible 'for a single gaze to see everything constantly' (Foucault, 1991a: 173). This is achieved with the **panopticon**. Bentham designed a structure for prisons that ensured that every cell was in plain sight of watch-towers placed at the centre of the building. The watchtower was also in plain sight of the prisoner, reminding him of his visibility and vulnerability. In the panopticon, 'visibility is a trap' (1991a: 200). Permanent visibility 'induce[s] in the inmate a state of conscious and permanent visibility that assures the automatic functioning of power' (1991a: 201). What is significant is not just the use of surveillance in the prison. It is how the panopticon can be thought of as a metaphor for the forms of surveillance in modern patterns of power in society as a whole. Through the panopticon, and the response of individuals to it, society itself has become 'disciplinary'.

Power capillaries and relations

In *History of Sexuality: Volume 1* (1990), Foucault's approach to power is further developed and is broadened to include resistant aspects. He adds to his analysis of power to stress that:

1 Power is relational rather than a thing that can be owned. A zero-sum resource model is replaced with one that sees power as the effect of particular configurations of relations and discourses.
2 Power is everywhere, not because it embraces everything, but because it comes from everywhere: '"Power" insofar as it is permanent, repetitious, inert, and self-producing, is simply the over-all effect that emerges from all these mobilities' (1990: 93).
3 Power is local, and can emerge from all levels of society. Power is part of our everyday relations, and as such it cannot be thought of as something that is exercised over us.
4 Power is productive. If power only ever denied us possibilities and opportunities, it would not be successful. Power relations open up as well as close off opportunities for particular forms of social relations, position and experience.
5 Resistance exists within power. Power relations produce the spaces and opportunities within which resistance appears. The use of legal statutes and psychiatric discourses to construct particular identities as incorrect (homosexuality, for example) produce the language in which to challenge that construction.

Knowledge

Foucault understands knowledge as socially-mediated; in particular, it is positioned as a product of discourse. Different discourses count different things as equating to valuable knowledge. The acceptance that is given to different kinds of knowledge reveals more about the legitimacy and power of the discourses they sit within, than it does about their inherent quality or truthfulness.

Foucault aims to challenge key Enlightenment claims about knowledge. First, that the development of knowledge is linear and progressive. Instead, the history of any branch of knowledge is a *complex relationship of successive displacements* (1991b: 53, original emphasis). Second, he rejected models of scientific inquiry that argue that there is a natural world over which science can generate true knowledge; instead he gave knowledge a generative, productive power. By providing a theory for the operation of the natural world, knowledge produces that world. Third, Foucault wanted to reject arguments that present knowledge as separate from and an antidote to power. Instead 'there is no power relation without the correlative constitution of a field of knowledge, nor any knowledge that does not presuppose and constitute at the same time power relations' (1991a: 27). Finally, he rejected the neutrality of knowledge because he saw in the Enlightenment a 'will to knowledge' (1984a: 162). In particular, knowledge has been turned towards the self and has generated a desire to know our true selves through the institutions and discourses of psychiatry, law and medicine. This knowledge is part of the modes of control and discipline through which power operates in modernity.

Subjectivity

An exploration of the production of subjectivity is central to Foucault's work, indeed in 'The Subject and Power' he claims that 'my objective ... has been to create a history of the different modes by which, in our culture, human beings are made subjects' (1982: 208). The sovereign subject is a social product of the modes of knowledge and discourse formed in the Enlightenment. The individual is 'itself only a parody: it is plural; countless spirits dispute its possession; numerous systems intersect and compete' (1984a: 161). The sovereign subject is inseparable from knowledge of him/her. As subjects we are contained, 'trapped in our own history' (1982: 210). Knowledge traps us by producing notions of authenticity and true selves that we can and should become. The will to knowledge of the self binds us to institutions such as psychiatry in order to interpret and discover our true – singular – nature. Because the scope of possible subject positions is delimited by the governing force of discourses, subjectivity is disciplinary.

The socially produced and disciplined subject is not a determined and passive subject. Individuals are actively involved in the processes of subjectification that discipline them. The issue is why and how 'a human being turns him – or herself into a subject' (1982: 208)? In part the answer is that when we adopt available subject positions, as well as being disciplined we also adopt a positive sense of self that is able to participate in the world. Individuality may be fictional and follow templates, but we have agency in the creative part we play in making that individual unique to us. Through adoption of particular containing templates we become individual selves. Power is exerted over free subjects. Power, if understood as a relationship between participants, must operate within a context where each participant has a space in which to respond and act. Where the actor is not free to act, it is force and violence – not power – that have taken place.

Aesthetics

In Foucault's (1985, 1986) last major works he explored an alternative ontology of the self which could be the foundation for an ethical framework capable of challenging disciplinary power. His desire was to find an alternative to universal moral frameworks imposed on people from above, by religion, morality or science (Thacker, 1993). Through an examination of ancient Greece he explored 'practices of the self' or 'techniques of the self' through which subjects can approach their subjectivity creatively. His conclusion was that an aesthetic approach focused on care and pleasure offers a radical rejection of truth. Truth is replaced by 'the will to live a beautiful life, and to leave to others memories of a beautiful existence' (Foucault, 1984b: 341).

The ethical framework within which the Greeks explored the aesthetics of their body, judged the person on how they adapted and lived moral guidelines which were seen as starting points for the development of an individual ethical life. Instead of rules and criteria from above there was a stress on liberty and autonomy. The subject who cares for themselves, who treats their life and their body as a 'work of art' (*ibid.*: 350), is far from the docile body passively adopting scripts. Foucault argued that he did not want to transpose the Greek system into contemporary life, there were problems with it – not least the role and position of women. Instead, his interpretation of their practices was meant to raise the possibility that modes of ethical life are possible without the disciplinary structure of moral or rational frameworks premised on beliefs about the authentic subjectivity of man.

Foucault produced a body of work which has taken analyses of power into new directions in order to think about the production of subjectivity, knowledge and resistance. For some feminists this has opened up new possibilities for exploring gender and identity. However, others have identified important weaknesses in his work which cast doubt on the validity of his approach for a feminist agenda.

Feminist critiques

Foucault has been the focus of many feminist debates about the potential of his ideas for feminist inquiry. The main problems revolve around the lack of gender in his accounts, the inconsistencies in his portrayal of power and the suitability of his ethical framework. The problems identified are a major barrier to using his ideas within feminist priorities.

Gender blind

Various feminist writers have argued that the almost complete silence within Foucault's work on questions of gender casts doubt on the validity of using his ideas for a feminist agenda (O'Brien, 1978). Much has been made of the use of the male pronoun in his work as a symbol for his lack of concern with gender processes, and within the work on sexuality it is particularly frustrating that gender is rarely raised. There is a suspicion that he is no more helpful to feminism than the ideas and discourses he aims to attack:

> Foucault's analysis is a tale told by the victors of Western culture, the power holders. If it is read as a prescription or as a basic mythic narrative of the West, it legitimates the androcentric view as THE perspective on Western culture. (Buker, 1990: 828)

However, does this oversight matter? Cannot someone else simply add gender to the narrative? The concern, however, is that the lack of gender creates fundamental weaknesses in the logic of his arguments (Braidotti, 1991). For example, his celebration of the aesthetics of the self, as an alternative to the discipline of the true self, fails to capture the gendered dynamics involved (Fraser, 1997). The metaphors used by Foucault to describe Greek aesthetic practice talk of 'self-mastery', 'virility' and the minimization of anything feminine. For Lois McNay (1994) this betrays a masculine approach to the body. Kate Soper argues that what Foucault finds attractive in ancient Greece is the processes of 'masculine self-regulation' (1993b: 41) he finds there. This attraction is an indication of his 'covert androcentricity' (Soper, 1993b: 29).

Carolyn J. Dean (1994) argues that Foucault fails to recognize the centrality of gender to the operation and development of modern concepts of subjectivity in modernity. An awareness of gender would have led to a very different story about sexual repression and liberation in the nineteenth and twentieth centuries than the one told in *History of Sexuality: Volume 1* (Foucault, 1990). An analysis of gender would have seen, within the development of modern sexual norms and identities, the production of a model of viral and controlled masculinity. However, Foucault's 'most spectacular failure' (Dean, 1994: 277) is the priority given to questions of dominance and discipline over questions of agency and resistance in his analysis of power.

Power

The first problem feminists have raised relating to Foucault's account of power is that it is overly deterministic. This criticism focuses on the account outlined in Foucault's *Discipline and Punish* (1991a). What Foucault describes here are institutions of power able to inflict harm on seemingly powerless subjects (docile bodies) (Cain, 1993). Disciplinary power is 'monolithic' and 'unidirectional', leading to 'problematic implications for an understanding of the relation between the body and gender identity' (McNay, 1991: 134). His concentration on the institutions of disciplinary power leaves little space to explore the responses of subjects to these institutions. It also leaves little space to explore other sources and sites of the operation of power. It is a form of reductionism that ignores the impact of 'legal, social and psychological constructs' (*ibid.*: 135), in order to construct a notion of centralized power that 'has the effect of pushing women back into this position of passivity and silence' (McNay, 1992: 47). If feminists adopt this model of power, and Davina Cooper argues some have, then what comes with this is 'the seeming inevitability of subordination and domination: of inequality' (Cooper, 1994: 445). Nancy Hartsock (1990) argues that it is nihilistic to assume that we cannot move beyond power relations that dominate to produce a qualitatively better and more egalitarian society. Monique Deveaux warns that 'we should not slip into fatalistic views about the omnipresence of power' (1994: 233).

What is missing in this picture is resistance. Foucault seems blind to how gender identities are constantly challenged and under assault (Soper, 1993a); he ignores actual experiences of resistance in order to maintain the image of docile bodies. Feminism cannot adopt this framework and focus on the 'delineation of women's oppression and the concrete transformation of society as central aims' (Deveaux, 1994: 223–4). Can resistance only ever appear as a result of dominant power relations? Cooper wishes to retain a notion that resistance can emerge from a 'set of values or long-term aspirations' (1994: 443), which are not solely relative to the particular power relationship under dispute or negotiation.

Foucault's revision of his theories of power in *History of Sexuality*, to allow for greater fluidity, resistance and contingency in the operation of power, has led to a separate set of criticisms. This account of power appears to imply that any notion of structural power – say patriarchy – is false. The call to move away from analyses of material and economic power relations appears to deny feminism the ability to discuss the systematic nature of women's oppression (Moi, 1985). The focus on fluid power relations amongst free agents implies that one cannot conclude that there are groups, individuals and structures which have more power. For many feminists, particularly those working with a materialist framework, 'power is not neutral, diffuse and freely available but fiercely protected by those who hold it and their agents' (MacCannell and MacCannell, 1993: 205). For example, Eloise A. Buker argues that Foucault fails to specify the role of male sexuality in the overall exploitation and social position of women. The freedom it suggests women have to produce and explore power within sexual relations, a material analysis would identify as illusionary. Power relations occur in a context where material and economic resources help position some actors as having more power. Inequalities within the ability to act powerfully are not given enough consideration in the capillaries of power

Foucault describes:

> His ban on contentious 'history' would make it impossible for women even to speak of the historically universal misogyny from which they have suffered and against which they have struggled, and would appear to reflect the blindness of a man who so takes for granted the persistence of patriarchy that he is unable even to see it. (Balbus, 1987: 120)

His proposal that power relations require the existence of free agents is a particular concern. He does not explore the processes – subjective and material – that deny some groups, in particular women, the space in which to be free agents. Instead he forecloses a discussion of the relationship between force and power (MacCannell and MacCannell, 1993). For example, Dean and Juliet F. MacCannell (1993) and Deveaux (1994) argue that there is a close relationship between the use of male force and the existence of male power, which suggests they operate as a continuum of techniques of subordination. He fails to recognize that the freedom of some agents often requires that someone else does not have freedom (Bell, 1991; Plaza, 1978).

The stress on contingency in the localized operation of power appears to make it more difficult to claim that some practices of power are more coercive than others (Dean, 1994). The placement of knowledge, truth, morality and just about everything else within power leaves little space for normative judgement or demands for rights. Each claim is itself implicated in exchanges of power. Nancy Fraser (1989) argues that there is an inconsistency in this. Foucault himself is clearly making normative judgements (at times Marxist, at others liberal) when he talks of domination, discipline and subjugation. Thus, he appears to carry on working with an unacknowledged normative framework, while denying others the legitimacy to make their own such claims. His final focus on the aesthetics of the self suggests a politics focused on individual experimentation. How does such a version of individual agency connect with wider political questions and strategies? How, without a wider normative framework, does a focus on the individual avoid simple individualism (McNay, 1994)?

Aesthetics

Foucault's (1986) final work on the aesthetics of self has been a source of varied criticisms. As indicated above, a significant concern is the retreat into individualism. Foucault's celebration of aesthetics appears ironically 'too bound up with the very self that he seeks to critique' (Fraser, 1997: 30). The focus on the individual's self-creation is a romantic retreat from the 'politics of solidarity', and as such it represents 'an atomized politics of introversion' (McNay, 1992: 158). The stress on the creativity and care of the self, as the alternative to disciplinary models of normative, top-down authoritarian morality, ignores relational and communal modes of ethics and care. In his ethical approach, care of self dominates over care of others. As such, the 'covert androcentricity' of his work influences his inability to imagine alternative ethical possibilities.

Rosalyn Diprose (1994) argues that he appears to have lost contact with his own arguments about the contexts within which individuals can be aesthetic. His own analysis of the social construction of subjectivity indicates that its formation occurs in relation to other subject positions that are viewed as more deviant, less normal. In his account of aesthetics he fails to acknowledge that particular bodies are valued, celebrated, in a context where other bodies are viewed as less valuable, less aesthetic. Therefore, the aesthetics of the self is flawed as an ethical approach because 'the value attributed to any body as "a work of art" is generated through comparison with, and often denigration of, the other' (Diprose, 1994: 31–2).

How can approaches to the self that are progressive be distinguished from ones that allow or encourage the 'maintenance of social hierarchies' (McNay, 1992: 77)? Joan S. Forbes (1996) argues that contemporary encouragement for women to experiment with and explore their sexual selves, to carve out their own sexual biographies and wants, can be recast as a form of discipline and compulsion. The woman-as-sexual-agent discourse belies the role of 'well worn themes and images within heterosexuality about male and female sexuality' (1996: 182) in shaping the boundaries and expression of female sexual exploration. Arguments for women to be free to enjoy and participate in pornography as a form of individual expression and liberation, free from disciplinary models of pure femininity, fall into a trap Foucault's project of self-experimentation appears unable to spot. Foucault's call for aesthetics of the self seems divorced from his own recognition that discourse regulates as well as generates identities.

In summary, feminists who are critical of a Foucauldian insertion into feminism argue that his perspective is fundamentally inadequate because it disallows:

- an analysis of gender;
- an analysis of inequalities between women and men;
- an analysis of the material structure of power;
- claims to rights on behalf of women; and
- moral judgements about harm and evil.

Feminist incorporations

Foucault's ideas emerged as feminists were exploring new ways to think about sexuality, the body, power and subjectivity. He shares feminism's disquiet with Enlightenment concepts of truth, reason and rationality (Aladjem, 1991; McNeil, 1993), and for these reasons it is not surprising that feminists working with a social constructionist agenda were attracted to some of his ideas. However, some of the early feminist appropriation of Foucault failed to recognize or respond to the inadequacies in his work. For this reason, feminist work using Foucault can be split into two groups; the first group simply adopts his arguments, in particular in relation to discipline, whilst the second takes a more critical approach, both using and interrogating his ideas to develop distinct claims. It is therefore problematic to talk in terms of 'Foucauldian feminism'; too much is altered by feminist incorporation to use a term that implies some strong allegiance to the original.

Gendering Foucault

Feminists interested in social constructionism looked to Foucault's ideas about discipline and surveillance to help explain the gendered dynamics of power in contemporary society. In particular, what interested this group was a focus on femininity and the body (McNay, 1991). Two influential accounts are provided by Sandra L. Bartky (1988) and Susan Bordo (1993), both examining 'techniques of femininity' (Deveaux, 1994: 225). Bartky begins by acknowledging the lack of gender in Foucault's work:

> Foucault treats the body throughout as if it were one, as if the bodily experiences of men and women did not differ and as if men and women bore the same relationship to the characteristic institutions of modern life. (1988: 63)

However, even though Foucault does not produce a gendered understanding of disciplinary power, Bartky asserts that feminists can. Using dieting and the diet industry as her exemplars, she proposes that the feminine body is a product of disciplinary power.

The projects aimed at women's bodies leave them in an impossible position, since the objectives they require are not achievable and women's attempts are seen as further proof of their frivolous nature. Women are criticized for spending time looking after their physical attributes, attributes which in a mainstream consumerist Western society since childhood they are constantly told are what makes them female and different from men:

> The disciplinary project of femininity is a 'set up.' It requires such radical and extensive measures of bodily transformation that virtually every woman who gives herself to it is destined in some degree to fail. Thus, a measure of shame is added to woman's sense that the body she inhabits

is deficient: she ought to take better care of herself; she might have jogged that last mile. (Bartky, 1988: 71)

Women who work with discourses of the perfect feminine body treat their body as the enemy, as something alien to them. Significantly Bartky argues that these invisible, individualized processes of self-discipline have replaced previous forms of patriarchal control in society. Like Foucault she argues that forms of domination have moved from the level of the population to the level of the individual and have incorporated the self into their operation.

Bordo (1993) argues that women take part in their own subjection by relating to their body and bodily needs as something to be controlled, monitored and altered. Disciplinary power is durable and adaptive and reaches out to most women regardless of their 'race', age, class or sexual orientation. For Bordo, Foucault's approach to the body improves existing feminist analysis by:

1 not looking for a villain or cause for the production of power;
2 allowing feminism to identify the constitution of subjects and bodies within the operation of power; and
3 recognizing the moments where resistance is subverted and halted.

The operation of discipline can be seen at its most stark in body disorders where femininity is produced 'in disturbingly concrete, hyperbolic terms' (1993: 16). In particular, Bordo examines anorexia as a condition containing a 'virtual, though tragic, parody of twentieth-century constructions of femininity' (*ibid.*: 17). Anorexia, when it begins in a diet, perhaps due to peer or family pressure, 'emerges out of what is, in our time, conventional feminine practice' (*ibid.*: 23). Femininity includes in its template the belief that women feed others – not themselves. Female hunger and containment is celebrated in the cultural symbols around women. At the same time women are also caught up in the fitness culture and the pursuit of control over one's body shape. The anorexic takes this self-mastery to a new level, where the level of power over one's body is paramount in the refusal to eat.

Traditional models of femininity may have changed, and women are now encouraged to take control, to be independent, but this independence and power has become focused on ensuring the perfect feminine – contained – body. The anorexic's refusal to eat can be thought of as an unconscious protest against femininity; by inscribing in her pain and body its costs and through that act removing all traces of femininity from it. At some level, control is taken and will is expressed via the subject's regime and refusal to acquiesce to the demands of others. However, the protest is subverted because the results of the act are the weakening of power and possibilities.

Protest turns into 'the utter defeat and capitulation of the subject to the contracted female world' (*ibid.*: 21).

The panopticon is used in work by Bartky and Bordo and other Foucauldian feminists to explore the role of the male gaze in the production of self-surveillance by women. Beauty magazines and images of femininity generate a disciplinary gaze within which women feel surveyed and evaluated. The power of the disciplinary gaze operates through women's self-monitoring of their own look against the templates available. No person, group or structure needs to be behind this process, or to have particular outcomes in mind, for the result to be the confinement of women's identities: as such the images become powerful through women's incorporation of them.

The arguments of Bartky and Bordo have been criticized by other feminists for failing to take a critical position on the inadequacies in Foucault's work. There is a concern that, like Foucault, their argument ends up treating women as passive robots, unable to challenge the forces of discipline around them. Deveaux argues that their work replaces an analysis of women's reasons and desires in undertaking dieting or exercise with a treatment that views them as 'robotic receptacles of culture' (1994: 227). McNay argues that adding gender to Foucault's analysis of disciplinary power makes the same mistake he did by creating 'an oversimplified notion of gender as an imposed effect rather than a dynamic process' (1992: 12). Partly as a response, other feminists choose to concentrate on Foucault's work on subjectivity, resistance and his later analysis of productive power, but in doing so they also revise his initial proposals and include processes invisible in his own accounts. This work includes an interrogation of the values of feminism, but moves on to consider the requirements for political resistance lacking in Foucault's arguments.

Power and resistance

Adapting some of Foucault's later ideas helps challenge particular types of feminist approach to resistance, power and identity. An important challenge is to resource models of power, which talk in terms of men having power and women lacking it. Such accounts, found in socialist and radical feminism, appear to imply that:

1 power is some intrinsic quality to men; and that
2 Black or working-class men have more power than white or middle-class women.

Feminists argue that this fails to identify the operations and effects of power and mistakenly attributes blame to particular individuals or groups

(Morris, 1988). Instead of talking of practices or groups that have power, it is more useful to examine how certain relations result in differentials of power through which some women, in particular contexts, are subordinated. One example is heterosexuality and masculinity; instead of viewing them as intrinsically powerful, heterosexuality and masculinity can be understood as socially-constructed practices that are contingently powerful, open to change and possible to resist. This suggests that the challenge to them does not lie in trying to invent a sphere outside their influence (Bailey, 1993; Cooper, 1994; Sawicki, 1991a); to do so remains within the existing framework of meaning that produced masculinity and heterosexuality. Instead, feminists can explore how masculinity and heterosexuality are played out in relations between individuals in such a way that power inequalities occur (Linder, 2001). It is the consideration of both heterosexuality and masculinity as processes that together influence power relations that Foucault himself failed to consider within his accounts of the development of subjectivity and sexuality, yet without doing so only a partial account is feasible.

A consideration of Foucault's capillaries of power leads to recognition of the diverse patterns of power within everyday relations, as an alternative to oppression understood as 'an opposition between a hegemonic, repressive force and an underclass possessing an unspoken truth' (Phelan, 1990: 427). Talking of power as contained in particular practices, which encourage rather than force us to do things, is a useful starting point for resistance (Barrett, 1991). Resistance is opened up by a relational model of power that suggests that 'wherever there is a relation of power it is possible to modify its hold' (Sawicki, 1991a: 437). The strategic focus it implies is 'that resistance must be carried out in local struggles against the many forms of power exercised at the everyday level of social relations' (Sawicki, 1991b: 222). These varied forms of resistance stress something Foucault failed to appreciate, that women are far more than docile bodies in their response to power relations. Freed from finding or identifying the revolutionary subject, feminism can focus on the practices of everyday resistance women already participate in.

Feminists critically engaging with Foucault are involved in doing more than deconstructing existing relations and discourses. The discussion of alternatives or realistic political forms of challenge is something Foucault categorically refused to involve himself in. This is not enough for feminists wishing to understand how things are in order for things to be different. The overall aim of deconstructing existing approaches is to open up the possibilities for alternative strategies to resist oppressive power relations (Martin, 1982). The categories of feminism may be less innocent, but contra to Foucault's views on feminism they are still usable. Knowledge can be part of political struggles, the mistake lies in thinking that knowledge, particularly of our selves, will set us free and move us beyond power and ambiguity. The category 'woman' is something feminism can use, but must also be something whose meaning and politics is open to intercession. As such, Shane Phelan (1990) argues that feminism should search for new frameworks for the moderation of rights, which are less naïve about knowledge and less open to domination by groups making claims to universal truth: a search that requires more than Foucault in order to take place.

Sexuality

For many of the feminists who wish to engage with Foucault's ideas, sexuality is the main area where some 'convergence' of interest and framework can take place (Braidotti, 1991: 90). Feminists do not need Foucault to know that notions of sexuality produced through discourse and identity have limited the rights of women. Carol Smart (1992) examines legal discourses in areas such as prostitution, divorce and pornography to explore how law has been a vehicle in defining correct and incorrect female sexuality. What Adrienne Rich (1986a) identified as 'compulsory heterosexuality' can be thought of as the discourses prevalent and dispersed throughout society, which produce templates for how women (and men) should be heterosexual. In each of these accounts women are given a role as actors capable of resistance they were not allowed in Foucault's accounts. In addition, issues of material resources and their role as a basis for challenge and containment are included in a way Foucault's lack of concern with the material allowed for. Smart does more than deconstruct legal texts; she considers the lives of the women such laws effected. Rich considers the material implications compulsory heterosexuality has had on women in terms of the diminished legal and economic rights of married women.

Feminists examining the sexual revolution note, as Foucault does, the hidden processes of regulation and containment maintained in myths of liberation and freedom. Such work goes on to point out that to examine changes in sexual norms and identities in society without a consideration of gender is fundamentally flawed. Lynne Segal (1994) and others have indicated the ways in which gender dynamics and power relations played a part in shaping the liberation on offer. Forbes notes that 'the "sexual revolution" depended on women freeing themselves of their inhibitions and enjoying (hetero)sex both in and outside of marriage' (1996: 181). While the contraceptive pill opened up possibilities for sexual experimentation and independence, it also brought with it assumptions about women's sexual availability. Both heterosexuality and masculinity remained powerful in the local and societal processes determining the possible form and scope of liberation. At the same time, the revolution also generated forms of resistance through greater awareness of the limits to women's sexual choices; this resistance took the shape of the second wave of feminism in the 1970s. Therefore, feminists are interested in Foucault's ideas about sexuality, but bring to the table a significant advance by prioritizing gender and considering material inequalities and issues around rights as part of the debate around the production of sexuality and subjectivity.

In summary, feminists argue that Foucault's ideas can be useful because they encourage feminism to consider:

- Sources of discipline in society and individual relations.
- Women's incorporation of surveillance.
- The role of discourses in the production of identity.
- The politics of knowledge and claims to truth.
- Resistant practices within everyday relations.

However, using some of his ideas requires an approach ready to move beyond his lack of interest in important areas, including:

- Gender.
- Political engagement.
- Economic inequality.
- Actions as well as discourses.

Political uses

An important area where feminists have used Foucault's ideas is in critical engagement with welfare policies in Europe, the United States and Australia. Here discursive analysis and notions of discipline and surveillance have been used to consider how women, particularly as clients, are monitored and regulated via the structures and objectives of welfare policy. The type of issues feminists include in their approach to discursive analysis indicates the degree to which they have moved his ideas forward.

Welfare policies

Feminists exploring welfare policies from a discursive position argue that welfare's influence on women's lives is not just through its role in providing financial and material benefits and penalties. It is also through the production of particular discourses about the deserving and non-deserving, rights and responsibilities, the private and public, and the normal family (Levitas, 1986). Such discourses affect women's lives through influencing the shape of policies and the organisation of support (Pringle and Watson, 1992). Discursive patterns of meanings can be traced throughout the operation of welfare, from the planning of policy at the central level to implementation at the local.

Fraser has produced a template for analysing the role and significance of discourses in welfare policies. She examines how the welfare system (in the United States) operates as a mechanism that helps construct the needs it then supplies. Powerlessness and dependency is solidified by the ability of the welfare system to interpret need in particular ways that individualize it and diminish its political and social dimension. Fraser uses JAT ('juridical–administrative–therapeutic state apparatus'; 1989: 154) to symbolize the three strategies that, she believes, are used in welfare interpretations of need. First, a need can be channelled into the juridical arena to narrow it to a question of legality (prostitution is illegal so is dealt with by the courts). Second, the need can be put into the administrative arena, which regards it as a question of efficient provision (how much money should the single mother get?). Finally, the therapeutic arena regards need as a product of individual failing, to be cured by counselling the 'sick' individual. Through the interpretation of social problems and the definition of what constitutes need, the welfare arena aims to channel discussion away from questioning the workings of the system itself. Certain identities and understandings of need are supported by the practices of welfare provision, while others are understood as private or deviant (Fraser and Gordon, 1994). The single mother is held up as the main symbol of all that is deviant: a legitimate reason to discriminate.

Fraser's final contribution to the debate is her suggestion that there are three different discourses existing in welfare debates attempting to define and interpret need:

1 Reprivatization discourse
2 Oppositional discourse
3 Expert discourse.

The reprivatization discourse is used to argue that the welfare arena is attempting to take over needs which are rightfully based within the private arena, within the family. The argument represents the family as a natural organization, a site of care and responsibility which, if left alone, would naturally assume the responsibility for needs that welfare is unjustifiably attempting to take over. The reprivatization discourse is used to assert that certain 'needs' should be returned to the private sphere 'where they belong'. The oppositional discourse is used to destabilize the boundaries between the private and public by focusing on politicizing need; need is understood as contestable, while the family is understood as a political body capable of change and critique. The expert discourse can be used by both those attempting to privatize and politicize need to legitimate their argument. The benefit of using experts and their discourses is the apparent superiority and objectivity of their 'knowledgeable' language and argument.

Welfare-to-work

In what follows I use this approach to consider the Clinton administration's 'welfare-to-work' reform. In 1996 the Personal Responsibility and Work Opportunity Reconciliation Act was passed (Walker, 1999) to:

1 Provide assistance to needy families so that children may be cared for in their own homes or in the homes of relatives.
2 End the dependence of needy parents on government benefits by promoting job preparation, work and marriage.
3 Prevent and reduce the incidence of out-of-wedlock pregnancies and establish annual numerical goals for preventing and reducing the incidence of these pregnancies.
4 Encourage the formation and maintenance of two-parent families (HR3734 *The Personal Responsibility and Work Opportunity Recon-ciliation Act* 1996).

The Act replaced Aid to Families with Dependent Children (AFDC) with the Temporary Assistance for Needy Families (TANF) Program. Instead of welfare support based on need and funded from general taxation, TANF requires that recipients will work in order to receive aid. In the words of the Administration for Children and Families: 'The law marks the end of federal entitlement to assistance' (ACF, 2001). Recipients must take a job and cannot stay in the programme for longer than two years without working. When recipients first apply for support they must undertake an initial assessment where a 'personal responsibility plan' is drawn up. If recipients do not take work their benefits can be reduced or terminated. Recipients cannot stay on the programme, even if working, beyond five years. Individual states, which are responsible for running TANF, must reach quotas for the number of recipients who are working. Working can include training and attending school, but there are limits on the percentage of claimants within states who can be working in this way. The states that administer the programme can also receive bonuses for reducing the number of births out of wedlock. They can also receive penalties if they do not penalize recipients for not taking work or let them receive benefits beyond the five years.

A discursive analysis can indicate some important exclusions and inclusions lying within the policy and the support that recipients receive.

The shift away from entitlement is significant. Entitlement positions welfare within a discourse of rights and citizenship; within such discourses entitlements are interpreted as things citizens have a right to without being seen as having failed or in need of charitable assistance. The identification of something as an entitlement or charity is socially constructed, has varied over time, and is politically important. Those who are seen as having entitlements to certain kinds of support also have rights – as citizens – to participate in the provision of that entitlement. Those who receive charity – clients – have much less right to participate. As such the clients of welfare, by being denied certain entitlements, have an identity as passive and dependent. To regain citizenship status they must work. In this way the Act reinterprets citizenship as something workers, rather than everyone, have. Work is defined as an intrinsic good, and is defined as waged work rather than, for example, raising a child. The Act also ensures that the state agencies have the right to heightened surveillance over clients, and the Personal Responsibility Plan ensures that recipients participate in and are aware of that surveillance.

Excluded from the discourses legitimating work as the key to the rights of citizenship are discussions of 'race' and gender. Yet 'race' and gender lie at the heart of the policy. The majority of recipients are women from ethnic minorities, often looking after children on their own. The rights to citizenship and entitlement this group has are the most tenuous and therefore the easiest to take away. The work most women are forced to take under the programme is low-skilled, and exploitative; it often means performing the care tasks that white middle-class people are happy to pay others to do (Albelda, 2001; Cancian, 2001). The welfare-to-work ethos and scheme thus represents, encourages and is a product of racial, class and gendered social divisions and hierarchies. It is not necessary to argue that policy actors are deliberately generating discourses that deny rights to Black women to understand that the emergence of these discourses and their articulation within policies such as TANF play a part in the maintenance and reproduction of those divisions.

Welfare-to-work emerges in a context where dependency has become the major rhetoric within which welfare assistance is interpreted by the state and by both conservative and liberal political actors. The dependency argument, replicated in the Act, claims that people on welfare become used to support, have little motivation to improve themselves and move off the cycle of welfare support, and pass on the dependency and attitude to their children. Contemporary welfare discourses about dependency 'serve to enshrine certain interpretations of social life as authoritative and to delegitimate or obscure others, generally to the advantage of dominant groups in society and to the disadvantage of subordinate ones' (Fraser and Gordon, 1997: 123). Dependency in contemporary welfare debates refers to individual weaknesses – either moral or psychological. The dominance of this pejorative, individual interpretation of dependency in welfare debates marks a significant *privitization* discourse at work in the shaping of welfare policy.

The pejorative usage of dependency is also aided by the development of various *expert* discourses, which have come along to explain the psychological failings of those receiving welfare. The use and legitimacy of these discourses can be explained by looking at the context of their use. For example, analysing the lives of black women as pathological has a long history in American psychiatry and social sciences; the infamous study by Daniel P. Moynihan in the 1960s argued that black women had 'emasculated' black men, leading to a cycle of poverty and crime in black families. Then black women were identified as 'pathologically independent'; today they are 'pathologically dependent'.

The use of psychiatric terminology and understandings of human motivation has increased in various areas of American lives. In 1980, for example, the American Psychiatric Association codified a condition called Dependent Personality Disorder (DPD); and new conditions are still being 'discovered' – sex addiction and attention deficit disorder, for example. Meanwhile, pop psychology explains that the only barrier to success is our inner self. This output is specifically targeted at women. In a context where psychology and psychiatry are used to interpret women's lives, it is unsurprising that it is used so freely and exclusively to understand those claiming welfare benefits. However, the problem is that the dominance of these psychiatric approaches privatizes the framework within which dependency is understood and removes any question of inequality or politics from the discussion. In psychiatric approaches to dependency 'the social relations of dependency disappear entirely into the personality of the dependent' (Fraser and Gordon, 1997: 137–8). Reading the processes behind poverty and its links to teenage pregnancy into a racialized and gendered notion of individual pathology helps calm cultural anxieties and produces easy – and cheap – recipes for tackling the 'problem'.

Reviewing this analysis one can argue that a feminist framework adapting Foucault's approach to discursive analysis to analyse contemporary welfare policies helps us to consider:

- the contexts in which new policies develop;
- the way in which the meaning of key terms of welfare can alter;
- the role of expert discourses in interpreting the users of welfare; and
- the socially constructed nature of notions of citizenship, entitlement and private and public responsibility.

It is also useful to contemplate, even with the alterations made by feminists, what the approach perhaps draws our attention away from:

- the economic priorities that lie behind welfare policy and reform;
- the material effects of being a welfare user;
- the practical processes of policy design and implementation; and
- the use of expert discourses to challenge the operation and effects of welfare policy.

Conclusion

Foucault's (1986) last work on aesthetics is the least useful to feminism; the focus on the creative self appears to be the result of forgetting his earlier arguments about the role of others and the other in the production of subjectivity. The argument he presents here indicates a tendency in his work to be removed from the implications of his ideas. A celebration of previous times is easier to contemplate than a full consideration of how an ethical life is possible in contemporary relations and society. The ethics of care debate has weaknesses but it offers a consideration of the political and relational qualities of both care and the self. This proposal is a less impoverished vision of alternative forms of subjectivity able to challenge individualistic models still dominant in Western society.

In other areas Foucault's ideas do provide a rich source of concepts that have been taken up by feminists wishing to explore both the local dimensions of power and the patterns of surveillance and discipline that infiltrate the everyday. Foucault directs feminism towards what it already does, and that is to dispute the frameworks within which freedom and rights are discussed. His ideas can be used to identify the intricacies of contemporary patriarchal power relations, but incorporating these ideas into feminism does have to respond to two difficulties. The first is the slight treatment Foucault himself gave gender and feminism; the second is his treatment of power, which leaves his work at times overly deterministic, and at others overly optimistic. Feminists have dealt with these problems by acknowledging the gender gaps in his work and by introducing feminist awareness of the contexts in which power relations are played out. This awareness helps avoid the significant ethical and theoretical problems in his work on power.

In moving on Foucault's ideas to new areas and priorities, feminists show once again an important criteria they continue to maintain in their work: the importance of generating and working with ideas that support political criticism and engagement. It is these criteria which have led many feminists to be concerned with the inclusion of the next set of ideas into feminist agendas: queer theory.

FURTHER READING

Rabinow, P. (ed.) (1984) *The Foucault Reader* (London: Penguin Books). This Reader brings together extracts from throughout Foucault's career and contains interviews not available elsewhere. The Introduction by Rabinow is also extremely useful.

Lois McNay (1994) *Foucault: A Critical Introduction* (Cambridge: Polity Press). McNay captures Foucault's important ideas and provides valuable critical commentary on their value.

Caroline Ramazanoglu (ed.) (1993) *Up against Foucault* (London: Routledge). Feminists interrogate Foucault's ideas and explore the changes necessary to make them applicable to gender issues.

Queer theory

CONTENTS

Michel Foucault's arguments about the social construction of sexuality and identity have been taken forward by a number of writers and disciplines. In particular they have become central within lesbian and gay studies. The perspective that has emerged from this work is often represented under the loose banner of queer theory. Queer theorists adapt Foucault to examine the production and representation of sexual meanings and identities in order to deconstruct notions of normality and fixed sexual orientation. In a short space of time queer theory has taken centre-stage in lesbian and gay, cultural, and literary studies. It now dominates contemporary examinations of sexuality, in particular those prioritizing questions of identity and difference.

For reasons, which echo those raised in relation to postmodernism and Foucault, feminists have questioned the way in which queer theory approaches the analysis of sexuality, in particular arguing that it does not appreciate issues relating to gender and materiality. Feminist suspicion has been heightened by the open hostility towards it that some queer writers display. Even so, important feminist writers have been key participants in queer theory's development. The opening section of this chapter will discuss the background to queer perspectives, its main claims and its critique of feminism. I will then move on to indicate how feminists have responded to this critique. The focus will then turn to Judith Butler as an example of someone attempting to bridge the gap between feminism and queer theory. The Political Uses section will identify differences in approach between radical and materialist feminists and queer feminists by comparing their analyses of the politics of butch and femme lesbians and relationships.

Outline of the key perspective

It is important to begin by considering the political and theoretical background to queer theory's emergence.

Political background

The 1970s saw the expansion of lesbian and gay politics in Western countries. A critique of homosexual reform groups and the rise of identity politics and counter-culture movements were important factors in its development. Prior to the late 1960s, reform groups in Britain, the United States and Europe defined homosexuality either as a psychological disorder or as a minority and inconsequential sexual desire. For young, politicized lesbian and gay activists this denied the possibility that homosexuality could be the source of a shared identity and/or something to feel proud of. The lesbian and gay groups of the early 1970s explicitly dropped the medical terminology of homosexuality and focused on a more assertive politics based on visibility and cultural identity (Altman, 1998; Cant and Hemmings, 1988). The aim was to assert lesbian and gay identity as something more than sexual desire; something shared and politically significant (Weeks, 1991).

By the middle of the 1970s, cultural expression and community-based values and identity were at the centre of lesbian and gay activism. However, it became increasingly difficult to maintain a unifying identity within 'the lesbian and gay community'. One of the most noticeable divisions was between women and men, and the tensions point to the difficulties with a politics based on a notion of a shared identity. Steven Seidman (1997) has identified four problems with the dominance of identity politics in lesbian and gay activism in this period:

1 Lesbian and gay identity was not placed under scrutiny.
2 Lesbian and gay politics did not question mainstream society's focus on gender as the key factor in sexual object choice. Bisexual writers argued that the importance given to gender in straight and lesbian and gay society denied the legitimacy of desires that had little to do with gender (Hutchins and Kaahumanu, 1991).
3 Hierarchies emerged about acceptable forms of sexual desire and object choice which conformed to wider sexual norms and laws, and in the process various categories of being sexual and of relationships were denied legitimacy (Rubin, 1993).
4 The shared identity at the centre of lesbian and gay politics betrayed a white, middle-class bias in its cultural enactment and representation (Fernandez, 1991).

Queer theories emerge out of disquiet with the politics of identity and a desire to widen the constituencies and issues explored in sexual politics. At the same time as these concerns emerged, theoretical ideas were developing to encapsulate the new constituencies and themes.

Theoretical background

As indicated above, theoretically, queer ideas find an important catalyst in the work of Foucault. His assertion that homosexuality is socially produced, and that the 'homosexual' is a relatively new figure formed in the legal and medical discourses of Victorian society, is central to queer theory's analysis of the relationship between homosexuality and heterosexuality. In addition, Jacques Derrida's analysis of the role of the other, and binary oppositions in securing language and social meaning, is also an important precursor. Some of the key writers who have adopted poststructuralist ideas to examine sexuality include Eve Kosofsky Sedgwick (1990), Diana Fuss (1989, 1991), Judith Butler (1990), Lee Edelman (1994) and Teresa de Lauretis (1984, 1994b). As this initial list indicates, feminist writers have been important participants in queer ideas from the beginning.

Queer perspectives can be identified by their:

- use of poststructuralism as a mode of analysis;
- analysis of the social as text;
- consideration of a wide group of sexual practices and minorities;
- adoption of psychoanalytic categories;
- focus on deconstruction.

One of the key queer texts is Sedgwick's *Epistemology of the Closet* (1990), which explores why:

> of the very many dimensions along which the genital activity of one person can be differentiated from that of another ... precisely one, the gender of object choice, emerged from the turn of the century, and has remained, as *the* dimension denoted by the now ubiquitous category of 'sexual orientation'. (1990: 8, original emphasis)

Sedgwick proposes that the binary opposition between homosexuality and heterosexuality is a vital element in securing order and structuring culture and ways of thinking in modernity. Drawing from both legal statutes and literary representations, she uses a deconstructionist approach to explore the development of the homosexual figure and the role of the closet in that development. Drawing on Foucault's analysis of the emergence of the modern homosexual, she argues that sexuality has become an important medium for the production of knowledge about what can (and should) be known.

The closet is an important element of lesbian and gay experience and a marker for the dominance of heterosexuality. The closet, and the legal and material implications that develop from it, is the 'defining structure of gay oppression in this century' (*ibid.*: 72). The contemporary gay experience – at least for some – of coming out provides a positive marking of sexuality. However, coming out is also problematic because in the articulation 'I am gay', 'I am lesbian', that part of self is secured as the defining and fixed element of the person's identity. The language and symbolic reference of coming out of the closet is now used to describe a variety of different visible positions. This does not imply that the closet has lost its gay resonance; instead it indicates 'that a whole cluster of the most crucial sites for the contestation of meaning in twentieth-century Western culture are consequentially and quite indelibly marked with the historical specificity of homosocial/homosexual definition' (*ibid.*: 72). As a 'master category', the homosexual/heterosexual opposition has the same status in Sedgwick's analysis that Marxism gives the proletariat/bourgeois opposition and feminist standpoint theory gives femininity and masculinity.

It is vital to deconstruct the operation of the opposition because an 'endemic crisis' (*ibid.*: 1) exists in its meaning and the processes it supports. The efforts and structures put in place to mark the line between heterosexuality and homosexuality indicates the perilous nature of that line. On some level most people may be open to the possibility that sexuality is a more fluid set of practices and desires than that allowed by the articulation of it as a type of person (homosexual or heterosexual). However, the articulation of homosexuality as equating to a minority category of people remains dominant in areas of representation and legal rights. Sedgwick aims to deconstruct the opposition between gay and straight as constituting 'distinct kinds of persons'. This involves highlighting forms of desire and notions of identity that transgress the opposition.

These ideas direct queer theory towards culture and the role of representation in the production of the division and for providing opportunities for transgression (Fuss, 1991). Alongside obvious cultural outlets (advertising, film and popular culture), queer writers argue that heterosexuality is produced and celebrated in law (the nuclear family model in welfare; Section 28 in the UK), medical discourses (the current search for the gay gene) and numerous social practices. Where homosexuality appears in cultural representation it often conforms to certain existing structures of representation within the hetero/homosexual binary (the camp man, the sporty lesbian). Other forms of sexuality and intimacy appear as freakish deviants, towards which straight society may show a certain level of voyeurism (hence the appeal of true-life sex confessional programmes in both the UK and the USA). Such figures are the contemporary exotic other who helps secure just how normal everyone else is, or thinks they are. Queer writings are thus concerned with the role the 'homosexual other' as a symbolic figure plays in maintaining **heteronormativity** in Western society. Rosemary Hennessy describes heteronormativity as 'an institution that organizes more than just the sexual: it is socially pervasive, underlying myriad taken-for-granted norms that shape what can be seen, said, and valued' (1995: 146).

Queer approaches can be summarized as pursuing the following claims:

- Both heterosexuality and homosexuality are social constructions.
- The binary opposition between the two is an important source of meaning and identity.
- The dominant legitimate identity requires the existence of the deviant category to make sense.
- The dominance of heterosexuality is fragile and produces the means for its decline.
- Transgression offers scope for resistance and challenge.

Queer critique of feminism

The tensions between women and men in the lesbian and gay movement in the 1970s led some lesbians to look to radical feminism as an explanatory framework, community and platform for activism (Jeffreys, 1994). Within this framework sexuality is viewed as a product and tool of patriarchy, and lesbianism is seen as a political choice as much as a sexual desire. At least implicit in this argument is a belief that feminism, in particular radical feminism, is the key site for exploring the operation of sexuality and its role in oppressing women (Rubin, 1975). Queer writers, including those who identify as feminist, have consciously set out to challenge and reject radical feminism's arguments (Bright, 1984; Califia, 1981).

Gayle Rubin's essay 'Thinking Sex: Notes for a Radical Theory of the Politics of Sexuality', first published in 1984, is an important contribution to this debate. The essay contains two important claims:

1 The radical feminist framework robs lesbian sexuality of any meaning other than as a marker of feminist and gender solidarity. Rubin and other writers such as Cheshire Calhoun (1995), Joan Nestle (1987) and Biddy Martin (1992) suggest that the only form of lesbian sexual expression allowed in this framework is monogamous, non-penetrative, long-term lesbian relations. The cost of producing notions of correct lesbian identity is to generate a notion of sexuality and identity that is fixed and essentialist. Martin argues that the reasons for lesbian feminists generating such rules are understandable as 'a defence against the continued

marginalization, denial and prohibition of women's love and desire for other women' (1992: 98). The problem is that the strategy has had too high a cost, excluding forms of pleasure and expression in the name of securing a lesbian identity.

2 Feminism should not be seen as the privileged site for the analysis of sexuality: 'The realm of sexuality also has its own internal politics, inequalities and modes of oppression' (Rubin and Butler, 1998: 100). This second point is fundamental to queer arguments about sexuality. Rubin argues that analysis of the 'sex/gender system' has taken gender to be the dominant factor and has seen sex as irrelevant or only as a product of patriarchy. This has led radical feminism to mistakenly view male homosexual practice as a product of male power, which plays a role in the oppression of women.

Rubin supports the feminist claim that sexuality is important to the oppression of women, but challenges radical feminism for what she identifies as anti-sex conservatism which views all forms of sexual expression as a symptom or product of male power and privilege. Carol S. Vance (1992) makes a similar point, arguing that feminism has become embarrassed to speak of sexual pleasures in its focus on sexual danger. Sexuality has became the source of 'unremitting victimization' (1992: 5). In the work of both Vance and Rubin, as well as other queer writers, feminist anti-pornography campaigns and hostility to Sado-Masochism (S/M) are seen as symptomatic of an approach to sexuality with little scope for pleasure, experimentation and fun (Christina, 1990).

Sedgwick is perhaps the most adamant that gender and sexuality need to be separated: 'The study of sexuality is not coextensive with the study of gender; correspondingly, antihomophobic inquiry is not coextensive with feminist inquiry' (1990: 27). Sedgwick identifies a number of inadequacies and problems in the analysis of sexuality within radical feminist work:

1 Sexuality is seen as operating as a function of gender relations, denying that the symbolic and individualized meanings that people may attribute to sexuality can revolve around other processes.

2 Feminist approaches to sexuality have, at times, betrayed a homophobic response to gay male desire (labelling it as more permissive, masculine and superficial than lesbian spirituality and connection).

3 Lesbian experiences of oppression are analysed through gender, rather than being linked to the experiences of gay men (and other sexual minorities).

4 The anti-sex approach towards pornography and S/M takes feminism back to 'the most repressive nineteenth-century bourgeois constructions of a sphere of pure femininity' (1990: 37).

5   The legitimacy of 'trans-gender role-playing and identification' is denied by feminist accounts that attribute butch–femme relationships and identities to replications of male oppression and hierarchy.

Rubin, Vance and Sedgwick all want to examine, from outside of what they see as the confines of feminism, the production of sexuality through norms and values that define good and bad sex. The alternative to 'sexual hierarchies' is a form of democratic pluralism, which sees all forms of sexual variations as part of the human condition. Many feminists from different perspectives have found this argument for pluralism deeply worrying.

Feminist critiques

Feminists have identified various problems, both political and theoretical, in the priorities of queer theory and the emphasis being given to it. Radical feminists are particularly visible in challenges to queer theorizing within feminism, and the criticism begins with weariness with the portrayal of feminism presented in queer theory.

Straw figure of feminism

It should be no surprise that feminists have critiqued queer ideas, given the persistent attack on their work. Feminists have grown weary of being presented in queer texts as not having a sense of humour and taking sexuality too seriously (Leidholdt and Raymond, 1990). They argue that queer writers represent feminism in a false light in order to make their ideas and politics appear more fun, new and sexy. While Martin believes that there is much of value within queer theory, she is concerned with the way the opposition between feminism and queer theory is projected. She notes that:

> celebrations of queerness rely on their own projections of fixity, constraint, or subjection onto a fixed ground, often onto feminism or the female body, in relation to which queer sexualities become figural, performative, playful, and fun. (1998: 11)

Stevi Jackson (1999) argues that it is simply not true that feminism is only interested in identifying women's victimization. Other feminists argue that in queer theory's rush to appear distinct from feminism it has lost sight of the ways in which gender remains a vital component in sexual inequalities. Writers such as Martin have also queried the dominance of queer theory within some areas of the academy. Theory, as does any other commodity, changes with the fashion; currently queer theories are simply more fashionable than feminism. Its 'hip' image and the star status of its proponents may say more about the commodification of ideas than it does about any theoretical quality or superiority.

Lesbianism

For lesbian feminists the need to remain focused on our distinct experiences has been more important than the playful fluidity of queer theorizing (Walters, 1996). De Lauretis, one of the first writers to use the term queer to refer to a particular body of work, now rejects the term in favour of exploring the specific processes involved in the construction and maintenance of lesbian identity. In explaining her decision to no longer use the term she notes:

> As for 'queer theory', my insistent specification lesbian may well be taken as a taking of distance from what, since I proposed it as a working hypothesis for lesbian and gay studies in this very journal, has quickly become a conceptually vacuous creature of the publishing industry. (1994a: 297)

The queer focus on deconstructing identity is seen by feminists working on lesbian issues as less useful than exploring the specifics, and at times benefits, of advocating lesbian identity.

There is a concern that differences between the processes influencing lesbians and gay men – discursive and material – are lost in the queer project. The political and theoretical divisions, which surfaced in the era of the Gay Liberation Front (GLF), have returned to queer politics with some feminists, radical in particular, suggesting that once again men have become dominant in defining the terms of queer debates. Sheila Jeffreys (1994) argues that queer theory is a theory of male homosexuality and cannot be used to explain the position of lesbians. Queer theory does not analyse the different position of lesbians and gay men because it would have to acknowledge that gay men – as men – are often in a better position than lesbians. It is problematic that as the term lesbian gains acceptance as a legitimate person and identity, queer theory loses that name to a sense of play.

A number of feminists point to the transgressive celebration of drag in queer theory, as evidence of the dominance of a male (bell hooks also argues white, 1992) perspective within it. Queer writers present drag as playful and subversive, whilst radical feminists suggest instead that drag is an act based in a misogynistic hatred of women. Other feminists do not see conscious misogyny at work, but do see a more complex process of appropriation and need in the drag act. Sara Ahmed suggests that the femininity parodied in drag is a product of patriarchy and commodity exchange, the drag performer's use of the symbols of these structures does not offer genuine resistance to 'the power divisions within which the gendered subject is always already negotiated' (1996: 83). Hennessy argues that it is naïve to represent drag – by drag queens or kings – as necessarily a desire to be unidentifiable in dominant codes of heterosexuality. Instead drag can emerge from attempts to realign sex with gender – I really am a woman/man inside – and can be 'a painful yearning for authenticity' (1995: 151).

Politics of transgression

For several reasons, both radical and materialist/Marxist feminists have found queer transgression a limited political tool (Wilson, 1993). Firstly, radical feminists have argued that some of the areas of sexuality that should be feminism's concern do not fit the queer agenda of playful transgression. Areas of sexual exploitation and harm such as rape, pornography, prostitution and child sex abuse require an awareness of power and oppression which is missing in queer arguments. Their celebration of denied sexual practices and minorities appears unable to distinguish between practices that are playful and ones that cause harm. Challenging heteronormativity by celebrating all forms of difference is not necessarily liberating for all. For example, it appears to assume that the issues in relation to lesbian and gay sex and intergenerational sex are the same (Matisons, 1998).

Second, the politics of cultural experimentation and aesthetics can easily turn into the politics of my expression, my interests and me. Elisa Glick (2000) argues, from a materialist feminist perspective, that queer politics offers and fails to deliver a strategy of 'fuck our way to freedom' (*ibid.*: 19). It appears caught in a contradiction where sex is both a key disciplinary vehicle for the regulation of the individual and also a key vehicle for the liberation of that individual. By being unable to move beyond individual acts of transgression and representation, queer theory separates these acts 'from their location in political and economic systems' (*ibid.*: 22). In the process it offers nothing more than the individualism of libertarianism.

It also appears to be unwilling to connect the development of alternative sexual practices with their historical and material roots (Clark, 1991). For example, queer discussion of the playfulness of S/M is unwilling to discuss the source of the symbols of that play – images and practices that originate in patriarchy, capitalism and fascism. Martha C. Nussbaum (1999a) proposes that queer theory is unable to make such connections because its proponents refuse to take any normative stance that might enable them to make claims about good and bad sexual practice or cultural experimentation.

The third problem surrounds the subjects that queer theory identifies as the transgressors. Is transgression an elitist activity available to a privileged minority who gets the joke? An act can only be transgressive if few participate; the more that join in, the less transgressive the act becomes. For some this suggests an elitist academic activity, separated from political engagement with the non-textual real world. Finally, there appears to be two central contradictions within at least some queer celebrations of the transgressive sexual practice or actor. The first is that, like postmodernism, queer theory rebels against a notion of the individual actor capable of agency, yet the acts celebrated within transgression are those made by individuals who stylistically mark their individual agency as queer. Second, queer theory begins with a critique of hierarchies of normality within sexual laws, only to go on to create its own sexual hierarchy where 'queer is good, queerer is better, but queerest is best of all' (Lloyd, 1999: 195). For example, is the person who labels herself as transgendered 'better' than the person who calls herself a transexual and feels trapped in the authentically wrong body? Is there a drift back into the very categories and boundaries of marked and celebrated identity in the praise given to those who 'belong' in the queer camp?

Is cultural analysis enough?

Various material aspects appear lost in a concern with cultural representation. One important material reality feminists and others find missing in queer theory is the body, which appears as the site of various discourses and representations, but itself has little significance (Bordo, 1993; Connell, 1995). The focus of materialist feminists is the lack of attention paid within queer theory to the institutional forces that are at play in the regulation of identity and material realities (Jackson, 1999). An awareness of institutions requires greater focus on the constraints on exploring different forms of sexual identities, rather than a celebration of the fluidity of forms of desire and identification (Gamson, 1998). Hennessy (1995) argues that without a historical materialist analysis capable of recognizing the material practices involved in the regulation of sexuality, any analysis becomes irrelevant.

Queer talk of the joy of fluid and playful identities does not include awareness of the material and social inequalities which enable some more than others to have the space in which to experiment (Fraser, 1995). An analysis of the link between contemporary sexual multiple identities and their economic context may highlight the role of new markets and arenas of commodity exchange (Delphy, 1993). Put broadly, if you have more than one identity you are going to need more clothes. Jackson (1995) sees a shying away from exploring male, white and middle-class dominance in the playing out of sexual roles, desires and identities. Where queer analysis does talk of institutional and material processes, the nature of their influence remains vague and primarily discursive. If an analysis of sexuality is going to take on board 'the distribution of wealth, resources, and power' it will have to 'address more than discourse' (Jackson, 1995: 153).

Is identity that bad?

Queer theory finds notions of fixed or shared identity confining and exclusionary. However, feminists and lesbian and gay activists who participate in identity politics question seeing identity as having only negative attributes and implications. Warning of the dangers of identity politics leaves the impression that identity, particularly one chosen and shared by others, cannot be a positive, affirming process. Rejecting the possibility that identity can be a basis of politics produces a series of questions:

- If identity leads to domination and is therefore a bad thing, what is it that can unite queer theorists or activists?
- Is opposition to 'normalizing social forces' (Seidman, 1997: 134) enough to bring theorists and activists together?
- Is any attempt to bring together even multiple and transitory ways of being and bonding with others into some form of identity inherently problematic?

Identity may create problems for feminism and other political projects, but it is also impossible to imagine politics without it.

In summary, feminists are wary of queer priorities because they appear to exclude analysis of important relationships between:

- material structures and sexual space and expression;
- gender and sexuality; and
- politics and identity.

It is these separations that feminists working with queer ideas work to resolve.

Feminist incorporations

A major theme of feminist work within queer theory is bringing the discussion of sexuality and gender back together. One of the key writers doing this is Judith Butler.

Judith Butler

Butler is loved and loathed in equal measure. She has had an unofficial fan club and been singled out as the main villain in the production of academic elitism within feminism. For some her work reflects, and has been a main trigger in the development of, feminist work able to respond to changing social and political dynamics around gender and sexuality. For others, her work is unnecessarily dense, convoluted and abstracted from real life. Her texts draw upon and significantly adapt psychoanalytic ideas, feminist reworkings of these ideas, philosophical concepts and poststructuralist arguments.

Her book *Gender Trouble* (1990) (*GT*) combines a queer perspective on the production of sexuality with a feminist concern with gender regulation and subordination. The ideas introduced from the book in Chapter 4 are that:

- The category of 'woman' cannot be the founding universal subject of feminism.
- The subject does not preexist modes of representation.
- Agency does not flow from the voluntary actions and intentions of the individual actor.
- Gender is a form of regulation that is produced through performativity.

The publication of *GT* generated a great deal of debate and many of the criticisms listed above of queer theory. In response, Butler wrote *Bodies that Matter* (1993) (*BTM*). The following summary of her argument will indicate its formulation in both texts.

Sex and gender

The division between sex and gender is one of the key notions of feminist thought. Sex equates to natural, biological differences between females and males; gender equates to the social construction of differences between women and men that are not essential, are the result of socialization and have been and continue to be a factor in inequality. Butler begins *GT* by deconstructing the division between sex and gender. The feminist strategy of using the division to challenge biologically deterministic arguments about femininity and masculinity has served to secure the notion that there are important, universal differences between women and men. Keeping sex and gender separate assumes that there is a prediscursive, natural realm of sex that is not the product of social interpretation and can be recovered from the bias of gender. Butler argues that, like all binary oppositions, each term is produced in relation to the other. The naturalness of sex only appears so in the context of the unnaturalness of gender.

In *BTM* the distinction between sex and gender is made more porous by her discussion of the materiality of the body. Butler suggests that she is open to the possibility that there are aspects of the body – pain, hunger, pleasure – that 'cannot be dismissed as mere construction' (1993: xi). However, the materiality of the body is not accessible without some process of interpretation and discursive involvement. The body may be real, but the moment we refer to it we embed social and cultural meaning into it. Our sense of what is material about the body is the 'effect of power', in particular the **heterosexual matrix** which is secured through the materialization of the body as sexed. Materialization of the body occurs through the discursive production of sexual difference, generated through regulated practices of repetition and reiteration.

Heterosexuality and gender

In *GT*, as part of her analysis of the relationship between heterosexuality and gender, Butler argues that constructivism must move away from the grammar of the subject. The focus on the subject is produced through the same structures of language and meaning that produce gender and heterosexuality. Her aim is to replace the focus on gendered subjects with a concentration on gender as 'a relative point of convergence among culturally and historically specific sets of relations' (1990: 10). The security of gender as a norm and category of subjectivity requires the equally secure notion of heterosexuality. What marks one as female or male, is one's attraction to the opposite sex. Heterosexuality operates through the construction of gendered notions of femininity and masculinity that secure the roles to be played out within social relations and the 'bipolar sex/gender system'. Gender and heterosexuality support each other, producing a perception of certainty and 'naturalness' that is fictional – 'a regulatory fiction'.

In *BTM*, the link between heterosexuality and gender is explored via a discussion of the processes through which the body is materialized. The outcome of the materialization of the body as sexed is the 'consolidation of the heterosexual imperative' (Butler, 1993: 2). We can see evidence of this through the importance given to knowing someone's sex; to be unclear about someone's sex is to question their 'very humanness' (*ibid.*: 8). The narrowing of bodily materiality to that which secures the dominance of heterosexuality occurs through 'the force of exclusion and abjection' (*ibid.*: 3). Bodies, which are not clearly marked as fitting within the heterosexual matrix, are important to its dominance. It is here that Butler (1999) explicitly rejects proposals to separate the analysis of gender from sexuality. Examining the processes through which 'if one identifies *as* a given gender, one must desire a different gender' (1993: 239, original emphasis) produces the shared agenda for queer and feminist theorizing.

In *BTM*, Butler returns to performativity to refute the claim that the analysis in *GT* implied that the subject is free to choose different performances through 'wilful appropriation' (1993: 7). The first stage is to stress again that the subject should not be placed at the centre of the analysis. The subject cannot be at the centre of the performance because the act only makes sense through its fit or lack of fit with the ongoing cultural codes and norms that make up the heterosexual matrix. Authority and power does not come through a single act or word or subject position, but through their **citation** of culturally understood regimes of meaning. When a baby is born and identified as female and given an identifiably female name, the ongoing process of citing cultural norms of femininity has begun. As she grows she is compelled to continue this citation and live up to (but never obtain, claims Butler) the symbolic ideal of femininity.

The symbolic

In both texts Butler adapts the psychoanalytic ideas of Lacan. In *GT* she uses Jacques Lacan to explore how the signifying processes embedded in language construct notions of the coherent, gendered and heterosexual subject. What Lacan refers to as the Symbolic, the linguistic structure of signification and the 'universal organizing principle of culture' (1990: 79), produces the boundaries within which the self develops. The conclusion of his perspective is that the division between sex and gender, femininity and masculinity, homosexuality and heterosexuality emerges through the Symbolic, which operates to repress certain desires and wants. Butler argues that norms of gender and heterosexuality are produced within the structure of signification within which meaning and notions of the self emerge. An analysis of the structure of signification indicates a 'radical dependency' between the terms of each binary pair. This dependency suggests a fragility, which is the space within which Butler aims to 'configure an alternative imaginary for the play of desires' (*ibid.*: 57).

In *BTM* Lacan is again drawn upon to make a link between the operation of the Symbolic and her notion of citationality. The development of a proper self emerges through citation of the Symbolic – the heterosexual matrix – through which the Symbolic itself has meaning. The development of subjectivity occurs through appearing to be the correct gender, for the correct body. Our sense of self should be thought of as an ongoing project, where we perform identificatory projections, influenced by the Symbolic, which is then itself made real by our continued citation of it.

Power

In both texts Butler uses a Foucauldian perspective on power to reposition prohibition as 'one formation of *power*, a specific historical configuration' (1990: 75, original emphasis), which produces both the correct and incorrect

object of desire and gender identification. Laws that prohibit particular sexual practices do not repress previously existing desires; they both produce
and regulate them in order to consolidate their own power. The implication
is that 'the category of sex and of identity ... [is] the effect and instrument
of a regulatory sexual regime' (*ibid.*: 101). Crucially this suggests that the
structures of prohibition, which impact the formation of identity, can be
challenged. In *BTM* Butler stresses that neither discourse nor subjects
are at the centre of things, being powerful. Power instead is a 'reiterated
acting that is power in its persistence and instability' (1993: 9).

Transgression

In *GT*, Butler identifies scope for agency and challenge as located within the
operation of the matrix or regime. The compulsion to be the correct gender
or sexuality cannot help but produce 'failures' who 'exceed and defy' the
sex/gender regime. Such failures can both transgress and destabilize the
operation of the regime that produces them. However, such failures should
not become a source of new fixed and secure alternative identities; instead,
the object is to explore 'disidentification'. What Butler calls for is 'a radical rearticulation of what qualifies as bodies that matter, ways of living
that count as "life", lives worth protecting, lives worth saving, lives worth
grieving' (1993: 16).

Butler looks to practices and identities that destabilise the sex/gender
regime through **parody** to make gender and heterosexuality '*radically incred-
ible*' (1990: 141, original emphasis). Three examples are focused on. The
first is the appropriation of heterosexual practices and symbolism within
same-sex relations; the masculine, leather-wearing gay man and the butch
dyke transgress the normalcy of sexual norms by creating a disjunction
between gender and femininity and masculinity. In the second example
the **redeployment** and **reappropriation** of terms of abuse – dyke, queer,
fag – as categories of identity destabilize the binary opposition that places
them as the deviant other of heterosexuality. The use of queer language is
a form of citation that works against the dominant chain of signification,
creating confusion and instability in the matrix itself. However, in *BTM*
Butler argues, perhaps in response to her critics, that the playful use of
queer language at times must 'yield' to other forms of politics and strategy.
There are issues and conflicts that are best-served by the politics of identity.

The third example of transgression has drawn the most controversy and
debate: Drag. Butler's choice of drag she acknowledges is heavily influenced
by previous anthropological work by Esther Newton (1972). In *GT*, drag is
transgressive because: '*In imitating gender, drag implicitly reveals the imitative
structure of gender itself – as well as its contingency*' (1990: 137, original

emphasis). Drag does not parody an original gender identity – but the notion that there is an original. The act of parody produces discontinuity between the naturalness of the repeated acts of gender and the fictions that support them. 'Parodic Proliferation' of the signs of hegemonic culture highlights the fragility that lies behind the symbols of gender and heterosexuality. The symbols of femininity that the drag queen plays with are derived from a misogynistic culture, but their performance here displays 'the myth of originality itself' (*ibid.*: 138). The laughter the drag queen generates is not at the expense of him or women, instead it is an acknowledgement of gender as 'an ideal that no one *can* embody ... laughter emerges in the realization that all along the original was derived' (1990: 139, original emphasis).

In *BTM*, Butler acknowledges that it is a mistake to assume that drag is necessarily transgressive. Drag can emerge from feelings of pain, exclusion and denial; it becomes transgressive when it is 'a site of a certain ambivalence' (1993: 125); where its performance indicates that what it parodies is already an imitation of something without an original. Butler explicitly rejects the radical feminist analysis of male drag as rooted in an expression of misogyny. Such an analysis fails to recognize the transformation the acts undertake when presented within drag (by drag queens or kings) which make them excessive to the heterosexual matrix, witness to imitation and capable of subversion. In assuming that the act is about women, aimed at hating them, feminist critics remain within a heterosexual mode of understanding, believing that gay men who are drag queens can only express themselves through a hatred of women.

To summarize, Butler's main claims are that:

- Sex and identity are not determined but are discursive.
- Heterosexuality, gender and the materiality of the body are interrelated regulatory fictions, and as such their analysis should be brought together.
- They are maintained through performance, repetition and citation.
- The processes of signification that create heterosexuality, gender and the correct body also produce their other, that which is outside signification.
- There is scope for challenge and resistance.
- Agency does not presuppose 'a choosing subject' (1993: 15).
- Transgression opens up the possibility of dispelling notions of the normal or real.

Butler's celebration of and call for subversive politics based on parody, theatre and transgression raises important questions about the scope and shape of such a political agenda, particularly for feminism.

Political uses

Queer strategies have become highly visible within lesbian and gay politics and feminist activism. One sign of their adoption has been the contentious changes in name of many lesbian and gay groups and Pride marches to lesbian, gay, bisexual and transgendered (LGBT), or simply Queer (Gamson, 1998; Humphrey, 1999). For those who have taken the queer route out of liberation politics, it offers a way forward for expressing a more encompassing politics of sexuality and sexual orientation (Rahman and Jackson, 1997; Smith, 1994).

The examples and strategies associated with queer politics concentrate on disruption (Halberstam, 1993; Martin, 1992). Whether this is language, political strategy, art forms or dress, the intent through play is to break apart the rules through which boundaries are made between the acceptable and unacceptable. The objective is to highlight the constructed nature of such rules and to highlight the winners and losers. Martin suggests that the aim is to 'open up the public realm to a discussion and appreciation of sexual diversity and variation' in a way that challenges 'the epistemological and political terms in which homosexuality and other "perversions" have been closeted' (1992: 95). Forms of activism that have been labelled queer include 'Queers bash Back, Queer Nights Out, Queer Kiss-Ins and Mall Zaps' (Hennessy, 1995: 146). Such events 'insert gay spectacle into the centers of straight consumption' (*ibid.*: 160). AIDS activists and groups are seen as important examples of queer politics in their strategies and outlook. Stanley Aronowitz's (1995) analysis of the activities of ACT-UP in New York highlights the strategies that have made this organization in particular so significant in accounts of queer politics. For Aronowitz the structure and strategies of ACT-UP are reflections of the failure of liberal politics to generate genuine change for groups suffering discrimination at the hands of the state.

Butch/femme lesbians

A useful way to outline the specifics of queer politics is to compare its analysis of butch/femme lesbians to that of radical and materialist feminists. The 1950s saw, in the United States, Canada and elsewhere, the emergence of a distinct urban lesbian subculture built around the butch/femme identity and role. This subculture, which has been recovered in historical analysis and retold in fiction, had a distinct iconography and strict rules of behaviour, both in courting and in relationships. It was particularly marked amongst working-class and Black lesbian communities. More recently, in the late 1980s and into the 1990s, the figures have returned to the limelight.

In particular, the femme has emerged as a legitimate lesbian and feminist figure. The peak of her rehabilitation saw the coining of the phrase **lipstick lesbian** and the (in)famous *Vanity Fair* cover of KD Lang and Cindy Crawford.

Radical and materialist feminist analysis

The 1950s/1960s butch/femme lesbian communities were criticized by radical feminism in the 1970s (Abbot and Love, 1972; Jeffreys, 1989), and this critique can be linked to the significance given to lesbianism within radical feminism. The decision to be with women and not men was a political choice as well as about individual desire (Radicalesbians, 1973; Rich, 1986a). The phrase 'woman-identified-woman' was coined to express the political nature of the relationships and community (Bunch, 1994). The political desire to develop a way of living, being and interacting with others distinct from male ways of acting was seen as crucial to building a collective feminist and lesbian future (Martin and Lyons, 1972; Rudy, 2001). This framework has influenced radical feminism's interpretation of the butch/femme relationship – past and present – as politically problematic.

The butch/femme relationship was and is criticized for replicating a heterosexual template, in particular the playing out of power inequalities. The fear, still articulated by contemporary radical feminists, is that the relationship brings the brutality of the straight, male dominant world into the lesbian world. During the 1970s some lesbians argued that they had been 'quasi chauvinists' (Shelley, 1976). For radical feminism the emergence of the butch/femme community and identity amongst working-class and/or Black women in the 1950s indicates a lack of choice and the dominance of strict gender roles in the surrounding culture. Gender imitation was the only available identity for such women (Faderman, 1991).

Criticisms of the contemporary lipstick lesbian point out that feminism has spent much time developing a critique of the disciplinary function of femininity only to see the identity reborn as chic lesbian style. Radical feminists retain a suspicion that what is attractive about the identity is the ability to be hidden, to go through straight society conforming to a particular feminine and straight ideal (Bell *et al.*, 1994). As such, unless indicating her connection to the butch lesbian, the femme is available to and appreciated by the male gaze and does little to challenge the supremacy of that gaze. Andrew Kirby (1995) argues that contemporary butch/femmes may aim to be playful and ironic in their use of the symbols and language of heterosexual meaning; however, this does not guarantee that transgression will occur. If, in everyday interactions, only those participating in the act of transgression read it as such, has transgression taken place? This is particularly so if political engagement does not move beyond questions of style to look at processes of commodification and material structure. Queer fascination with tracing the butch/femme through history betrays for radical feminists a form of nostalgia, fascinated with style but unable to discuss or recognize the complex social and economic processes that helped generate such roles in particular moments.

Materialist feminist critics of the reemergence of butch/femme relationships and lipstick lesbians argue that their popularity in mainstream media is evidence of the roots of their rebirth. Toned down butch/femmes or lipstick lesbians are manipulated and constructed within capitalism as safe versions of 'exotic' sexuality and as products of consumption. Hennessy (1995) is concerned that celebration of lesbian chic through the iconography of the butch/femme focuses on their cultural resonance in such a way that it 'keep[s] invisible the violent social relations' (*ibid.*: 147) from which they can emerge. Feminists concerned with the contemporary rejection of the ideals of radical feminism see the reemergence of butch/femme identities and the focus on style and individual experimentation as a symptom of the individualism and superficiality of the queer political agenda. Glick suggests that queer analysis 'retreats from materiality' into symbolism in order to celebrate the butch/femme figure. Celebration of lesbian chic has 'emptied the political and economic content of our analysis only to legitimate a commodification of lesbian culture for both gay and straight consumers' (2000: 29).

Queer feminist analysis

Queer approaches to the butch/femme relationship and identity begin by suggesting that the radical feminist approach to their 1950s emergence is trapped within an essentialist attitude towards gender. Judith Roof argues that identifying oppression or inequality within butch/femme relationships as due to imitating masculinity conflates 'masculinity, maleness, butchness and oppressive power' (1998: 25) in such a way as to assume that one cannot be male or act male without acting oppressively. The radical lesbian analysis seems to suggest that power inequalities in a lesbian relationship can only come from the introduction of masculinity through the butch role. This assertion denies the possibility of domestic violence and power inequalities in lesbian relationships in contexts where butch roles are absent. The radical feminist approach produces a straightjacket of rules about sexual behaviour and desire that 'locked its adherents into a species of puritanical sexual policing' (*ibid.*: 27).

Queer writers have reinterpreted the 1950s subculture as a resistant product of the complex class and 'race' politics of the time (Lapovsky Kennedy and Davis, 1993). In this analysis the focus is on the development of the culture and community and its playful use of gender symbolism, in a context offering few avenues of challenge and escape (Feinberg, 1993). Nestle's (1987) fictional, historical and autobiographical work has been influential for her celebration of her femme identity, relationship to butch lesbians and community. She argues that 1950s femmes were far from passive or weak in their adoption of feminine attire and look, instead they worked hard at 'our styles – our outfits, our perfumes, our performance' (1992: 233).

Queer analysis of the contemporary butch/femme places their reemergence within the exploration and celebration of difference in lesbian and gay studies and politics in the 1980s and 1990s. The contemporary reemergence of butch/femme identities at a time of greater fluidity in identity has influenced both its style and the analysis of it. In particular, under the queer gaze the contemporary butch/femme relationship is seen as an important site for the destabilization of the gender/sex regime. The parodies that both the butch and the femme can play out separately or together do not weakly imitate an original; instead they make more clear the social production and fictional elements of the supposed original (de Lauretis, 1994b). Ruth Holliday (1999) draws out a similar analysis in her discussion of the role of performativity in the style choices of lesbians (butch and femme) and of gay men. The stylistic statements of the lesbian women playing with butch or femme imagery is a source of comfort – a connection to a community, to a way of life that feels real – a deliberate transgression, and a source of discipline. It can be thought of as disciplinary because performing the role of butch or femme can emerge, in part, from a need to fit with codes of dress within the lesbian community one wishes to join.

Holliday's last point highlights that queer approaches to butch/femme identity do not necessarily see it as always or only transgressive and playful. Limits to style and transgression, pain and historical processes are identified alongside notions of fun and play. What marks out the queer approach is the assertion that even if the roots of butch/femme style and attitude may lie in particular class and 'race'-based heterosexual modes of meaning, their appropriation by lesbians *can* offer challenge to them. Kristin G. Esterberg argues that 'this is serious play because it has to do with deeply important aspects of the self ... At the same time, lesbian performances are not unconstrained. We do not choose freely from an unlimited set of possibilities' (1996: 261). Sally R. Munt suggests that butch/femme identity may be a response to pain, but that 'we do not languish there' (1998: 3). The transgressive potential within the relationship comes not from 'being' butch or femme, but from 'doing butch/femme, to try to ensure that posing doesn't become dozing, to make the self work. And play' (*ibid.*: 11).

An important element of the queer approach to butch/femme identity is to remove the focus from individual butch/femme lesbians to, instead, concentrate on context as the source of meaning, transgression and limitation (Knopp, 1995; Walker, 1995). Elspeth Probyn (1995) argues that to understand the transgressive potential of the femme you have to see her with her butch lover. In queer terms this joint visibility disrupts the gender/sex regime, which dictates that people identified as biologically female and male should enact the roles. To read the femme image as a straight wannabe is to leave heterosexuality as the matrix within which symbols are interpreted. The lipstick lesbian, who looks like she conforms to a heterosexual male gaze, but in fact looks that way to pleasure another woman 'skewer[s] the lines of force that seek to constitute woman as Woman, as object of the masculine gaze' (1995: 81). Women obtaining pleasure from each other may be a male fantasy, but it can also be a lesbian/queer fantasy. For 'making out in a straight space can be a turn-on, one articulation of desire that bends and queers a masculine place allowing for a momentarily sexed

---

Box 6.1   Butch/femme lesbians

Radical/materialist feminist analysis

1   Butch/femme relationships and sexual practices are politically suspect.
2   The femme remains an object of the male gaze.
3   The butch appropriates masculinity and brings it into the lesbian relationship.
4   The butch/femme relationship is unequal.
5   The femme remains hidden.
6   The contemporary emergence of butch and femme representations is a product of commodification.

Queer feminist analysis

1   The relationship is a challenge to the 'straitjacket' of lesbian feminism.
2   The femme challenges the notion that only heterosexual women can be feminine.
3   The butch challenges the notion that only men can be masculine.
4   The relationship can be a product of violence and pain, but is productive as a response.
5   Together the butch and femme challenge the gender norms of heterosexuality.
6   Queer butches and femmes use commodities and commodity cultures as political tools.

lesbian space' (*ibid.*). Lisa Duggan and Kathleen McHugh (1996) explore the fun and transgressive scope of the femme identity in similar terms:

> Refusing the fate of Girl-by-Nature, the fem(me) is Girl-by-Choice. Finding in androgyny (the rejection of all femininity) too much loss, too little pleasure, and ugly shoes, the fem(me) takes from the feminine a wardrobe, a walk, a wink, then moves on to sound, the death knell of an abject sexuality contorted and subjected to moral concerns. (Quoted in Halberstam, 1998: 60)

Such refusal to respond to the male gaze and to instead seek out the gaze of the butch is a form of political agency. The femme disturbs the straight world by making it more difficult for the straight man to identify and reject the dyke (Hemmings, 1999). The differences in how the feminist perspectives interpret the politics of the butch/femme identity and relationship are summarized in Box 6.1.

Conclusion

Queer ideas raise a number of difficulties for feminism. They aim to separate the analysis of sexuality and gender; to destabilize notions of shared and individual identity; to legitimize various forms of sexual practices feminists find oppressive; and to focus on cultural transgression over material politics. For many feminists the difficulties these priorities generate are too significant to be overcome by adaptation. For others the difficulties can be at least partially resolved by refusing to separate sexuality and gender. By keeping these two factors together feminists such as Butler are shedding new light on their interrelationship, in particular the support normalizing notions of heterosexuality and gender draw from each other. The focus on both allows for an analysis of regulation as well as play; constraint as well as fluidity; and materiality as well as culture – areas of recognition that queer theory itself at times fails to acknowledge.

In many ways I am happy to see ideas drawn from queer, postmodern and poststructuralist frameworks influence feminist theorizing. Each are broadening out the concerns of feminism, and the contribution feminists are making to them is taking them into new areas. At the same time I increasingly share the scepticism of other feminists who question the value and validity of queer perspectives. It is difficult to escape the conclusion that they represent little more than the celebration of the play and experimentation of particular individuals. However, proposing that feminist participants in queer ideas, such as Butler, are concerned only with the joys of play is a limited reading of their work. A desire to highlight regulation lies at the heart of Butler's project. What she can benefit from is greater recognition of the role of material issues in the regulation she wishes to testify to.

I next turn to the final area of feminist engagement with social and political thought discussed in this book: social studies of technology.

FURTHER READING

Judith Butler (1994) 'Gender as Performance', *Radical Philosophy* (Summer): 32–9. This interview with Butler is an opportunity to see what lies behind some of her argument and is more approachable in comparison to her other texts.

Mandy Merck, Naomi Segal and Elizabeth Wright (eds) (1998) *Coming Out of Feminism* (Oxford: Blackwell). Very useful collection of different feminist perspectives on the relationship between lesbian and gay studies and feminism. The chapter by Martin and the discussion between Rubin and Butler are particularly relevant to the discussions in this chapter.

'More Gender Trouble: Feminism Meets Queer Theory', special edition of *Differences*, Summer–Fall 1994. Contributions by Butler, de Lauretis and others make this an excellent source for feminist responses to queer theory which are friendly but cautionary.

Social studies of technology

CONTENTS

The last chapter considered the influence social constructionist frameworks are having on lesbian and gay studies. There are a number of other areas where these frameworks are also being taken up, and one important area which has caught the attention of feminists is analyses of the social impact of technology. The application of social constructionism to technology questions has led to the development of a new subdiscipline of sociology: Social Studies of Technology (SST).

SST explores the historical and contemporary relationships between society and technology. It adopts a constructionist approach to challenge commonsense assumptions that it is technology that shapes society; instead it proposes that society and social interpretations shape technology. Feminists have both participated in the development of this work and have at times been critics of its preoccupations and arguments. In particular, feminists have expressed surprise that SST writers have failed to acknowledge the role of gender as an important social variable that contributes to the social shaping of technologies. After exploring the development of SST and feminist concerns with it, this chapter details how feminists have adapted the perspective to understand how technology is shaped by gender inequalities. The Political Uses section will outline what SST can add to feminist analyses of reproductive technologies.

Outline of the key perspective

Technology is hardly a new topic for social science. However, beginning in the 1960s and influenced by wider shifts in sociology, history and philosophy, SST has emerged as a specific discipline concerned with theorizing the relationship between society and technology.

Influences on its emergence in the late 1960s are numerous. The first catalyst was the development of the sociology of scientific knowledge from writers such as Thomas Kuhn (1996). Kuhn argues that science can, at least in part, be understood as a social and rhetorical enterprise, and SST has gone on to apply the same understanding to analyses of technological innovation. The second catalyst was various critiques of technology and technological rationality. In the 1960s, New Left and environmental activists linked technology to both physical and spiritual decay in the fabric of society. SST is interested in these links, but problematizes how we think about **impacts** and notions that technology has certain **effects**. The third catalyst was a political push from activists and educationalists to encourage engineers and scientists to become interested in the environments in which their inventions and artefacts are situated and used. This led to changes in education, state regulation and practice which advocate participatory and socially-responsible design. SST supports this kind of shift, but it also goes on to explore and critique the ways in which designers incorporate the social into their work. Finally, the development of social constructionism and postmodernism has provided new frameworks for conceptualizing the relationship between technology and society.

SST begins with an explicit rejection of accounts of societal change that identify technology as the autonomous driver. Telling history through technological inventions such as the wheel or the printing press is problematic because it is grounded in **technological determinism**. Determinism presents humans as passive, unable to shape the technologies around them; the path of development is linear, following a rational path akin to 'natural laws'. Technologies appear to have their own momentum, but surely they must come from somewhere? In varied ways SST attempts to capture how social factors come to influence and be embedded in technology.

A key founding principle in SST is that the line between the social and the technological is blurred. Talk of 'impacts' is problematic because it presents society and technology as separate independent spheres, which at times become influenced by the other. Instead, SST argues that the relationship between the two is so thorough that they each play a constitutive role in the emergence of the other. This is summarized by the claim that what SST looks at is the *mutual shaping of technology and society*. Another way of thinking of this is to consider the social and the technological as a *seamless web* (Hughes, 1986) of meanings and practices. Exploring this web involves getting inside the *black box* of apparently finished technologies to uncover their social origins and workings.

SST has developed into a range of perspectives, and the main two focused on here are those that explicitly sit within a social constructionist framework and have been taken up by feminists. Other important SST frameworks not discussed here include technological systems (Hughes, 1983) and the politics of technology (Winner, 1980).

Social construction of technology – SCOT

SCOT begins with the explicit acquisition of the social constructionist approach used in the sociology of scientific knowledge (SSK). SSK advocates an important **principle of symmetry**; social explanations should be sought for both true and false scientific claims (Bloor, 1976); scientific explanations seen as true are those that fit with dominant social understandings of the world at the time. In terms of technology, whether a particular artefact fails or succeeds is the end result of a social process. Wiebe E. Bijker warns do 'not, in explaining the success or failure of an artifact, refer to the working or non-working of that artifact as explanation' (Bijker, 1995b: 242). (In both SCOT and ANT (Actor Network Theory) approaches, artefact is often spelt with an i – artifact.) An artefact's meaning, its identity and purpose, whether it is interpreted as working or not, is the result of the activities of **relevant social groups**. Artefacts emerge in the interactions between different groups; indeed the same 'thing' may be different artefacts in different interactions. The implication is that there are no intrinsic properties to the thing itself, and Bijker refers to this as **interpretative flexibility**:

> The meanings given by a relevant social group actually *constitute* the artifact. There are as many artifacts as there are relevant social groups; there is no artifact not constituted by a relevant social group. (1995a: 77, original emphasis)

Bijker uses the example of different bike designs in the late nineteenth century to explain the approach. Briefly, the Ordinary design of bicycle (very large front wheel, known more commonly as the Penny Farthing) was dominant in bike design in the early part of the nineteenth century. By the end of the century it had lost out to the safety design of bike, which remains the template for bike design today (a diamond frame and same-sized wheels). This is not the case of a failed technology being taken over by a better design; there was a complex negotiation between different relevant social groups over what a bike was for, what its key properties should be and what it would look like. For young men, the Ordinary was an exciting sporting machine; for women and older men it was dangerous. Only through complex processes did the safety bike become the stable **obdurate** design.

SCOT writers (although not all – Grint and Woolgar, 1992; Woolgar, 1991) became concerned that the focus on identifying the social within the technological appeared to imply that things are social 'all the way down' and that the technical itself is irrelevant. If SST is concerned with mutual shaping, then it must be concerned with the role that technical properties have in social relations and negotiations. In various ways we can think of the technical as having a non-deterministic effect on the processes of meaning and negotiation. We can think of this as unintended consequences or **affordances** (Hutchby, 2001). At its most basic, once a technology has taken on a particular shape and properties it becomes harder to reinterpret it as being about something else: you can use your washing machine to cook your dinner if you want, but it will be a tad cold and mixed up! Ensuring that the technical continues to play a role has been taken forward by another area of social constructionist analysis in SST: actor network theory (ANT).

Actor network theory – ANT

ANT approaches argue that SCOT privileges the 'social' in its analysis. ANT rejects this in favour of arguing that 'any division we make between society on the one hand and scientific or technical content on the other is necessarily arbitrary' (Latour, 1991: 106). One cannot assume beforehand that it is the social processes that will dominate the development of technology and explain change (Law, 1987), and therefore a key aim of ANT is to treat technology and society symmetrically in the analysis (Callon, 1986; Latour, 1996).

Both technology and human actors are positioned in networks of technical and social relations. Michel Callon defines the network as 'a coordinated set of heterogeneous actors which interact more or less successfully to develop, produce, distribute and diffuse methods for generating goods and services' (1991: 133). Actors (human and non-human) form a set of practices, shared language and common meanings for each other; the technical components of the network help keep it together. Various aspects of the operation of the network are relative, the product of the network itself. You cannot predict what actors will do in a network based on some prior knowledge of them, and this means that *a priori* judgements cannot be made. This includes judgements about the operation of power, and Bruno Latour argues: 'Power is not a property of any one of those elements but of a chain' (1991: 110). This implies a relativistic agenda for ANT, where actors, processes and meanings are relative to the temporal workings of the network:

> There is never any need to leave our networks, even if we are talking about defining the truth, the exactitude, the coherence, the absurdity, or the reality of a statement. The judgement of reality is immanent in, and not transcendent to, the path of a statement. (*Ibid.*: 128)

ANT focuses on the role of particular key actors, **heterogeneous engineers** (Law, 1987), often scientists or inventors, in bringing together a network around a particular artefact. A key element of network formation is the *translation* of different interpretations into a stable set of meanings for the network and its components. The actors in the network *align* themselves to what Madeleine Akrich (1992) has referred to as **scripts** that produce frameworks of action and which link current translations to prior existing frameworks. One way to help ensure that different actors follow the script is to *incorporate* or *enrol* them. One way of doing this is to make use of **immutable mobiles**, usually some form of map or set of rules, for example an instruction manual.

Various different technologies have been analysed from an ANT perspective – military aircraft, electric vehicles, missile guidance systems, and doors. One famous account is Latour's analysis of the heavy weights attached to hotel keys (Latour, 1991); the weight is the product of a network aimed at encouraging guests to leave their keys at reception, rather than carry them with them. The network consists of the designers who make the weight, the customers who use the key, the key and weight and the hotel manager who wanted a solution to the problem that customers do not return their keys. The weighted key works where a request fails. Statements are not enough, technology and innovators are called upon, and are allied to the aim of not losing hotel keys. As such the manager's original request to 'please return your key' is translated – via the key – in the social world of the customer into 'hand in key because their weight and size makes them a nuisance'. This translation into the physicality of a key ensures a durable network and stable set of meanings.

The implications of the type of SST analysis that SCOT and ANT represent can be summarized in the following way:

- Definitions of successful and failed technologies are socially mediated and relative.
- Power relations emerge in socio-technical relations, rather than determine their shape.
- The distinction between the social and the technical is unclear and discursively produced.
- The interactions between actors (including non-human) are the key process to examine when exploring socio-technical relations.

Feminist critiques

Feminists are important participants in the development of SST. However, many argue that they have had to make important changes to its empirical and theoretical priorities in order to make it suitable to feminist agendas. I will examine each priority in turn.

Empirical priorities

In both SCOT and ANT there is a tendency to focus on large-scale techno-logical systems, military technologies and leisure technologies. Significantly less time has been given to domestic technologies and the everyday tools and objects that women come into contact with (Cockburn and Fürst-Dilic, 1994; Faulkner, 1998). SST appears more concerned with design and the laboratory than with manufacturing and use. The people who work on the assembly line of technology production rarely appear as relevant social groups or as nodes in the network; indeed, technical artefacts are more likely to appear as actors than are factory workers.

As well as ignoring part of the process of social shaping, the dominance of design studies of a narrow range of technologies often means that women are absent in SST analyses. Women are more likely to be found outside the lab-oratory, as production workers on computer assembly lines or as purchasers and users of technologies. The actors ANT follows are the 'white-coated sci-entists, the hard-hatted engineers, the grey-suited business executives' (Cockburn and Ormrod, 1993: 9). An awareness of the patterns of exclusion women face from technology is paramount for feminists, in particular mate-rial and transnational feminists. Globalized patterns of production of high-tech goods is what lies behind many women's role as exploited assembly worker of goods aimed for markets elsewhere. In this analysis the important network, missed completely by both SCOT and ANT (and some argue by feminist reinterpretations), is global capitalism and its generation of inequality and exploitation.

A final concern with the empirical agenda of SST is the focus on 'thick descriptions', detailed accounts of singular moments in an artefact's develop-ment. This focus lacks a link to wider processes or structures that may contribute to the local events under investigation. Can or how does one move beyond the specific in order to make general statements about socio-technical relations? In part the answer for SCOT and ANT is that such general state-ments should be avoided, but feminists argue that this agenda is politically insufficient. For the analysis to be of value it must allow for connections to wider relations and hold open the possibility of change at that level.

Theoretical priorities

SCOT and ANT hold on to a claim of scepticism about power and conse-quence; the analyst should wait to see what develops out of a particular network. Materialist feminists have been particularly unhappy with this strategy and the dominance of social constructionist approaches in SST (Clegg, 2001). Cynthia Cockburn and Susan Ormrod (1993) argue that used too loosely the notion of interpretative flexibility becomes an excuse to ignore or deny the material obstacles to particularly placed users being able to shape technologies into new things. The negotiable, social and transient qualities given to artefacts make it more difficult to argue that particular technologies are dangerous. The fear is that the move away from these kinds of arguments, perhaps unintentionally, ends up as conservative and supportive of the current situation.

The focus on the actors present in networks and relevant social groups is problematic for many feminists. Both SCOT and ANT acknowledge that there are people outside the relevant groups and marginal to the network, but argue they are not their concern; their role as analysts is to describe what is present. Underneath the rejection of a normative framework in SCOT and ANT, various writers identify the use of a pluralist model of power. Such a model can and has been criticized for failing to recognize the operation of power in how people and issues are not present in the first place. For example, feminists of various persuasions have long been concerned with the ways in which the rules of participation – in the design of technology, in the running of the state – operate in such a way that women's participation and their interests just never appear on the agenda. This level of power appears invisible in SCOT and ANT approaches (Wajcman, 2000).

As with other perspectives examined in this book, the lack of discussion about gender creates problems for using SST to explore women's relationship to technology. The empirical gap has led to the theoretical mistake of assuming that where only men are present, gender is not an element of the social processes embedded in artefacts. One does not need to find women to find gender within the social shaping of technology (Berg and Lie, 1995; Lohan, 2000); it can play a part in women's non-appearance and what happens amongst the gender that remains. For most feminists looking to work with the ideas of SST it is not enough to add gender to the mix; some of the key categories of SST have to be rethought once questions of gender differences are taken into account.

ANT has proved particularly troublesome for feminists. Its explicit disinterest with matters outside the network and claims to neutrality on questions of power leave it very difficult to identify the wider context within which networks or alliances form, and some rather than others become the significant 'heterogeneous engineers' (Harding, 1991):

> I am still sociologically interested in understanding why and how some human perspectives win over others in the construction of technologies and truths, why and how some human actors will go along with the will of other actors, and why and how some human actors resist being enrolled ... I want to take sides, to take stands. (Joan H. Fujimura, quoted in Star, 1991: 29)

Judy Wajcman argues that ANT 'can make it awkward to address the obduracy of the link between men and technology' (2000: 453). The symmetry between humans and non-humans is theoretically interesting and valuable, but appears to make it difficult to talk of the ways in which the relationship between technology and humans can create barriers and exclusion.

For some feminists, ANT neutrality to things beyond the immediacy of the network has become a form of conservative positivism (Saetnan, 1997). It presumes that the analyst can describe what is there, without their own position influencing where in the network they chose to begin and who they nominate as their heterogeneous engineers. Maria Lohan (2000) argues that feminist theorizing has long made us aware that if you do not look for certain things, have an eye for certain processes, then you are unlikely to see their emergence. Hence ANT's inability to see gender at work in the networks they examine (Silva, 2000). Considering power as an effect or consequence of the workings of the network is not sufficient an explanation for consistent patterns of dominance and exploitation (Faulkner, 2001); why is it that 'some networks are remarkably enduring' (Gill and Grint, 1995: 21)?

Feminists involved in adapting SST argue that its empirical and theoretical priorities need to shift for its approach to be both critical of the current situation and politically engaged with constructing an alternative future. This feminist approach is summed up by Anne-Jorunn Berg who argues that 'when we [feminists] criticize technology, broadly speaking we do so with a focus on the possibilities for change in gender relations – or the ending of male dominance in and over technology' (1994b: 95). The discussion below indicates how this consideration influences feminist adaptation of SST.

Feminist incorporations

Feminist interest in SST is influenced by the long heritage of work concerned with technology in feminist studies. Marxist and materialist feminists were and are concerned with the role of technology in women's exploitation within capitalism. Cockburn's (1983) work in the 1980s was hugely influential in indicating how male workers and managers used technology to exclude women from particular jobs and areas of skill, and radical feminists were amongst the first to identify technology as one of the components of the binary opposition that celebrated masculinity over femininity. Eco-feminists developed this criticism to identify technological values in the widespread destruction of nature within modernity (Griffin, 1984). In each of these areas technology became associated with masculinity and man's exploitation of nature and women. This quote from Petra Kelly, who was one of the leaders of the environmental movement in Western Germany in the

1980s, describes the conceptual connections made:

> If we trace the myths and metaphors associated with the conquest of
> nature, we will realize how much we are under the sway of masculine
> institutions and ideologies. Masculine technology and patriarchal values
> have prevailed in Auschwitz, Dresden, Hiroshima, Nagasaki, Vietnam,
> Iran, Iraq, Afghanistan and many other parts of the world. The ultimate
> result of unchecked, terminal patriarchy will be ecological catastrophe or
> nuclear holocaust. (1997: 113)

Different feminist approaches have developed to tackle the existence of
masculine values in technology:

1 To encourage women to participate in technology; and
2 To celebrate the non-technological and women's alternative connection
  to nature.

The first strategy is associated with liberal approaches to technology (Ely
and Meyerson, 2000). Here the issue is seen as getting more women as individuals involved in technology to remedy the numerical inequality in participation. The additional benefit is that women's participation may 'soften' the
masculinity of technology. The second strategy has developed within radical
feminism and eco-feminism, where a critique of technology is fuelled by
interpreting key technologies such as guns and bombs and problems such as
environmental destruction as direct products of masculinity (Merchant,
1980). Eco-feminists argue that women have vital and distinct knowledge of
nature that can be used to avert the present ecological crisis (Shiva, 1989).

Both the liberal and the eco-feminist/radical approach to technology have
come under criticism from other feminists. The liberal approach is faulted
for interpreting gender as a numbers game, where just having equal numbers
of women and men designing or using technology means that the problem
is resolved. In such strategies and accounts technology is interpreted as
gender-neutral and something women just need to be introduced to, to
realize what a good thing it is. In this sense, women are the problem; if only
they would grasp the wonders and pleasures of working with technology.
Liberalism fails to go beyond the surface to see how gendered values are
embedded in the culture of technology (Clegg, 2001). Where gender is identified in liberal discourse it is identified as a 'distortion' (Henwood, 2000:
210); remove the distortion and remove the problem (Gilbert, 2001). In this
way, liberal approaches do not conceptualize the importance of gender in
the constitution of identity, both for technology and users, and the wider
structures and cultures of gender within which identity forms.

In eco-feminist/radical approaches to gender and technology there has been a tendency to support the binary division by presenting technology as inherently masculine. Only men could come up with nuclear weapons and not safe contraception. The danger in this line of argument is that 'there is a tendency to present technology as deterministically patriarchal (or capitalist) and to portray women as victims of men's technology' (Faulkner, 2001: 80). Essentialist language for either gender or technology entails a failure 'to uncover the *social* processes by which many men come to have an intimacy with technology while women largely experience estrangement from it' (Webster, 1996: 45, original emphasis). Such arguments present technology as large-scale systems and fail to acknowledge that the everyday artefacts that fill our lives are also significant. By remaining focused on technologies read through a male gaze, feminists help retain a vision of technology as masculine, big and overpowering (Hirschauer and Mol, 1995).

The disquiet with equating masculinity with technology has led feminists to the social constructionism within SST as an alternative tactic for thinking about the relationship between gender and technology. If technologies and their meanings are thought of as embedded with social and cultural norms and values, it seems reasonable to assume that gender, as a particularly prevalent cultural and social norm, will be an important vehicle for bringing meaning to objects (Webster, 1996). On one level this process can be thought of as flexible and performative in individual interactions with technology (Lohan, 2000). The issue is how such individual interactions come to replay consistent patterns of gendering. There is, in the words of Flis Henwood, 'some mechanism at work which continues to reassert dualistic gender categories and identities in gender–technology relations' (2000: 222).

We can explore dualistic gender categories in relation to skill and technological know-how. Women may use technologies, but they are not always recognized as skilful users (McLaughlin *et al.*, 1999; Tancred, 1995). This identification has less to do with actual technical ability and more to do with the dominance of masculine models of skill and design (Murphy, 1990; Webster, 1996). The issue is how norms for different types and levels of skill become gendered in such a way that they end up being played out in individual and group interactions with technology (Volman and Ten Dam, 1998). How is it that gender 'sticks' (Faulkner, 2000) to certain types of skill, occupation, user and technology – even to the extent that it becomes true that women and men appear to score better in different types of skill and technological know-how test.

The answer lies in looking at the gendered worlds within which individual artefacts develop (Cohn, 1986; McLaughlin, 1999). This can be in a straightforward empirical way; for example, might gender differences in computer use relate to differences in training and education, rather than to some essential quality of women and men? It can also be explored through a concern with why and how gender becomes significant to the performance and reproduction of individual and group identity. The ways in which cultures form around gender can become, not necessarily intentionally, a factor in encouraging the maintenance of gendered patterns of technological design, engagement and use (Benston, 1992; Stepulevage, 2001). Wendy Faulkner argues that:

> the continued male dominance of engineering is due in large measure to the enduring symbolic association of masculinity and technology by which cultural images and representations of technology converge with prevailing images of masculinity and power. (2001: 79)

For example, the culture of computing and hacking at times celebrates its image as male, nerdish and unsociable, and this image provides a language and camaraderie for the young men who take up the activity. The unintended consequence is that this image presents computing as an enterprise a girl cannot participate in without losing an aspect of her gender identity (Turkle, 1988).

To summarize, a feminist SST perspective examines gender by:

- Looking beyond numbers: the gender question in technology is about more than how many use a particular technology or how many women want to be engineers or scientists.
- Including men as well as women in the analysis: the concern is with the embedding of femininities and masculinities into particular technologies and approaches to design and use.
- Being conscious of the wider contexts in which interpretative flexibility can occur: an individual artefact can be reinterpreted as something else, while existing gender patterns of inequality remain less malleable to reinterpretation.
- Thinking about the gender of individuals (identity), groups (culture) and structures (Harding, 1986; Scott, 1988b): there is a need to be conscious of wider patterns of gender meaning and structure in society, within which gender is negotiated.

Some of the particular areas of feminist SST work include:

- Historical work, which traces the impact – at times unexpected – that new technologies have had on gender relations in the home and at work (Coffin, 1996).
- Historical work that uncovers the role of women inventors and designers (Rothschild, 1983).

- Contemporary analysis of the implications of excluding (Karpf, 1987) and including women users in design.
- Historical and contemporary work that looks at the role women users play after design (Berg, 1994b; Fischer, 1991; Martin, 1991; Sundin, 1998).
- Contemporary analysis of key technologies: for example, domestic technologies (Silva, 2000), reproductive technologies (Davis-Floyd and Dumit, 1998), technologies in development contexts (Agarwal, 1992) and office technology (Webster, 1996).

In particular, both SCOT and ANT have been adopted and adapted.

SCOT

SCOT appeals to feminists because it can be used to capture both local negotiations and global contexts at different moments in the life of technology:

> Once technology is seen as a process instead of an already-made thing, the *user* of technology is no longer its passive recipient but can come into view as an important actor in its shaping. Intentions baked into technology may restrict the flexibility of a given artefact, but they cannot altogether determine its use or meaning. (Berg, 1994b: 96, original emphasis)

In feminist hands the mutual shaping of technology and society maxim is reinterpreted as 'it is impossible fully to understand technologies if genders are not taken into account, and it is impossible to understand genders if technologies are not taken into account' (Lohan, 2000: 902).

Berg (1994a) uses the example of a smart house to show how gender becomes part of design. In her example, the lack of engagement with women users leads to prototypes that are 'masculine construct[s]' (1994a: 176) and indicates 'lack of support for changes in the domestic sexual division of labour' (*ibid.*: 177). Jeanette Hofmann (1999) analyses the gendering of word-processor software design, through considering how designers ascribe particular qualities to their presumed users. Early software design developed restricted and basic templates for user interfaces, based on expectations about female, secretarial users. Gill Kirkup (1992) makes a similar argument in relation to home PCs, indicating that their route into the home was via the male hobby market. This route influenced their initial design which focused on the fun of making it work as a gadget in itself, rather than a machine to be used for something. This male heritage continued into the first uses found for home PCs: games, in particular military simulation games. The empirical outcome of this pattern of gendering is clear in the differential use of PCs in the home, which continues to show a bias towards male use. Here SCOT is being used to examine gendering in design; it has also been used to consider gender in use. Both Michèle Martin (1991) and Claude Fischer (1991) have indicated the vital role women users have played in translating the telephone from a business to a domestic technology. Berg examines MINITEL (French telephone text-based service for providing information to individual homes) to indicate how creative engagement with using artefacts continues to incorporate gender into 'technology-in-the-making' (1994b: 100) once design is complete.

Cockburn and Ormrod's (1993) account of the development of the domestic microwave oven brings design and use into the one analysis. The microwave began life as a radar military technology in the 1940s, and to understand its journey from there into the kitchen they identify and examine a wider range of relevant social groups than is normally included in SCOT analysis. Their focus includes design and production engineers, low-paid assembly workers, marketing actors, international and national safety codes and regulations, cookery writers, manufacturers who produce components, foods and products such as plastic containers to be used in the oven, shop workers, retail companies, purchasers and finally users. All the actors are part of the 'microwave world' that generates the artefact: microwave cooking. It was not until the 1980s that this world was formed sufficiently enough for the microwave to become an everyday domestic product. Gendered structures, locations, representations and identities influence the involvement and outlook of each of these groups and actors. Gendering begins in the design lab, but continues into the everyday world of the microwave's place in the domestic realm (Ormrod, 1994).

Cockburn and Ormrod indicate how technology becomes a 'differentiating principle' (1993: 102) in the gender structure of product design, retail selling and the domestic division of labour. Some domestic goods are designed and sold as 'brown goods' and are identified by their leisure and entertainment uses (TV, video and so forth). These goods are more likely to be designed and sold by and to men. Other goods are identified as 'white goods' and are identified by their domestic work properties (washing machine, cooker and so on). These goods, while still designed by men, are more likely to be sold by and to women (although men may be the ones who pay for the product). Brown goods are often sold as complex technologies (which only men can understand), while the technological aspects of white goods are discussed less and instead reliability is the focus. A hierarchy surrounds the distinction, one where 'the relative appreciation of men and the masculine' and the 'relative depreciation of women and the feminine' (1993: 160) plays an important part.

Looking at the brown–white distinction from a feminist SCOT perspective leads to the conclusion that what makes an artefact brown or white is not its technical properties; how an artefact looks, how it is sold and who the consumer is expected to be is what identifies it. When microwaves were first designed and sold, they were presented as brown goods; they were marketed as technological innovations and were sold by men to men. Over time this changed as the technology became part of the everyday world and less innovative, and other new 'high-tech' leisure toys took its place as it moved solidly into the world of the white good and expectations about the female consumer. The retail environment domesticated the microwave and shaped it into 'a socially wanted and accessible object' (*ibid.*: 109).

Although once microwave ovens leave the factory, a certain level of obduracy has become part of their shape and functionality, advertising and the retail world retain interpretative flexibility. This carries onto domestic use:

> A modicum of flexibility is retained right up to the moment of use and beyond. ... We have seen that in the highly gendered arena of the domestic kitchen the microwave is shaped by the relations in to which it is obliged to fit. Often it is put to a use that is not quite the one its manufacturers intended for it. (*Ibid.*: 156)

For example, the relevant social group of producers (the majority of whom are men) has continued to interpret the microwave oven as a high-tech product by incorporating further advances into its capabilities (grills, spits, digital interfaces and so on). In the domestic realm, the relevant social groups are women with children and sometimes partners who carry out the double burden of paid and domestic labour, and single professional women and men who want varied, quick and single-portioned meals. Both these groups identify the product as a time-saving device, which influences their lack of use of the new add-ons to the product. The artefact generated by the social groups of varied domestic actors is responded to by the spread of ready-made meals on supermarket shelves and the reemergence of cheap microwaves stripped of uses that consumers do not want.

Taking a SCOT approach to the gendering of a technology in the way developed here allows for an identification of how gender 'gave this technology a particular social identity' (*ibid.*: 155). Relevant social groups, design, selling, purchasing and use can all be gendered in varied ways, which at times leads to shifts in the artefact. Each shift suggests a level of interpretative flexibility that continues well into its use. However, interpretative flexibility does not inhibit gendered structures, representations and locations playing a role in shaping the flexibility on offer, leading to the replication of gender inequalities in the artefacts produced.

ANT

Feminist approaches to ANT display a distinct approach to power and politics. For Ormrod (1995) the benefit of ANT is that it can reposition gender inequalities as the result of particular arrangements rather than of some stable structure, such as patriarchy:

> Male dominance may be the end result of particular operations of power, but this is not simply imposed on women (and some men). Rather gender relations are a *process* involving strategies and counter-strategies of power. (1995: 36, original emphasis)

ANT can bring history and time into the repetition of particular patterns of power relationship. Instead of viewing historical patterns of inequality and power as structures that determine the future shape of technology and gender, these patterns can be thought of as rhetorical resources that actors 'interpret and reinterpret ... to effect' (*ibid.*: 39).

Ruth Schwartz Cowan (1987) uses an ANT approach to focus on the consumer (rather than the designer) to examine how she or he is 'embedded in a network of social relations that limits and controls the technological choices that she or he is capable of making' (1987: 262). Cowan argues that this neglected element of network relations is important; it is here that the user either supports or disrupts the network translation. Here the boundary object of the technology must move between very different social worlds. When looking at the consumer they must be defined both through their relationship to the technology and to the other networks they exist within. Incorporating consumption in this way brings in actors usually invisible in ANT.

Ann Scott (2001) draws on ANT arguments to explore the networks and socio-technical artefacts that make up feminist social activism. She examines electronic feminist activism to capture how the incorporation of electronic resources help 'construct the *character* of these movements' (2001: 409, original emphasis) through the 'multiple technosocial networks grounding material practice' (*ibid.*: 418). The ANT approach is useful because it allows for a consideration of the material, without assuming that it has a determining influence. Instead the materiality of technology is understood as negotiable, through the scripts it enables (and dis-ables) in the network relations that evolve within it and around it. For example, new patterns of communication are emerging through the Internet and e-mail which allow new styles of feminist activism. Scott also considers the networks evolving around electronic media, which are creating new problems and dilemmas for women. For example, new forms of commodified electronic information and heightened surveillance are emerging as important aspects of the Information Society. Seeing both these different network possibilities (democratic and authoritarian) as contained in the relations emerging with technology, gives feminism an agenda for engaging in these processes.

Susan Leigh Star (1991) has produced one of the most influential feminist rearticulations of ANT. Her approach stresses the need to move away from analysing singular technologies to focus on the ensemble of socio-technical artefacts that operate within social networks. Technologies sit within a network of rules, decisions, exclusions and actors held together by an unarticulated agreement that certain priorities are correct and exclusions justified. Star alters the ANT framework by suggesting that to understand the operation of the network, and its ability to standardize, you do not study the network itself. You begin outside the network, with the other, the stranger: 'multiple personality and marginality – are the point of departure for feminist and interactionist analyses of power and technology' (1991: 29). We need to examine the invisible workers of the network, those who are 'the delegated *to*, the disciplin*ed*' (*ibid.*: 29, original emphasis). This is because ANT writers 'know how to discuss the process of translation from the point of view of the scientist, but much less from that of the laboratory technician, still less from that of the lab's janitor' (*ibid.*: 33). It is useful to begin with the marginalized, because it is only from their perspective that one can see that a particular network brings with it standardization of life and socio-technical relations.

The standardizing activities of networks create a form of loss where the ambiguous is not allowed. This loss includes 'destruction of the world of the non-enrolled' (*ibid.*: 49). Binary divisions resurface in the conventions and translations that allow the network to grow and expand, and in the process 'uncertainties are translated into certainties: old identities discarded, and the focus of the world narrowed into a set of facts' (*ibid.*: 47). A feminist form of ANT stresses not just the labour involved in securing the network, it also seeks to identify the sources of disruption. The other always forms in the context of the standardized, and always contains resistant possibilities. For Star (1991), ANT must do more than describe what is present, it needs to imagine other possible networks and interactions between humans and non-humans that can value multiplicity and flexibility. Uniform consensus is not the only form of network that is possible.

Feminist SST can be summarized as being concerned with:

- Both the existence and limits to interpretative flexibility.
- The flexible and varied embedding of gendered identities, cultures and structures into socio-technical relations.
- The relations inside, outside and on the margins of politically and socially significant relevant social groups and networks.

- Disrupting exploitative and standardizing socio-technical relations and networks, with the aim of helping produce alternative forms of human–machine interactions.

Political uses

Various technologies that feminist theorists are concerned with are invisible in SST accounts. In particular, reproductive technologies have always been a political and theoretical concern for feminism, but find no place in SST. One distinct advantage of feminist participation in SST is its intent to widen the scope of empirical interest. The issue is whether spreading SST's interests to include reproductive technologies helps bring new light and value to existing feminist approaches in this area.

Reproductive technologies

The liberal feminist approach in the past and present focuses on campaigns to ensure that women have access to fertility control, in particular the right to an abortion. In contrast, radical (Oakley, 1993; Rich, 1986b) and Marxist feminists (O'Brien, 1981) have concentrated on the role of men and technology in the medicalization of fertilization, pregnancy and birth. This body of work is very important in shattering the illusion that more technology automatically equals better and healthier pregnancies, births and babies. For example, it challenges notions that hospital births involving the use of drugs and technology are inherently safer than births at home assisted by a midwife. The significant emotional, psychological and physical costs of the involvement of medical practice and technologies in pregnancy and birth have been documented through women's testimony (Stanworth, 1987).

Important feminist campaign groups have formed to reclaim pregnancy and birth from the clutches of medicine and doctors. This has led to changes in state and medical practice. In the UK, maternity care in the 1990s is significantly altered from the large impersonal, obstetrician-dominated, labour wards of the 1970s (Hunt and Symonds, 1995). Women have greater choice over their treatment and birth method, midwives are given a more significant and independent role, and wards themselves are smaller and more personalized. However, there are still concerns over the ready use of medical technology. For example, currently one in four births in the UK are delivered via a caesarean section. In the USA, home births are virtually unheard of (apart from amongst the poor and rural populations). SST approaches have begun to become part of feminist responses to the continued, perhaps increasing role of reproductive technologies in women's experiences of fertility, infertility, pregnancy and labour.

Feminist SST approaches to reproductive technologies are marked by a concern with how, in different contexts, technology and pregnancy can come to mean different things (Ortiz, 1997; Way, 1998). There is a shift away from talking of bad technologies. The effects of technology are understood as the products of the social processes in which they are embedded. Bonnie Fox and Diana Worts argue that rather than see technologies as inherently bad, analysis should concentrate on the 'social context and intervening circumstances in which women give birth' (1999: 328). The socio-technical ensemble, made up of the technologies commonly used, the cultural meanings associated with pregnancy and birth, and the professional hierarchies of hospital care can generate feelings of powerlessness and dependency. By getting beyond generalized statements and assumptions about bad technologies and empowering natural births, analysis can uncover the ways in which women can be active in defining the terms of medical intervention and its significance to their experience of pregnancy and birth. Where women have strong social networks around them they are more likely to be able to engage with technology and intervention in a way that does not lead to feelings of powerlessness. Where social support is lacking, some acquiescence to the medical model can be understood as 'a means of strengthening personal resources to meet the challenges ahead' (*ibid*.: 343). There is no single experience or result from the use or non-use of technology during birth; instead it is the socio-technical ensemble and the woman's social world that contribute to the end result.

Of particular interest in feminist SST discussion of reproductive technologies is the influence of visual technologies, in particular ultrasound, in reshaping the fetus, the pregnant woman and pregnancy (Haraway, 1997). Fox (2000) argues that the appearance of the fetus on a screen (new ultrasound technologies offer both colour and 3D images) helps generate a discourse that gives the fetus an identity 'as a separate entity' (2000: 173). The visualization on screen becomes an intermediary between the pregnant woman's body and the fetus (Weir, 1998). The power of ultrasound to become such an intermediary is connected to the importance of the visual in Western culture and the ability of this image to fit in with discourses of personhood. In the process the woman as a person with a body becomes less visible (Condit, 1995; Stabile, 1994). Ultrasound cannot be thought of as the cause of these dilemmas for women; instead it allows for a set of affordances that lead to 'an erasure of the woman by a constellation of factors, including foetal imaging techniques, representations within popular culture, Pro-Life rhetoric, and the discourses of law and science' (Fox, 2000: 174).

The role of ultrasound in pregnancy is to detect potential conditions, such as Down's syndrome and Spina Bifida, in the fetus. Usually, if the ultrasonographer interprets the image as suspicious, the prospective parent or parents will be encouraged to take further tests, including amniocentesis, to identify with greater certainty whether the fetus does have the condition. For problems such as Down's syndrome, a positive result (the screening terminology for the identification of a condition) will lead to the offer of an abortion. Disability activists in the UK and the USA argue that the aim of screening is to reduce the number of babies born with such conditions (Hubbard, 1997; Shakespeare, 1998).

Feminists have used ANT in a variety of ways to think about screening. Ann R. Saetnan (1996) uses ANT to consider debates about the ethics and value of ultrasound screening in Norway, arguing that gender becomes part of the social shaping of ultrasound through its rhetorical role in the debates. Different influential actors who are pro and anti ultrasound screening make use of gendered language and association to attempt to incorporate others in their network. Gendered rhetoric in the debates helps secure medical frameworks as dominant. Saetnan notes that when an important doctor argues that 'women need reassurance during pregnancy, that physicians can provide it through expert diagnostics ... he can expect most people to simply nod and accept the arguments' (1996: 70).

One can think of antenatal screening as a socio-technical network stabilizing the social and political priorities that lie behind the *dis*-valuing of disabled people and the incorporation of pregnant women into that process (Willis, 1998). Non-disabled and disabled women are incorporated into the policing of normality via offering screening as a routine part of antenatal care (Saxton, 2000). Nancy Press argues 'the offer of prenatal testing itself is the message and the institutional structures through which the offer is made constitute the senders of the message' (2000: 217). Women are incorporated into a role of policing the 'quality' of the population, justified in a repertoire of empowerment and free choice. Individual choice becomes a repertoire within screening networks, which means that choice is at the foreground 'while backgrounding the social matrix of a technoscientific marketplace to whose requisites individual choices are increasingly enrolled' (Rapp, 1999: 38). The repertoire constructs notions of health, illness, disability and normality through a 'binary model which posits them as disruptive but ultimately containable forces' (Shildrick, 1997: 215). This suggests a process of standardizing forms of life, via the stability of the technology and the process it sits within. Screening technologies are significant because they 'take their place in the field of forces that constitute the construction/(re)production of identity' (Shildrick, 1997: 197).

Can these ideas provide strategies for challenging the dilemmas around visualization and screening? Are they politically useful? One avenue, advocated by feminist SST is to adopt the language and perspective of

Donna J. Haraway's cyborg (1991). Haraway's cyborg reflects the blending and blurring of humans and technologies, out of which can come new subjectivities and meanings. In ultrasound the 'mode of knowing and feeling the fetus through the coupling of human and machine' (Mitchell and Georges, 1997: 373) generates a 'cyborg fetus'. The embryo frozen in a hospital lab and the fetus on an ultrasound screen are products of and embedded in complex technological, social, economic and political networks which belie the division between nature and technology, human and non-human (Franklin, 1999). The embryo is a 'laboratory artefact which exists only through technology' (Fox, 2000: 182). Rather than look to a space of human meaning and identity outside of technological mediation, those working with the cyborg metaphor embrace the notion that 'Modern bodies are made and remade through science and technology; they too are technological artefacts' (Wajcman, 2000: 458). Rather than see this bond as a nightmare made real, SST feminists look at it as offering new possibilities for how we might embrace relations between humans and machines:

> Situating it [the embryo] within this complex matrix of biotechnological entities, rather than considering the abstract question of whether or not it matters in isolation from the context in which it is produced, forces us to confront the more important question of how much cryo-preserved embryos matter relative to other creatures. (Fox, 2000: 182)

New reproductive technologies may make it more difficult to hold onto neat distinctions between humans and non-humans, but rather than view this as inherently bad, adopting the world view of the cyborg can allow a positive interpretation. This can lead us to envision new ways of thinking about the relations between humans, other animals and technologies that foster interconnections. The challenge to the framework that has produced networks and technologies that survey, dissect, commodify and destroy can come from developing alternative relationships between humans and technologies that encompass those people and identities positioned in the margins.

In practical terms the agenda for political engagement provided by feminist SST includes:

- Challenging the networks and actors who produce particular stable configurations of damaging reproductive socio-technical relations.
- Proposing contexts and environments within which women retain power and choice.
- Identifying forms of knowledge, identity, subject position, coalition and human–technology relation excluded in the current order of things.

The possible dilemmas of this strategy of engagement are whether it risks:

- Drifting away from the useful certainty of existing feminist campaigns.
- Denying the benefits of minimizing the role of technology in reproduction.
- Confusing and complicating individual women's right to choice and integrity over their bodies.

Conclusion

Technology is an important area for feminism because the social and material relations that emerge with it have significant implications for gender norms, values, identities and areas of discrimination. Feminists have taken the ideas of SST and adopted them to particular priorities and concerns. This has led to a greater concern with the user and uses of technology, the limits to interpretative flexibility, the margins of networks and the possibility of developing new kinds of network and relation. SST has been embraced because it offers the opportunity to reject technological determinism and opens up the space to acknowledge and use women's agency and creativity in their relations with technology.

It has been useful to examine SST in this final substantive chapter for a number of reasons. First, it is a useful example of social constructionism being used by feminists to bring a new approach to existing areas of concern. Second, as with the other ideas and frameworks feminists adapt, the adaptation brings new life to SST. Third, in thinking over whether it is valuable to use SST within feminist analyses, the political benefits remain important criteria in making the judgement. In this last area some feminists remain cautious about the political benefits of SST when examining important areas such as reproductive technologies. This caution, evidenced so often in this book, helps ensure that the mode of engagement feminists have with SST is measured and critical. Here, as elsewhere, feminists are not dutiful daughters in their relationships with other ideas, and to me this is strong evidence of the health and vigour of contemporary feminist social and political thought.

FURTHER READING

Science, Technology and Human Values is a leading journal of social studies of technology that captures the main debates and highlights important research in the field.

Donald MacKenzie and Judy Wajcman (eds) (1999) *The Social Shaping of Technology*, 2nd edn (Buckingham: Open University Press). A very useful edited collection which contains extracts from important SST texts and authors. Contains a variety of chapters looking at the relationship between gender and technology.

Keith Grint and Rosalind Gill (eds) (1995) *The Gender–Technology Relation* (London, Taylor & Francis). This collection contains important theoretical and empirical work on gender and technology; written from an explicitly SCOT and ANT approach.

CHAPTER 8

Conclusion

To conclude this book I wish to briefly capture the current agendas of feminist theorizing and give a defence of those agendas by proposing how they match current times and indicate a healthy scepticism about what theories can say. What these ideas also show is the importance of the contribution feminist theorizing makes to wider social and political thought. The book began by arguing that feminist ideas do not have enough presence in teaching; what has been explored in this book is testimony to the need to retain or perhaps renew the presence feminist ideas are given in the academy.

Contemporary social and political thought is marked by a concern with subjectivity, identity and difference. Existing frameworks have been rearticulated and new concepts developed to capture the theoretical significance of acknowledging the differences in people's histories, experiences and identities. The new issues are bringing with them new areas of contest and resistance, such as the body, cultural representations and sexual experimentation.

The scope of rights is also being rearticulated to include wider demands relating to cultural recognition, historical inequalities and the private sphere. Feminist arguments are a vital catalyst to the inclusion of these issues into social thought, and they also play an important role in evaluating the ways in which social and political thought has responded to difference and identity. An important element of the evaluation role that feminist ideas play lays in situating theoretical ideas in their social and historical contexts. Do ideas for responding to differences fit with how these differences are played out in the social world? In this way feminist writings ensure that social and political relevance is an important criterion for evaluating the credibility of theoretical work. Feminism's engagement with the wider body of social and political thought is important for the gaps it identifies and the alternatives it proposes. The role that feminist ideas play in critiquing other works and in developing their own frameworks indicates that they remain a vital component of social and political thought, enriching its scope and providing an important political litmus test to its priorities.

As indicated above, beyond the evaluation role, feminist ideas continue to develop their own distinct and necessary perspectives for conceptualizing difference and identity. In early work on difference there was a tendency to treat it as a problem, as an obstacle to be resolved in the path towards a shared viewpoint. This approach has been replaced by writings that configure differences as positive and enriching. Recognition is now an important principle, alongside equality, in feminist theories. These new principles have brought into sharper focus issues and subject positions which had been excluded from earlier feminist writings. Each of the areas of feminist thought discussed in this book bring something distinct to how we think about difference in a context of uncertainty and fluidity; in particular how we conceptualize knowledge, experience, and identity requires reinvention. The stress in feminist writing is to conceptualize in a context where the imperative is to acknowledge:

- variations in people's experiences and histories;
- the situated and contested quality of claims to knowledge; and
- the temporal and multiple complexity of identities.

In each of the feminist approaches summarized in the book, a critique or engagement with an existing theoretical perspective has been the source of a new strategy for dealing with difference, knowledge and identity. The end result of each of these interrogations and new articulations is an enrichment of both wider social and political thought and feminist theorizing. Below is a brief summary of the ideas outlined in each chapter:

1   Equal-rights feminists take the agenda of liberalism and citizenship forward by proposing new grounds for the operation of rights. In particular, strategies are developing for divorcing rights from the abstract individual in order to explore collective, group and gendered versions of citizenship. The scope of rights is broadening to encapsulate identity and cultural expression, and this has implications for the scope of political activism and the demands that women make as equal citizens. Feminist writers are exploring versions of rights which are able to embody the private sphere and cultural recognition.

2   Feminist-standpoint perspectives adapt Marxist arguments to ground theoretical knowledge in collective experiences of marginalization and exploitation. The collective experiences that count in standpoint theory are broader than the paid labour that became the focus of Marxism; in particular, feminists include reproduction and child-rearing. The inclusion of feminist critiques of science into standpoint theory has led to new ideas about the situated nature of any claim to objectivity, truth and knowledge.

3   Ethics of care perspectives began in feminist rejections of psychological models of moral hierarchies which identified women as lesser moral actors. In their place the perspective has sought to appreciate the contextual basis of varied moral visions and worlds. Reason and rationality

are displaced with a celebration of human particularity and care for the known and unknown other. At times, like some articulations of stand-point theory, it has placed women's experiences of child-rearing at the centre of this varied moral world. More recently, ethics of care ideas have concentrated on the political dimensions to shared visions of human interconnection and relationship. This latter articulation pro-duces an increased demand for the state and the public sphere to care responsively for its different citizens.

4   Postmodern approaches identify binary oppositions within language as important in the structuring of difference, subjectivity and meaning. Feminists have used this idea to explore how the opposition between femininity and masculinity secures and reproduces gender differences and inequalities. Subjectivity is particularly important to postmodern feminists; the main strategy is to deconstruct fixed and gendered subject positions in order to imagine multiple and fluid identities. Feminists adapt the postmodern agenda in order to think about the politics of iden-tity, and this includes the development of alternative subject positions suitable to contemporary experiences of ambiguity and political coali-tion.

5   Foucault's work highlights the importance of discourse in the develop-ment of knowledge, in particular about the self and sexuality. He identi-fies power as disciplinary, local, contingent and regulatory. Feminists have applied these ideas to explore the disciplinary operation and repro-duction of gender in culture and identity. This focus repairs troubling gaps in Foucault's work and rejects his later aesthetic ethical agenda. Feminists also adapt his arguments about power to identify forms of resistant identities and everyday political activity.

6   Queer perspectives are vital in contemporary explorations of sexuality and identity. This perspective represents a challenge to any notion of fixed sexual identities, even those presented by the lesbian and gay movement, and instead offers a celebration of transgression and playful-ness. Feminists work with and take this agenda forward by identifying heteronormativity as the result of linguistic and cultural processes that secure some identities as normal, while others are demonized. In doing so, feminists reunite discussions of gender and sexuality. Feminists are intrigued by the queer politics of parody and transgression, and are using it to disclose the fictional qualities of gender. At the same time they are more willing to work with, rather than against, identity politics.

7   Social studies of technology is a relatively new area of theoretical activ-ity. It explores the mutual shaping of technology and society, and using social constructionist ideas, the focus is on stressing the interpretative flexibility maintained in technologies and people's use of them.

Feminists work with and adapt these ideas to explore the role of gender in shaping technology and the identity of users. In the process they broaden SST to think more centrally about the role of the user and social structures in influencing the processes under examination. This work is producing political agendas which stress the role that women users can play in redirecting technology, in the context of gender structures that aim to reduce that role.

The prominence of difference and fluidity in contemporary theoretical activity at times implies that living in an uncertain, ambiguous world of contingency and contest is a joyful experience. In recent feminist work there is recognition that fluidity and uncertainty also bring problems and anxiety, both at the level of the individual and the level of theorizing. What differentiates the feminist approaches discussed in this book is their response to uncertainty.

For equal-rights, standpoint and ethics of care feminist approaches the focus is on finding a political and/or experiential basis to ground some claim to certainty and knowledge. For postmodern, Foucauldian, queer and SST feminist approaches the focus is on pushing forward with the possibilities of transgressive and playful identities and politics. Each of these different strategies sees danger in the other. Those adopting the first strategy worry about the elitism and scope of playful transgression; those working with the latter strategy worry about the exclusions and judgements made in claims to truth and experience. The worry each has with the other has blurred the line between the two. Equal-rights feminists acknowledge the fictional nature of the sovereign subject, standpoint theories are open to the contested nature of objectivity and knowledge, and ethics of care writers talk of the role of language in our interpretation of responsive care. Meanwhile, most postmodern, Foucauldian, queer and SST feminists, in order to engage with practical politics, acknowledge the political benefits of ceasing to deconstruct identity and instead work with collective knowledge claims. The importance of identity politics remains; what perhaps is given greater emphasis in all feminist theory is the need to be less 'comfortable' in those identities when speaking of them.

The debates explored in the book indicate that there is an important body of work which identifies itself as feminist, and which is still engaged with conceptualizing the varied processes that generate gender inequalities and identities. However, can we say that these different ideas still share something that we can call feminist? Does prioritizing difference mean that all that makes an idea feminist is that it identifies itself as such? What criteria can we use to measure the degree to which something is feminist? The postmodern approaches I have discussed would warn of the dangers of such a move. Self-identification should be seen as an important marker, it still implies a political intent and purpose that few feminists advocate turning away from: *imagining and working towards alternative social and personal relationships and structures which do less harm to women*. It is legitimate to interrogate ideas that claim feminist intent based on the political benefits of using them to examine particular problems for different groups of women. Such interrogation is an ongoing activity and something that moves outside the theoretical stage to include the women whose lives are being examined.

I would like to end with two cautionary points about the narrative that the book has produced. First, a focus on the new should not deny the validity and continued importance of existing work. The long legacy of feminist theorising is a continuum of overlapping ideas and priorities. Feminists are right to warn against caricaturing people's work; we do need to retain an awareness of all feminist ideas, to have good memories. Second, the ideas discussed in the book are strong evidence that feminist theorizing is alive, that in some areas it prospers and that it remains an important contributor to social and political thought. However, this should not be seen as an outright rejection of the concerns feminists have raised about the health of feminist theory. There are difficulties created by the context within which feminist ideas develop, in particular current institutional contexts create uncertainty and appear to encourage divorce from the non-academic world. If there is anything that should make ideas feminist, it is that the worlds outside the academy remain important to their development. There is a need to maintain and in places rebuild connections with various kinds of political, personal, academic and social communities in order to create an environment within which feminist work is relevant, meaningful and useful.

Bibliography

Abbot, S. and Love, B. (1972) *Sappho Was a Right-on Woman*. New York: Stein & Day.

ACF (2001) *Fact Sheet: Welfare*: www.acf.dhhs.gov/news/facts/tanf.html.

Acker, J. (1989) 'The Problem with Patriarchy'. *Sociology*, 23: 235–40.

Adams, M.L. (1994) 'There's No Place Like Home: On the Place of Identity in Feminist Politics', in M. Evans (ed.), *The Woman Question*. London: Sage.

Agarwal, B. (1992) 'Cold Hearths and Barren Slopes: The Woodfuel Crisis in the Third World', in G. Kirkup and L.S. Keller (eds), *op. cit.*

Ahmed, S. (1996) 'Beyond Humanism and Postmodernism'. *Hypatia*, 11(2): 71–93.

——(2000) *Strange Encounters*. London: Routledge.

Ahmed, S. *et al.* (2000) 'Introduction: Thinking through Feminism', in S. Ahmed *et al.* (eds), *op. cit.*

—— (eds) (2000) *Transformations: Thinking Through Feminism*. Routledge, London.

Akrich, M. (1992) 'The De-Scription of Technical Objects', in W. E. Bijker and J. Law (eds), *Shaping Technology/Building Society: Studies in Sociotechnical Change*. Cambridge, Mass: MIT Press.

Aladjem, T.K. (1991) 'The Philosopher's Prism: Foucault, Feminism, and Critique'. *Political Theory*, 19(2): 277–91.

Alarcón, N. *et al.* (1999) 'Introduction: Between Woman and Nation', in C. Kaplan *et al.* (eds), *op. cit.*

Albelda, R. (2001) 'Welfare-To-Work, Farewell to Families? US Welfare Reform and Work/Family Debates'. *Feminist Economics*, 7(1): 119–35.

Alcoff, L. (1997) 'The Politics of Postmodern Feminism Revisited'. *Cultural Critique*, 36: 5–27.

Alcoff, L. and Potter, E. (eds) (1993) *Feminist Epistemologies*. London: Routledge.

Alexander, M. J. and Mohanty, C. T. (1997) 'Introduction: Genealogies, Legacies, Movements', in M. J. Alexander and C. T. Mohanty (eds), *op. cit.*

——(eds) (1997) *Feminist Genealogies, Colonial Legacies, Democratic Futures*. London: Routledge.

Altman, D. (1998) 'The End of the Homosexual?', in P.M. Nardi and B.E. Schneider (eds), *op. cit.*

Amos, A. and Parmar, P. (1984) 'Challenging Imperial Feminism'. *Feminist Review*, 17: 3–19.

Anzaldúa, G. (1999) *Borderlands = La Frontera*. San Francisco: Aunt Lute Books.

Aronowitz, S. (1995) 'Against the Liberal State: Act-up and the Emergence of Postmodern Politics', in L.J. Nicholson and S. Seidman (eds), *op. cit.*

Aronson, J. (1998) 'Lesbians Giving and Receiving Care: Stretching Conceptualizations of Caring and Community'. *Women's Studies International Forum*, 21(5): 505–19.

Baden, S. and Goetz, A.M. (1997) 'Who Needs [Sex] When You Can Have [Gender]?' *Feminist Review*, 56: 3–25.

Baier, A. (1997) 'Trust and Antitrust', in D.T. Meyers (ed.), *op. cit.*

Bailey, M.E. (1993) 'Foucauldian Feminism: Contesting Bodies, Sexuality and Identity', in C. Ramazanoglu (ed.), *op. cit.*

Balbus, I.D. (1987) 'Disciplining Women: Michel Foucault and the Power of Feminist Discourse', in S. Benhabib and D. Cornell (eds), *Feminism as Critique*. Minneapolis: University of Minneapolis.

Bannerji, H. (1995) *Thinking Through: Essays on Feminism, Marxism and Anti-Racism*. Toronto: Women's Press.

Barnes, C. (1992) 'Institutional Discrimination and Disabled People and the Campaign for Anti-Discrimination Legislation'. *Critical Social Policy*, Summer: 5–22.

Barrett, M. (1980) *Women's Oppression Today: Problems in Marxist Feminist Analysis*. London: NBL/Verso.

——(1991) *The Politics of Truth: From Marx to Foucault*. Cambridge: Polity Press.

——(1992) 'Words and Things: Materialism and Method in Contemporary Feminist Analysis', in M. Barrett and A. Phillips (eds), *op. cit.*

Barrett, M. and Philips, A. (eds) (1992) *Destabilising Contemporary Feminist Debates*. Cambridge: Polity Press.

Bartky, S.L. (1988) 'Foucault, Femininity, and the Modernization of Patriarchal Power', in I. Diamond and L. Quinby (eds), *op. cit.*

Barwell, I. (1994) 'Towards a Defence of Objectivity', in K. Lennon and M. Whitford (eds), *Knowing the Difference: Feminist Perspectives in Epistemology*. London: Routledge.

Bauman, Z. (1993) *Postmodern Ethics*. Oxford: Blackwell.

Bell, D. *et al.* (1994) 'All Hyped up and No Place to Go'. *Gender, Place and Culture*, 1(1): 31–47.

Bell, D. and Klein, R. (eds) (1996) *Radically Speaking: Feminism Reclaimed*. London: Zed Books.

Bell, V. (1991) 'Beyond the Thorny Question – Feminism, Foucault and the Desexualisation of Rape'. *International Journal of the Sociology of Law*, 19(1): 83–100.

——(2000) 'Owned Suffering: Thinking the Feminist Political Imagination with Simone De Beauvoir and Richard Wright', in S. Ahmed *et al.* (eds), *op. cit.*

Benhabib, S. (1992) 'The Generalized and the Concrete Other', in E. Fraser *et al.* (eds), *Ethics: A Feminist Reader*. Oxford: Blackwell.

——(1995) 'Feminism and Postmodernism', in L. Nicholson (ed.), *op. cit.*

Benston, M.L. (1992) 'Women's Voices/Men's Voices: Technology as Language', in G. Kirkup and L.S. Keller (eds), *op. cit.*

Berg, A.-J. (1994a) 'A Gendered Socio-Technical Construction: The Smart House', in C. Cockburn and R. Fürst-Dilic (eds), *op. cit.*

——(1994b) 'Technological Flexibility: Bringing Gender into Technology or was it the Other Way Around'?, in C. Cockburn and R. Fürst-Dilic (eds), *op. cit.*

Berg, A.-J. and Lie, M. (1995) 'Feminism and Constructivism: Do Artifacts Have Gender?' *Science, Technology and Human Values*, 20(3): 332–51.

Berlant, L. (2000) 'The Subject of True Feeling: Pain, Privacy and Politics', in S. Ahmed *et al.* (eds), *op. cit.*

Bhabha, H.K. (2000) 'Postcolonial Criticism', in D. Brydon (ed.), *op. cit.*

Bhavnani, K.-K. and Coulson, M. (1997) 'Transforming Socialist Feminism: The Challenge of Racism', in H.S. Mirza (ed.), *op. cit.*

Bijker, W.E. (1995a) *Of Bicycles, Bakelites, and Bulbs.* Cambridge, Massachusetts: MIT Press.

—— (1995b) 'Sociohistorical Technology Studies', in S. Jasanoff *et al.* (eds), *Handbook of Science and Technology Studies.* London: Sage.

Bijker, W.E. *et al.* (eds) (1987) *The Social Construction of Technological Systems.* Cambridge, MA: MIT Press.

Block, G. and James, S. (1992a) 'Introduction: Contextualizing Equality and Difference', in G. Block and S. James (eds), *op. cit.*

—— (eds) (1992b) *Beyond Equality and Difference.* London: Routledge.

Bloor, D. (1976) *Knowledge and Social Imagery.* London: Routledge & Kegan Paul.

Blum, L.A. (1993) 'Gilligan and Kohlberg: Implications for Moral Theory', in M.J. Larrabee (ed.), *op. cit.*

Boling, P. (1991) 'The Democratic Potential of Mothering'. *Political Theory*, 19(4): 606–25.

Bondi, L. and Domosh, M. (1992) 'Other Figures in Other Places: On Feminism, Postmodernism and Geography'. *Environment and Planning D: Society and Space*, 10: 199–213.

Bordo, S. (1992) 'Postmodern Subjects, Postmodern Bodies'. *Feminist Studies*, 18 (Spring): 159–75.

—— (1993) 'Feminism, Foucault and the Politics of the Body', in C. Ramazanoglu (ed.), *op. cit.*

Brabeck, M. (1993) 'Moral Judgement: Theory and Research on Differences between Males and Females', in M.J. Larrabee (ed.), *op. cit.*

Bradshaw, A. (1996) 'Yes! There is an Ethics of Care: An Answer for Peter Allmark'. *Journal of Medical Ethics*, 22(1): 8–12.

Braidotti, R. (1987) 'Envy: Or with Your Brains and My Looks', in A. Jardine and P. Smith (eds), *op. cit.*

—— (1991) *Patterns of Dissonance.* Cambridge: Polity Press.

—— (1994) *Nomadic Subjects.* New York: Columbia University Press.

Breenan, T. (1989) (ed.) *Between Feminism and Psychoanalysis.* London: Routledge.

Bright, S. (1984) 'The Year of the Lustful Lesbian'. *New York Native*, 30 July– 12 August.

Brodribb, S. (1992) *Nothing Mat(T)ers: A Feminist Critique of Postmodernism.* New York: New York University Press.

Brooks, A. (1997) *Postfeminisms. Feminisms, Cultural Theory and Cultural Forms.* London: Routledge.

Broverman, I. *et al.* (1972) 'Sex-Role Stereotypes: A Current Appraisal'. *Journal of Social Issues*, 28: 59–78.

Brown, L.M. and Gilligan, C. (1992) *Meeting at the Crossroads: Women's Psychology and Girls' Development.* London: Harvard University Press.

Brown, W. (1992) 'Finding the Man in the State'. *Feminist Studies*, 18 (Spring): 7–13.

—— (1993) 'Wounded Attachments'. *Political Theory*, 21(3): 390–410.

—— (1995) *States of Injury: Power and Freedom in Late Modernity*. Princeton, N.J.: Princeton University Press.

Brydon, D. (ed.) (2000) *Postcolonialism: Critical Concepts in Literary and Cultural Studies*. London: Routledge.

Bryson, V. (1999) *Feminist Debates: Issues of Theory and Political Practice*. New York: New York University Press.

Buker, E.A. (1990) 'Hidden Desires and Missing Persons: A Feminist Deconstruction of Foucault'. *The Western Political Quarterly*, 43 (December): 811–32.

Bunch, C. (1994) 'Learning from Lesbian Separatism', in K. Jay and A. Young (eds), *Lavender Culture*. New York: New York University Press.

Burchell, G. *et al.* (eds) (1991) *The Foucault Effect: Studies in Governmentality*. London: Harvester/Wheatsheaf.

Butler, J. (1990) *Gender Trouble: Feminism and the Subversion of Identity*. London: Routledge.

—— (1992) 'Contingent Foundations: Feminism and the Question of "Postmodernism"', in J. Butler and J.W. Scott (eds), *op. cit.*

—— (1993) *Bodies That Matter: On The Discursive Limits of 'Sex'*. London: Routledge.

—— (1999) 'Revisiting Bodies and Pleasures'. *Theory, Culture and Society*, 16(2): 11–20.

Butler, J. and Scott, J.W. (eds) (1992) *Feminists Theroize the Political*. London: Routledge.

Cain, M. (1993) 'Foucault, Feminism and Feeling', in C. Ramazanoglu (ed.), *op. cit.*

Calhoun, C. (1988) 'Justice, Care, Gender Bias'. *Journal of Philosophy*, LXXXV(9): 451–63.

—— (1995) 'The Gender Closet: Lesbian Disappearance under the Sign "Women"'. *Feminist Studies*, 21(1): 7–34.

Califia, P. (1981) 'What is Gay Liberation?' *Heresies*, 3(12): 30–4.

Callon, M. (1986) 'The Sociology of an Actor-Network: The Case of the Electric Vehicle', in M. Callon *et al.* (eds), *Mapping the Dynamics of Science and Technology: Sociology of Science in the Real World*. Basingstoke: Macmillan – Palgrave.

—— (1991) 'Techno-Economic Networks and Irreversability', in J. Law (ed.), *op. cit.*

Cancian, M. (2001) 'Rhetoric and Reality of Work-Based Welfare Reform'. *Social Work*, 46(4): 309–14.

Cant, B. and Hemmings, S. (eds) (1988) *Radical Records*. London: Routledge.

Card, C. (1990) 'Caring and Evil'. *Hypatia*, 5(1): 101–8.

—— (ed.) (1991) *Feminist Ethics*. Lawrence, Kansas: University Press of Kansas.

—— (1997) 'Gender and Moral Luck', in D.T. Meyers (ed.), *op. cit.*

Carling, A. (1994) 'The Strength of Historical Materialism – A Comment'. *Science and Society*, 58(1): 60–72.

Cavarero, A. (1992) 'Equality and Sexual Difference: Amnesia in Political Thought', in G. Block and S. James (eds), *op. cit.*

Chancer, L.S. (1998) *Reconcilable Differences*. Berkeley: University of California Press.

Charlesworth, H. (1996) 'Women as Sherpas: Are Global Summits Useful for Women?' *Feminist Studies*, 22(3): 537–47.

Chodorow, N. (1978) *The Reproduction of Mothering: Psychoanalysis and the Sociology of Gender*. London: University of California Press.

Christina, G. (1990) 'Drawing the Line'. *On Our Backs*, 6: 14–15.

Clark, D. (1991) 'Commodity Lesbianism'. *Camera Obscura*, 25–26: 181–201.

Clegg, S. (2001) 'Theorising the Machine: Gender, Education and Computing'. *Gender and Education*, 13(3): 307–24.

Clough, P.T. (1994) *Feminist Thought*. Oxford: Blackwell.

Cockburn, C. (1983) *Brothers: Male Dominance and Technological Change*. London: Pluto Press.

Cockburn, C. and Fürst-Dilic, R. (1994) (eds) *Bringing Technology Home: Gender and Technology in a Changing Europe*. Buckingham: Open University Press.

Cockburn, C. and Ormrod, S. (1993) *Gender and Technology in the Making*. London: Sage.

Coffin, J.G. (1996) *The Politics of Women's Work*. Princeton, New Jersey: Princeton University Press.

Cohen, J.L. (1995) 'Critical Social Theory and Feminist Critiques: The Debate with Jürgen Habermas', in J. Meehan (ed.), *op. cit.*

Cohn, C. (1986) 'Sex and Death in the Rational World of Defence Intellectuals'. *Signs*, 12(4): 687–718.

Collins, P.H. (1989) 'The Social Construction of Black Feminist Thought'. *Signs*, 14: 745–73.

——(1991) *Black Feminist Thought: Knowledge, Consciousness and the Politics of Empowerment*. London: Routledge.

——(1995) 'The Social Construction of Black Feminist Thought', in B. Guy-Sheftall (ed.), *op. cit.*

——(1997) 'Comment on Hekman's "Theory and Method: Feminist Standpoint Theory Revisited": Where's the Power?' *Signs*, 22: 375–81.

——(2000) 'Gender, Black Feminism, and Black Political Economy'. *Annals of the American Academy of Political and Social Science*, 568: 41–53.

Conaghan, J. (2000) 'Reassessing the Feminist Theoretical Project in Law'. *Journal of Law and Society*, 27(3): 351–85.

Condit, D.M. (1995) 'Fetal Personhood: Political Identity under Construction', in P. Boling (ed.), *Expecting Trouble: Surrogacy, Fetal Abuse and New Reproductive Technologies*. Boulder: Westview Press.

Connell, R.W. (1995) 'Democracies of Pleasure: Thoughts on the Goals of Radical Sexual Politics', in L. Nicholson and S. Seidman (eds), *op. cit.*

Connor, S. (1993) 'The Necessity of Value', in J. Squires (ed.), *Principled Positions*. London: Lawrence & Wishart.

Coole, D. (1994) 'Wither Feminisms?' *Political Studies*, 42: 128–34.

Cooper, D. (1994) 'Productive, Relational and Everywhere – Conceptualizing Power and Resistance within Foucauldian Feminism'. *Sociology*, 28(2): 435–54.

Cornell, D. (1992) 'Gender, Sex and Equivalent Rights', in J. Butler and J.W. Scott (eds), *op. cit.*

Cornell, D. (1998) *At the Heart of Freedom: Feminism, Sex, and Equality*. Princeton, N.J.: Princeton University Press.

Cowan, R.S. (1987) 'The Consumption Junction: A Proposal for Research Strategies in the Sociology of Technology', in W.E. Bijker *et al.* (eds), *op. cit.*

Crary, A. (2001) 'A Question of Silence: Feminist Theory and Women's Voices'. *Philosophy*, 76(297): 371–95.

Daly, M. (1978) *Gyn/Ecology: The Metaethics of Radical Feminism*. Boston: Beacon Press.

Daly, M. and Lewis, J. (2000) 'The Concept of Social Care and the Analysis of Contemporary Welfare States'. *British Journal of Sociology*, 51(2): 281–98.

Davis, K. (1992) 'Towards a Feminist Rhetoric: The Gilligan Debate Revisited'. *Women's Studies International Forum*, 15(2): 219–31.

—— (1997) 'What's a Nice Girl Like You Doing in a Place Like This? The Ambivalences of Professional Feminism', in L. Stanley (ed.), *op. cit.*

Davis-Floyd, R. and Dumit, J. (eds) (1998) *Cyborg Babies: From Techno-Sex to Techno-Tots*. London: Routledge.

de Lauretis, T. (1984) *Alice Doesn't: Feminism, Semiotics and Cinema*. Bloomington: Indiana University Press.

—— (1990) 'Eccentric Subjects: Feminist Theory and Historical Consciousness'. *Feminist Studies*, 16(1): 115–49.

—— (1994a) 'Habit Changes'. *Differences*, 6 (Summer–Fall): 296–313.

—— (1994b) *The Practice of Love: Lesbian Sexuality and Perverse Desire*. Bloomington: Indiana University Press.

Dean, C.J. (1994) 'The Productive Hypothesis – Foucault, Gender, and the History of Sexuality'. *History and Theory*, 33(3): 271–96.

Delphy, C. (1977) *The Main Enemy*. London: Women's Research and Resource Centre.

—— (1984) *Close to Home: A Materialist Analysis of Women's Oppression*. Amherst: University of Massachusetts Press.

—— (1993) 'Rethinking Sex and Gender'. *Women's Studies International Forum* 16: 1–9.

Derrida, J. (1985) *The Ear of the Other*. London: Bison Books.

—— (1998) *Of Grammatology*. Baltimore and London: The Johns Hopkins University Press.

Deveaux, M. (1994) 'Feminism and Empowerment: A Critical Reading of Foucault'. *Feminist Studies*, 20(2): 223–47.

—— (2000) 'Conflicting Equalities? Cultural Group Rights and Sex Equality'. *Political Studies*, 48(3): 522–39.

Diamond, I. and Quinby, L. (eds) (1988) *Feminism and Foucault: Reflections on Resistance*. Boston: Northeastern University Press.

Di Stefano, C. (1990) 'Dilemmas of Difference: Feminism, Modernity and Postmodernism', in L.J. Nicholson (ed.), *op. cit.*

Dietz, M.G. (1985) 'Citizenship with a Feminist Face: The Problem with Maternal Thinking'. *Political Theory*, 13(1): 19–37.

Dinnerstein, D. (1987) *The Rocking of the Cradle and the Ruling of the World*. London: Women's Press.

Diprose, R. (1994) *The Bodies of Women: Ethics, Embodiment and Sexual Difference*. London: Routledge.

Doezema, J. (2001) 'Ouch! Western Feminists' "Wounded Attachment" to the "Third World Prostitute"'. *Feminist Review*, 67 (Spring): 16–38.

Dreyfus, H.L. and Rabinow, P. (1982) (eds) *Michel Foucault: Beyond Structuralism and Hermeneutics*. Chicago, Ill.: University of Chicago Press.

Duggan, L. and McHugh, K. (1996) 'A Femm(Me)Inist Manifesto'. *Women and Performance*, 16.

Dutt, M. (1996) 'Some Reflections on U.S. Women of Color and the United Nations Fourth World Conference on Women and NGO Forum in Beijing, China'. *Feminist Studies*, 22(3): 519–28.

Dworkin, R. (1985) *A Matter of Principle*. London: Harvard University Press.

—— (1990) 'Foundations of Liberal Equality', in G.B. Peterson (ed.), *Tanner Lectures on Human Value Volume 11*. Salt Lake City: University of Utah Press.

Edelman, L. (1994) *Homographesis*. New York: London.

Edwards, P.K. (1986) *Conflict at Work*. Oxford: Blackwell.

Eisenstein, Z.R. (1981) *The Radical Future of Liberal Feminism*: London: Longman.

—— (1997) 'Women's Publics and the Search for New Democracies'. *Feminist Review*, 57 (Fall): 140–67.

Elam, D. (1994) *Feminism and Deconstruction*. London: Routledge.

Ely, R.J. and Meyerson, D.E. (2000) 'Advancing Gender Equity in Organizations: The Challenge and Importance of Maintaining a Gender Narrative'. *Organization*, 7(4): 589–608.

Engels, F. (1985) *The Origin of the Family, Private Property and the State*. Harmondsworth: Penguin.

Espinosa, M.F. (1997) 'Indigenous Women on Stage: Retracing the Beijing Conference from Below'. *Frontiers*, 18(2): 237–55.

Esterberg, K.G. (1996) '"A Certain Swagger When I Walk": Performing Lesbian Identity', in S. Seidman (ed.), *Queer Theory/Sociology*. Oxford: Blackwell.

Faderman, L. (1991) *Odd Girls and Twilight Lovers: A History of Lesbian Life in the Twentieth Century*. New York: Penguin.

Faulkner, W. (1998) 'Extraordinary Journeys around Ordinary Technologies in Ordinary Lives'. *Social Studies of Science*, 28(3): 484–9.

—— (2000) 'The Power and the Pleasure? A Research Agenda for "Making Gender Stick" to Engineers'. *Science Technology & Human Values*, 25(5): 87–119.

—— (2001) 'The Technology Question in Feminism: A View from Feminist Technology Studies'. *Women's Studies International Forum*, 24(1): 79–95.

Fawcett, B. (2000) *Feminist Perspectives on Disability*. Harlow: Prentice Hall.

Feinberg, L. (1993) *Stone Butch Blues: A Novel*. Ithaca, NY: Firebrand Books.

Ferguson, K.E. (1984) *The Feminist Case against Bureaucracy*. Philadelphia: Temple University Press.

Fernandez, C. (1991) 'Undocumented Aliens in the Queer Nation: Reflections on Race and Ethnicity in the Lesbian and Gay Movement'. *Democratic Left*, May/June.

Ferree, M.M. *et al.* (2002) 'Four Models of the Public Sphere in Modern Democracies'. *Theory and Society*, 31: 289–324.

Finch, J. (1989) *Family Obligations and Social Change*. Cambridge: Polity Press.

Firestone, S. (1972) *The Dialectic of Sex*. New York: Bantam.

Fischer, C. (1991) 'Touch Someone: The Telephone Industry Discovers Sociability', in M.C. Lafollette and J. Stine (eds), *Technology and Choice: A Technology and Culture Reader*. Chicago, Ill.: The University of Chicago Press.

Flanagan, O. and Jackson, K. (1987) 'Justice, Care and Gender: The Kohlberg–Gilligan Debate Revisited'. *Ethics*, 97: 622–37.

Flax, J. (1976) 'Do Feminists Need Marxism?' *Quest*, III(1): 46–58.

—— (1992a) 'Beyond Equality and Difference: Justice in Feminist Postmodernism', in G. Bock and S. James (eds), *op. cit.*

—— (1992b) 'The End of Innocence', in J. Butler and J.W. Scott (eds), *op. cit.*

—— (1993) *Disputed Subjects: Essays on Psychoanalysis, Politics and Philosophy*. London: Routledge.

Fleming, M. (1995) 'Women and the "Public Use of Reason"', in J. Meehan (ed.), *op. cit.*

Forbes, J.S. (1996) 'Disciplining Women in Contemporary Discourses of Sexuality'. *Journal of Gender Studies*, 5(2): 177–89.

Foucault, M. (1971) 'Orders of Discourse'. *Social Science Information*, 10 (April): 7–31.

—— (1972) *The Archaeology of Knowledge*. London: Routledge.

—— (1982) 'The Subject and Power', in H. Dreyfus and P. Rabinow (eds), *op. cit.*

—— (1984a) 'Nietzsche, Genealogy, History', in P. Rabinow (ed.), *op. cit.*

—— (1984b) 'On the Genealogy of Ethics: An Overview of Work in Progress', in P. Rabinow (ed.), *op. cit.*

—— (1985) *History of Sexuality Volume 2: The Use of Pleasure*. Harmondsworth: Penguin.

—— (1986) *History of Sexuality Volume 3: The Care of the Self*. Harmondsworth: Penguin.

—— (1990) *The History of Sexuality Volume 1: An Introduction*. New York: Vintage Books.

—— (1991a) *Discipline and Punish*. New York: Vintage Books.

—— (1991b) 'Politics and the Study of Discourse', in G. Burchell *et al.* (eds), *op. cit.*

—— (1991c) 'Questions of Method', in G. Burchell *et al.* (eds), *op. cit.*

—— (1991d) *Remarks on Marx*. New York: Semiotext(e).

Fox, B. and Worts, D. (1999) 'Revisiting the Critique of Medicalized Childbirth'. *Gender and Society*, 13(3): 326–46.

Fox, M. (2000) 'Pre-Persons, Commodities or Cyborgs: The Legal Construction and Representation of the Embryo'. *Health Care Analysis*, 8(2): 171–88.

Franklin, S. (1999) 'Making Representations: The Parliamentary Debate on the Human Fertilisation and Embryology Act', in J. Edwards *et al.* (eds), *Technologies of Procreation: Kinship in the Age of Assisted Conception*. London: Routledge.

Fraser, M. (1997) 'Feminism, Foucault and Deleuze'. *Theory Culture & Society*, 14(2): 23–37.

Fraser, N. (1989) *Unruly Practices: Power, Discourse, and Gender in Contemporary Social Theory*. Minneapolis: University of Minnesota.

——(1990) 'The Uses and Abuses of French Discourse Theories for Feminist Politics'. *Boundary 2-an International Journal of Literature and Culture*, 17(2): 82–101.

——(1994) 'After the Family Wage'. *Political Theory*, 22: 591–618.

——(1995) 'Pragmatism, Feminism, and the Linguistic Turn', in L. Nicholson (ed.), *op. cit.*

——(1997a) 'Heterosexism, Misrecognition and Capitalism: A Response to Judith Butler'. *Social Text*, 52/53(15): 3–4.

——(1997b) 'Rethinking the Public Sphere: A Contribution to the Critique of Actually Existing Democracy', in N. Fraser (ed.), *op. cit.*

—— (ed.) (1997) *Justice Interruptus: Critical Reflections on the 'Postsocialist' Conditions*. London: Routledge.

——(2001) 'Recognition without Ethics?' *Theory Culture & Society*, 18(2–3): 21–42.

Fraser, N. and Gordon, L. (1994) '"Dependency" Demystified: Inscriptions of Power in a Keyword of the Welfare State'. *Social Politics*, Spring: 4–31.

——(1997) 'A Genealogy of "Dependency": Tracing a Keyword of the U.S. Welfare State', in N. Fraser (ed.), *op. cit.*

Fraser, N. and Nicholson, L.J. (1990) 'Social Criticism without Philosophy: An Encounter between Feminism and Postmodernism', in L. J. Nicholson (ed.), *op. cit.*

Freedberg, S. (1993) 'The Feminine Ethic of Care and the Professionalization of Social Work'. *Social Work*, 38 (September): 535–40.

Freidman, M. (1997) 'Beyond Caring: The De-Moralization of Gender', in D.T. Meyers (ed.), *op. cit.*

Freud, S. (1961) 'Some Psychological Consequences of the Anatomical Distinction between the Sexes', in J. Strachey (ed.), *Standard Edition of the Complete Psychological Works of Sigmund Freud: Vol 19*. London: Hogarth.

Friedan, B. (1965) *The Feminine Mystique*. Harmondsworth: Penguin.

Friedman, M. (1987) 'Care and Context in Moral Reasoning', in E.F. Kittay and D.T. Meyers (eds), *op. cit.*

Fuss, D. (1989) *Essentially Speaking*. New York: London.

——(1991) 'Inside/Out'. New York: London.

Gagnier, R. (1990) 'Feminist Postmodernism: The End of Feminism or the Ends of Theory', in D.L. Rhode (ed.), *Theoretical Perspectives on Sexual Difference*. New Haven: Yale University Press.

Gagnon, J. and Simon, W. (1974) *Sexual Conduct*. London: Hutchinson.

Gallop, J. (1987) 'French Theory and the Seduction of Feminism', in A. Jardine and P. Smith (eds), *op. cit.*

Gamson, J. (1998) 'Must Identity Movements Self-Destruct? A Queer Dilemma', in P.M. Nardi and B.E. Schneider (eds), *op. cit.*

Gatens, M. (1992) 'Power, Bodies and Difference', in M. Barrett and A. Phillips (eds), *op. cit.*

Gedalof, I. (2000) 'Identity in Transit'. *European Journal of Women's Studies*, 7(3): 337–54.

Gibson-Graham, J.K. (1996) *The End of Capitalism (as We Know it): A Feminist Critique of Political Economy*. Oxford: Blackwell.

Gilbert, J. (2001) 'Science and its "Other": Looking Underneath "Woman" and "Science" for New Directions in Research on Gender and Science Education'. *Gender and Education*, 13(3): 291–305.

Gill, R. and Grint, K. (1995) 'The Gender-Technology Relation: Contemporary Theory and Research', in K. Grint and R. Gill (eds), *op. cit.*

Gilligan, C. (1987) 'Moral Orientation and Moral Development', in E.F. Kittay and D.T. Meyers (eds), *op. cit.*

——(1993a) *In a Different Voice*. London: Harvard University Press.

——(1993b) 'Reply to Critics', in M.J. Larrabee (ed.), *op. cit.*

Gilligan, C. and Wiggins, G. (1987) 'The Origins of Morality in Early Childhood Relationships', in J. Kagan and S. Lamb (eds), *The Emergence of Morality in Young Children*. Chicago: University of Chicago Press.

Gimenez, M.E. (2000) 'What's Material About Material Feminism? A Marxist Feminist Critique'. *Radical Philosophy*, 101 (May–June): 18–28.

Glick, E. (2000) 'Sex Positive: Feminism, Queer Theory and the Politics of Transgression'. *Feminist Review*, 64: 19–45.

Goss, J. (1996) 'Postcolonialism: Subverting Whose Empire?' *Third World Quarterly*, 17(2): 239–50.

Graham, H. (1983) 'Caring: A Labour of Love', in J. Finch and D. Groves (eds), *A Labour of Love: Women, Work and Caring*. London: Routledge & Kegan Paul.

Gremmen, I. (1999) 'Visiting Nurses' Situated Ethics: Beyond "Care Versus Justice"'. *Nursing Ethics*, 6(6): 515–27.

Grewal, I. and Kaplan, C. (1994) 'Introduction: Transnational Feminist Practices and Questions of Postmodernity', in I. Grewal and C. Kaplan (eds), *Scattered Hegemonies: Postmodernity and Transnational Feminist Practices*. Minneapolis and London: University of Minnesota Press.

Griffin, S. (1984) *Woman and Nature: The Roaring inside Her*. London: The Women's Press.

Grint, K. and Gill, R. (eds) (1995) *The Gender-Technology Relation*. London: Taylor & Francis.

Grint, K. and Woolgar, S. (1992) 'Computers, Guns and Roses: What's Social About Being Shot?' *Science, Technology and Human Values*, 17(3): 366–80.

Grosz, E. (1999) 'Contemporary Theories of Power and Subjectivity', in S. Gunew (ed.), *Feminist Knowledge: Critique and Construct*. London: Routledge.

Guerrina, R. (2001) 'Equality, Difference and Motherhood: The Case for a Feminist Analysis of Equal Rights and Maternity Legislation'. *Journal of Gender Studies*, 10(1): 33–42.

Guy-Sheftall, B. (1995) (ed.) *Words of Fire*. New York: The New Press.

Habermas, J. (1989) *The Theory of Communicative Action, Volume Two: The Critique of Functionalist Reason*. Cambridge: Polity Press

——(1990) *Moral Consciousness and Communicative action*. Cambridge: Polity Press.

——(1991) *The Theory of Communicative Action, Volume One: Reason and the Rationalization of Society*. Cambridge: Polity Press.

——(1996) *Between Facts and Norms: Contributions to a Discourse Theory of Law and Democracy*. Cambridge, Mass.: MIT Press.

Hacker, S. (1989) *Pleasure, Power and Technology: Some Tales of Gender and Technology*. Boston: Unwin Hyman.

Halberstam, J. (1993) 'Imagined Violence/Queer Violence: Representation, Rage, and Resistance'. *Social Text*, 37: 187–201.

——(1998) 'Between Butches', in S.R. Munt (ed.), *op. cit.*

Hallstein, D.L.O. (1999) 'A Postmodern Caring: Feminist Standpoint Theories, Revisioned Caring, and Communication Ethics'. *Western Journal of Communication*, 63(1): 32–56.

Haraway, D.J. (1988) 'Situated Knowledge: The Science Question in Feminism as a Site of Discourse on the Privilege of Partial Perspective'. *Feminist Studies*, 14(3): 575–99.

——(1991) *Simians, Cyborgs and Women: The Reinvention of Nature*. New York: Routledge.

——(1997) 'The Virtual Speculum in the New World Order'. *Feminist Review*, 55 (Spring): 22–72.

Harding, S. (1986) *The Science Question in Feminism*. Ithaca, NY: Cornell University Press.

——(1991) *Whose Science? Whose Knowledge*. Buckingham: Open University Press.

——(1993a) 'Reinventing Ourselves as Other; More New Agents of History and Knowledge', in L. Kauffman (ed.), *American Feminist Thought at Century's End Reader*. Oxford: Blackwell.

——(1993b) 'Rethinking Standpoint Epistemology: What Is "Strong Objectivity"', in L. Alcoff and E. Potter (eds), *op. cit.*

——(1995) '"Strong Objectivity": A Response to the New Objectivity Question'. *Synthese*, 104(3): 331–49.

——(1997) 'Comment on Hekman's "Theory and Method: Feminist Standpoint Theory Revisited": Whose Standpoint Needs the Regimes of Truth and Reality?' *Signs*, 22(2): 382–91.

Hartmann, H. (1979) 'The Unhappy Marriage of Marxism and Feminism: Towards a More Progressive Union'. *Capital and Class*, 8: 1–34.

Hartsock, N. (1983) 'The Feminist Standpoint: Developing the Ground for a Specifically Feminist Historical Materialism', in S. Harding, and M.B. Hintikka (eds), *Discovering Reality: Feminist Perspectives on Epistemology, Metaphysics, Methodology, and Philosophy of Science*. Dordrecht, Holland: D. Reidel.

—— (1990) 'Foucault on Power: A Theory for Women?', in L. Nicholson (ed.), *op. cit.*

——(1997) 'Comment on Hekman's "Truth and Method: Feminist Standpoint Theory Revisited": Truth or Justice'. *Signs*, 22(2): 367–74.

——(1998) *'The Feminist Standpoint Revisited' and Other Essays*. Boulder, Colorado: Westview.

Harvey, D. (1989) *The Condition of Postmodernity*. Oxford: Blackwell.

Hawkesworth, M. (1999) 'Analyzing Backlash: Feminist Standpoint Theory as Analytical Tool'. *Women's Studies International Forum*, 22(2): 135–55.

Heidegger, M. (1962) *Being and Time*. Oxford: Blackwell.

Hekman, S.J. (1997) 'Truth and Method: Feminist Standpoint Theory Revisited'. *Signs*, 22(2): 341–74.

Hekman, S.J. (2000) 'Beyond Identity: Feminism, Identity and Identity Politics'. *Feminist Theory*, 1(3): 289–308.

Held, V. (1984) *Rights and Goods: Justifying Social Action*. New York: Free Press, Macmillan – Palgrave.

—— (1997) 'Feminism and Moral Theory', in D.T. Meyers (ed.), *op. cit*.

Hemmings, C. (1999) 'Out of Sight, Out of Mind? Theorizing Femme Narrative'. *Sexualities*, 2(4): 451–64.

Hennessy, R. (1993) *Materialist Feminism and the Politics of Difference*. London: Routledge.

—— (1995) 'Queer Visibility in Commodity Culture', in L.J. Nicholson and S. Seidman (eds), *op. cit*.

Hennessy, R. and Ingraham, C. (1997) 'Introduction: Reclaiming Anticapitalist Feminism', in R. Hennessy and C. Ingraham (eds), *op. cit*.

—— (eds) (1997) *Materialist Feminism: A Reader in Class, Difference, and Women's Lives*. London: Routledge.

Henwood, F. (2000) 'From the Woman Question in Technology to the Technology Question in Feminism – Rethinking Gender Equality in IT Education'. *European Journal of Women's Studies*, 7(2): 209–27.

Hirschauer, S. and Mol, A. (1995) 'Shifting Sexes, Moving Stories – Feminist Constructivist Dialogues'. *Science Technology and Human Values*, 20(3): 368–85.

Hoagland, S.L. (1988) *Lesbian Ethics*. California: Institute of Lesbian Studies.

—— (1991) 'Some Thoughts About "Caring"', in C. Card (ed.), *op. cit*.

Hofmann, J. (1999) 'Writers, Texts and Writing Acts: Gendered User Images in Word Processing Software', in D. MacKenzie and J. Wajcman (eds), *The Social Shaping of Technology*. Buckingham: Open University Press.

Holliday, R. (1999) 'The Comfort of Identity'. *Sexualities*, 2(4): 475–91.

hooks, b. (1982) *Ain't I a Woman*. London: Pluto.

—— (1984) *Feminist Theory: From Margin to Center*. Boston: South End Press.

—— (1990) *Yearning: Race, Gender and Cultural Politics*. Toronto: Between the Lines.

—— (1992) *Black Looks: Race and Representation*. Boston: South End Press.

—— (1995) 'Black Women: Shaping Feminist Theory', in B. Guy-Sheftall (ed.), *op. cit*.

Howell, J. (1997) 'Post-Beijing Reflections: Creating Ripples, but Not Waves in China'. *Women's International Forum*, 20(2): 235–52.

HR3734 (1996) *Personal Responsibility and Work Opportunity Reconciliation Act*.

Hubbard, R. (1997) 'Abortion and Disability: Who Should and Who Should Not Inhabit the World?', in L.J. Davis (ed.), *The Disability Studies Reader*. London: Routledge.

Hughes, D.M. (1995) 'Significant Differences: The Construction of Knowledge, Objectivity, and Dominance'. *Women's Studies International Forum*, 18(4): 395–406.

Hughes, T.P. (1983) *Networks of Power: Electrification in Western Society, 1880–1930*. Baltimore: Johns Hopkins University Press.

—— (1986) 'The Seamless Web: Technology, Science, Etcetera, Etcetera, Etcetera'. *Social Studies of Science*, 16: 281–92.

Humphrey, J.C. (1999) 'To Queer or Not to Queer a Lesbian and Gay Group? Sexual and Gendered Politics at the Turn of the Century'. *Sexualities*, 2(2): 223–46.

Hunt, S. and Symonds, A. (1995) *The Social Meaning of Midwifery*. London: Macmillan – Palgrave.

Hutchby, I. (2001) 'Technologies, Texts and Affordances'. *Sociology*, 35(2): 441–56.

Hutchins, L. and Kaahumanu, L. (1991) 'Bicoastal Introduction', in L. Hutchins and L. Kaahumanu (eds), *Bi Any Other Name*. Boston: Alyson.

Irigaray, L. (1985) *Speculum of the Other Woman*. Ithaca, NY: Cornell University Press.

Jackson, S. (1995) 'Gender and Heterosexuality: A Materialist Feminist Analysis', in M. Maynard and J. Purvis (eds), *(Hetero)Sexual Politics*. London: Taylor & Francis.

——(1998) 'Feminist Social Theory', in S. Jackson and J. Jones (eds), *Contemporary Feminist Theories*. Edinburgh: Edinburgh University Press.

——(1999) 'Feminist Sociology and Sociological Feminism: Recovering the Social in Feminist Thought'. *Sociological Research Online*, 4(3): U337–56.

——(2001) 'Why a Materialist Feminism is (Still) Possible – and Necessary'. *Women's Studies International Forum*, 24(3–4): 283–93.

Jagger, A.M. (1991) 'Feminist Ethics: Projects, Problems, Prospects', in C. Card (ed.), *op. cit.*

Jagose, A. (1997) '"Feminism without Women": A Lesbian Reassurance', in D. Heller (ed.), *Cross Purposes: Lesbians, Feminists and the Limits of Alliance*. Bloomington and Indianapolis: Indiana University Press.

James, J. (1996) 'Experience, Reflection, Judgement and Action: Teaching Theory, Talking Community', in D. Bell and R. Klein (eds), *op. cit.*

——(1999) 'Radicalising Feminism'. *Race and Class*, 40(4): 15–31.

James, S. (1992) 'The Good-Enough Citizen: Citizenship and Independence', in G. Block and S. James (eds), *op. cit.*

Jameson, F. (1991) *Postmodernism or, the Cultural Logic of Late Capitalism*. Durham: Duke University Press.

Jardine, A. and Smith, P. (eds) (1987) *Men in Feminism*. New York: Methuen.

Jeffreys, S. (1989) 'Butch and Femme, Now and Then', in L.H. Group (ed.), *Not a Passing Phase: Reclaiming Lesbians in History*. London: Women's Press.

——(1994) 'The Queer Disappearance of Lesbians: Sexuality in the Academy'. *Women's Studies International Forum*, 17(5): 459–72.

Jiaxiang, W. (1996) 'What are Chinese Women Faced with after Beijing?' *Feminist Studies*, 22(3): 497–501.

Jinngwei, Y. (1996) 'Enlightenment'. *Feminist Studies*, 22(3): 508–10.

Jones, K.B. (1996) 'What is Authority's Gender?', in N.J. Hirschmann and C. Di Stefano (eds), *Revisioning the Political*. Boulder, Colorado: Westview Press.

Kallianes, V. and Rubendeld, P. (1997) 'Disabled Women and Reproductive Rights'. *Disability and Society*, 12(2): 203–21.

Kaplan, C. (1996) *Questions of Travel: Postmodern Discourses of Displacement*. Durham, N.C. and London: Duke University Press.

Kaplan, C. *et al.* (eds) (1999) *Between Woman and Nation: Nationalisms, Transnational Feminisms, and the State*. Durham, N.C. and London: Duke University Press.

Kapur, R. (2001) 'Imperial Parody'. *Feminist Theory*, 2(1): 79–88.

Karpf, A. (1987) 'Recent Feminist Approaches to Women and Technology', in M. McNeil (ed.), *Gender and Expertise*. London: Free Association Books.

Keller, E.F. and Longino, H.E. (eds) (1996) *Feminism and Science*. Oxford: Oxford University Press.

Kelly, P. (1997) 'Women and Power', in K.J. Warren (ed.), *Ecofeminism: Women, Culture and Nature*. Bloomington: Indiana University Press.

Kenny, A. (ed.) (1994) *The Wittgenstein Reader*. Oxford: Blackwell.

Kerber, L.K. (1993) 'Some Cautionary Words for Historians', in M.J. Larrabee (ed.), *op. cit.*

King, D.K. (1995) 'Multiple Jeopardy, Multiple Consciousness: The Context of Black Feminist Ideology', in B. Guy-Sheftall (ed.), *op. cit.*

Kirby, A. (1995) 'Straight Talk on the Pomohomo Question'. *Gender, Place and Culture*, 2(1): 89–95.

Kirkup, G. (1992) 'The Social Construction of Computers: Hammers or Harpsichords', in G. Kirkup and L.S. Keller (eds), *op. cit.*

Kirkup, G. and Keller, L.S. (eds) (1992) *Inventing Women: Science, Technology and Gender*. Cambridge: Polity Press.

Kittay, E.F. (1995) 'Taking Dependency Seriously: The Family and Medical Leave Act Considered in Light of the Social Organization of Dependency, Work and Gender Equity'. *Hypatia*, 10(1): 8–29.

Kittay, E.F. and Meyers, D.T. (eds) (1987) *Women and Moral Theory*. Savage, MD: Rowman & Littlefield Publishers, Inc.

Knight, K. (ed.) (1998) *The MacIntyre Reader*, Oxford: Polity Press.

Knopp, L. (1995) 'If You're Going to Get All Hyped up You'd Better Go Somewhere!' *Gender, Place and Culture*, 2(1): 85–8.

Kohlberg, L. (1981) *Essays on Moral Development Vol1: The Philosophy of Moral Development*. San Francisco: Harper & Row.

Kohlberg, L. and Gilligan, C. (1971) 'The Adolescent as a Philosopher: The Discovery of the Self in the Post-Conventional World'. *Daedalus*, 100: 1051–86.

Kohlberg, L. and Kramer, R. (1969) 'Continuities and Discontinuities in Child and Adult Moral Development'. *Human Development*, 12: 93–120.

Kristeva, J. (1984) *Revolution in Poetic Language*. New York: Columbia University Press.

Kuhn, A. and Wolpe, A. (1978) (eds) *Feminism and Materialism: Women and Modes of Production*. London: Routledge.

Kuhn, T. (1996) *The Structure of Scientific Revolutions*. Chicago, IL: University of Chicago Press.

Kuhse, H. (1995) 'Clinical Ethics and Nursing – Yes to Caring, but No to a Female Ethics of Care'. *Bioethics*, 9(3–4): 207–19.

Lacan, J. (1968) *The Language of the Self: The Function of Language in Psychoanalysis*. Baltimore: Johns Hopkins University Press.

Laclau, E. and Mouffe, C. (1985) *Hegemony and Socialist Strategy*. London: Verso.

—— (1987) 'Postmodernism without Apologies'. *New Left Review*, 39: 79–106.

Landes, J.B. (1995) 'The Public and Private Sphere: A Feminist Reconsideration', in J. Meehan (ed.), *op. cit.*

Landry, D. and MacLean, G. (1993) *Materialist Feminisms*. Oxford: Blackwell.

Lapovsky Kennedy, E. and Davis, M.D. (1993) *Boots of Leather, Slippers of Gold: The History of a Lesbian Community*. New York: Routledge.

Lappalainen, R.E. and Motevasel, I.N. (1997) 'Ethics of Care and Social Policy'. *Scandinavian Journal of Social Welfare*, 6(3): 189–96.

Larrabee, M.J. (ed.) (1993) *An Ethic of Care; Feminist and Interdisciplinary Perspectives*. London: Routledge.

Latour, B. (1991) 'Technology is Society Made Durable', in J. Law (ed.), *op. cit.*

——(1996) *Aramis, or the Love of Technology*. Cambridge, Mass.: Harvard University Press.

Law, J. (1987) 'Technology and Heterogeneous Engineering: The Case of Portuguese Expansion', in W.E. Bijker *et al.* (eds), *op. cit.*

——(ed.) (1991) *The Sociology of Monsters*. London: Routledge.

Leidholdt, D. and Raymond, J. (eds) (1990) *The Sexual Liberals and the Attack on Feminism*. New York: Pergamon Press.

Levine, C. *et al.* (1985) 'The Current Formulation of Kohlberg's Theory and a Response to Critics'. *Human Development*, 28(2): 94–100.

Levitas, R. (1986) 'Ideology and the New Right', in R. Levitas (ed.), *The Ideology of the New Right*. Cambridge: Polity Press.

Lie, M. (1995) 'Technology and Masculinity: The Case of the Computer'. *European Journal of Women's Studies*, 2(3): 379–94.

Linder, F. (2001) 'Speaking of Bodies, Pleasures, and Paradise Lost: Erotic Agency and Situationist Ethnography'. *Cultural Studies*, 15(2): 352–74.

Lister, R. (1997) *Citizenship: Feminist Perspectives*. London: Macmillan – Palgrave.

Lloyd, M. (1999) 'Performativity, Parody, Politics'. *Theory, Culture and Society*, 16(2): 195–213.

Lohan, M. (2000) 'Constructive Tensions in Feminist Technology Studies'. *Social Studies of Science*, 30(6): 895–916.

Lorber, J. (2000) 'Using Gender to Undo Gender'. *Feminist Theory*, 1(1): 79–95.

Lorde, A. (1984a) 'Age, Race, Class, and Sex: Women Redefining Difference', in A. Lorde (ed.), *op. cit.*

——(1984b) 'The Master's Tools Will Never Dismantle the Master's House', in A. Lorde (ed.), *op. cit.*

——(1984c) 'An Open Letter to Mary Daly', in A. Lorde (ed.), *op. cit.*

——(ed.) (1984) *Sister Outsider*. New York: The Crossing Press.

Lugones, M.C. (1991) 'On the Logic of Pluralist Feminism', in C. Card (ed.), *op. cit.*

Lurie, S. *et al.* (2001) 'Restoring Feminist Politics to Poststructuralist Critique'. *Feminist Studies*, 27(3): 679–707.

Lyotard, J.-F. (1984) *The Postmodern Condition*. Minneapolis: University of Minnesota Press.

MacCannell, D. and MacCannell, J.F. (1993) 'Violence, Power and Pleasure', in C. Ramazanoglu (ed.), *op. cit.*

Mann, S.A. (2000) 'The Scholarship of Difference: A Scholarship of Liberation?' *Sociological Inquiry*, 70(4): 475–98.

Mann, S.A. and Kelley, L.R. (1997) 'Standing at the Crossroads of Modernist Thought: Collins, Smith, and the New Feminist Epistemologies'. *Gender and Society*, 11(4): 391–419.

Martin, B. (1982) 'Feminism, Criticism, and Foucault'. *New German Critique*, 27: 3–30.

Martin, B. (1988) 'Feminism, Criticism and Foucault', in I. Diamond and L. Quinby (eds), *op. cit.*

—— (1992) 'Sexual Practice and Changing Lesbian Identities', in M. Barrett and A. Phillips (eds), *op. cit.*

—— (1998) 'Sexualities without Genders and Other Queer Utopias', in M. Merck *et al.* (eds), *op. cit.*

Martin, D. and Lyons, P. (1972) *Lesbian/Woman*. San Francisco: Glide.

Martin, M. (1991) *'Hello Central?' Gender, Technology, Technology and Culture in the Formation of Telephone Systems*. Montreal and Kingston: McGill-Queens University Press.

Marx, K. and Engels, F. (1976) *Collected Works, Volume 5*. London: Lawrence & Wishart.

Matisons, M.R. (1998) 'The New Feminist Philosophy of the Body'. *The European Journal of Women's Studies*, 5: 9–34.

McClintock, A. (1992) 'The Angel of Progress: Pitfalls of the Term "Post-Colonialism"'. *Social Text*, 32(33): 84–99.

McEwan, C. (2000) 'Engendering Citizenship: Gendered Spaces of Democracy in South Africa'. *Political Geography*, 19(5): 627–51.

McIntosh, M. (1968) 'The Homosexual Role'. *Social Problems*, 16(2): 189–92.

McLaughlin, J. (1997) 'Feminist Relations with Postmodernism: Reflections on the Positive Aspects of Involvement'. *Journal of Gender Studies*, 6(1): 5–15.

—— (1999) 'Gendering Occupational Identities and IT in the Retail Sector'. *New Technology, Work and Employment*, 14: 143–56.

McLaughlin, J. *et al.* (1999) *Valuing Technology: Organisations, Culture and Change*. London: Routledge.

McLellan, D. (1999) 'Then and Now: Marx and Marxism?' *Political Studies*, 47(5): 955–66.

McNay, L. (1991) 'The Foucauldian Body and the Exclusion of Experience'. *Hypatia*, 6(3): 125–39.

—— (1992) *Foucault and Feminism: Power, Gender and the Self*. Cambridge: Polity Press.

—— (1994) *Foucault: A Critical Introduction*. Cambridge: Polity Press.

McNeil, M. (1993) 'Dancing with Foucault: Feminism and Power-Knowledge', in C. Ramazanoglu (ed.), *op. cit.*

Meehan, J. (ed.) (1995) *Feminists Read Habermas: Gendering the Subject of Discourse*. London: Routledge.

Merchant, C. (1980) *The Death of Nature: Women, Ecology, and the Scientific Revolution*. London: Wildwood House.

Meyers, D.T. (ed.) (1997) *Feminist Social Thought: A Reader*. London: Routledge.

Merck, M. *et al.* (eds) (1998) *Coming out of Feminism*. Oxford: Blackwell.

Minh-ha, T.T. (1989) *Women, Native, Other*. Bloomington: Indiana University Press.

Mirza, H.S. (1986) 'The Dilemma of Socialist Feminism: A Case for Black Feminism'. *Feminist Review*, 22: 103–5.

—— (ed.) (1997) *Black British Feminism*. London: Routledge.

Mitchell, L.M. and Georges, E. (1997) 'Cross-Cultural Cyborgs: Greek and Canadian Women's Discourses on Fetal Ultrasound'. *Feminist Studies*, 23(2): 373–402.

Moallem, M. (1999) 'Transnationalism, Feminism and Fundamentalism', in C. Kaplan *et al.* (eds), *op. cit.*

Modleski, T. (1991) *Feminism without Women*. New York: Routledge.

Mohanty, C.T. (1995) 'Feminist Encounters: Locating the Politics of Experience', in L. Nicholson and S. Seidman (eds), *op. cit.*

Moi, T. (1985) 'Power, Sex and Subjectivity: Feminist Reflections on Foucault'. *Paragraph*, 5: 95–102.

Moi, T. and Redway, J. (1994) 'Editors' Note'. *South Atlantic Quarterly*, 93(4).

Moody-Adams, M.M. (1991) 'Gender and the Complexity of Moral Voices', in C. Card (ed.), *op. cit.*

——(1997) 'Gender and the Complexity of Moral Voices', in D.T. Meyers (ed.), *op. cit.*

Moore, M. (1999) 'The Ethics of Care and Justice'. *Women and Politics*, 20(2): 1–16.

Moore, S. (1988) 'Getting a Bit of the Other – the Pimps of Postmodernism', in R. Chapman and J. Rutherford (eds), *Male Order: Unwrapping Masculinity*. London: Lawrence & Wishart.

Morris, J. (1993) 'Feminism and Disability'. *Feminist Review*, 43 (Spring): 57–70.

Morris, M. (1988) *The Pirate's Fiancée: Feminism, Readings, Postmodernism*. London: Verso.

Mouffe, C. (1992) 'Feminism, Citizenship and Radical Democratic Politics', in J. Butler and J.W. Scott (eds), *op. cit.*

Moya, P. (1997) 'Postmodernism, "Realism," and the Politics of Identity', in M.J. Alexander and C.T. Mohanty (eds), *op. cit.*

Munt, S.R. (1998) 'Introduction', in S.R. Munt (ed.), *op. cit.*

——(ed.) (1998) *Butch/Femme: Inside Lesbian Gender*. London: Cassell.

Murphy, P. (1990) 'Gender Differences in Pupils' Reactions to Practical Work', in B.E. Woolnough (ed.), *Practical Science: The Role and Reality of Practical Work in School Science*. London: Taylor & Francis.

Nails, D. (1983) 'Social Scientific Sexism: Gilligan's Mismeasure of Man'. *Social Research*, 50(Autumn): 490–513.

Naples, N.A. (1999) 'Towards Comparative Analyses of Women's Political Praxis: Explicating Multiple Dimensions of Standpoint Epistemology for Feminist Ethnography'. *Women and Politics*, 20(1): 29–57.

Nardi, P.M. and Schneider, B.E. (eds) (1998) *Social Perspectives in Lesbian and Gay Studies*. London: Routledge.

Narrayan, U. (1995) 'Colonialism and Its Others: Considerations on Rights and Care Discourses'. *Hypatia*, 10(2): 133–40.

Nelson, L.H. (1993) 'Epistemological Communities', in L. Alcoff and E. Potter (eds), *op. cit.*

Nestle, J. (1987) *A Restricted Country*. Ithaca, NY: Firebrand Press.

——(1992) 'The Fem Question', in C.S. Vance (ed.), *op. cit.*

Newton, E. (1972) *Mother Camp: Female Impersonators in America*. Chicago and London: The University of Chicago Press.

Nicholson, L. (ed.) (1995) *Feminist Contentions: A Philosophical Exchange*. London: Routledge.

Nicholson, L.J. (ed.) (1990) *Feminism/Postmodernism*. London: Routledge.
—— (1993) 'Women, Morality, and History', in M.J. Larrabee (ed.), *op. cit.*
—— (1994) 'Interpreting Gender'. *Signs*, 20: 79–105.
Nicholson, L.J. and Seidman, S. (eds) (1995) *Social Postmodernism: Beyond Identity Politics*. Cambridge: Cambridge University Press.
Nietzsche, F. (1990) *Beyond Good and Evil*. London: Penguin.
Nussbaum, M.C. (1992) 'Human Functioning and Social Justice: In Defence of Aristotelian Essentialism'. *Political Theory*, 20: 202–46.
—— (1999a) 'The Professor of Parody'. *The New Republic*, 45 (22 February).
—— (1999b) *Sex and Justice*. New York: Oxford University Press.
Nye, A. (1988) *Feminist Theory and the Philosophies of Man*. London: Routledge.
Oakley, A. (1993) *Essays on Women, Medicine and Health*. Edinburgh: Edinburgh University Press.
—— (1998) 'Science, Gender and Women's Liberation: An Argument against Postmodernism'. *Women's Studies International Forum*, 21(2): 133–46.
O'Brien, M. (1981) *The Politics of Reproduction*. London: Routledge & Kegan Paul.
O'Brien, P. (1978) 'Crime and Punishment'. *Journal of Social History*, 23: 508–20.
Okin, S.M. (1989) *Justice, Gender and the Family*. New York: Basic Books.
—— (1991) 'John Rawls: Justice as Fairness for Whom?', in M.L. Shanley and C. Pateman (eds), *op. cit.*
—— (1992) *Women in Western Political Thought*. Princeton, N.J.: Princeton University Press.
—— (1994) 'Gender Inequality and Cultural Differences'. *Political Theory*, 22(1): 5–24.
Opotow, S. (1990) 'Moral Exclusion and Injustice: An Introduction'. *Journal of Social Issues*, 46(1): 1–20.
Ormrod, S. (1994) 'Let's Nuke Dinner': Discursive Practices of Gender in the Creation of a New Cooking Process', in C. Cockburn and R.A. Fürst-Dilic (eds), *op. cit.*
—— (1995) 'Feminist Sociology and Methodology: Leaky Black Boxes in Gender/Technology Relations', in K. Grint and R. Gill (eds), *op. cit.*
Ortiz, A.T. (1997) '"Bare-Handed" Medicine and its Elusive Patients: The Unstable Construction of Pregnant Women and Fetuses in Dominican Obstetrics Discourse'. *Feminist Studies*, 23(2): 263–88.
Parens, E. and Asch, A. (eds) (2000) *Prenatal Testing and Disability Rights*. Washington, D.C.: Georgetown University Press.
Pateman, C. (1988) *The Sexual Contract*. Cambridge: Polity Press.
—— (1992) 'Equality, Difference, Subordination: The Politics of Motherhood and Women's Citizenship', in G. Block and S. James (eds), *op. cit.*
Perry, S. (1998) 'Holding up Half the Sky: Women in China'. *Current History*, September: 279–84.
Phelan, S. (1990) 'Foucault and Feminism'. *American Journal of Political Science*, 34(2): 421–40.
Phillips, A. (1993) *Democracy and Difference*. Cambridge: Polity Press.
—— (1999) *Which Equalities Matter?*, Cambridge: Polity Press.
Piaget, J. (1932) *The Moral Judgement of the Child*. London: Routledge & Kegan Paul.

Plaza, M. (1978) 'Phallomorphic Power and the Psychology of Woman'. *Ideology and Consciousness*, 4: 4–36.

Pollert, A. (1996) 'Gender and Class Revisited; or, the Poverty of "Patriarchy"'. *Sociology*, 30(4): 639–59.

Porter, E. (1999) *Feminist Perspectives on Ethics*. London: Longman.

Press, N. (2000) 'Assessing the Expressive Character of Prenatal Testing: The Choices Made or the Choices Made Available?', in E. Parens and A. Asch (eds), *op. cit.*

Pringle, R. and Watson, S. (1992) '"Women's Interests" and the Post-Structuralist State', in M. Barrett and A. Philips (eds), *op. cit.*

Probyn, E. (1995) 'Lesbians in Space, Gender, Sex and the Structure of Missing'. *Gender, Place and Culture*, 2(1): 77–95.

Puka, B. (1993) 'The Liberation of Caring: A Different Voice for Gilligan's "Different Voice"', in M.J. Larrabee (ed.), *op. cit.*

Quayson, A. (2000) *Postcolonialism: Theory, Practice or Process?*, Cambridge: Polity Press.

Quillen, C. (2001) 'Feminist Theory, Justice, and the Lure of the Human'. *Signs*, 27(1): 87–122.

Rabinow, P. (ed.) (1984) *The Foucault Reader*. London: Penguin Books.

Radicalesbians (1973) 'The Woman-Identified Woman', in A. Koedt, E. Levine and A. Rapone (eds), *Radical Feminism*. New York: Times Books.

Rahman, M. and Jackson, S. (1997) 'Liberty, Equality and Sexuality: Essentialism and the Discourse of Rights'. *Journal of Gender Studies*, 6(2): 117–29.

Rai, S. and Lievesley, G. (eds) (1996) *Women and the State, International Perspectives*. London: Taylor & Francis.

Ramazanoglu, C. (1986) 'Ethnocentrism and Socialist-Feminist Theory: A Response to Barrett and McIntosh'. *Feminist Review*, 22: 83–6.

—— (1989) *Feminism and the Contradictions of Oppression*. London: Routledge.

—— (ed.) (1993) 'Feminism, Foucault and the Politics of the Body', *Up Against Foucault*. London: Routledge.

Ramazanoglu, C. and Holland, J. (1993) 'Women's Sexuality and Men's Appropriation of Desire', in C. Ramazanoglu (ed.), *op. cit.*

—— (2000) 'Still Telling it Like it is? Problems of Feminist Truth Claims', in S. Ahmed *et al.* (eds), *op. cit.*

Rapp, R. (1999) *Testing Women, Testing the Fetus: The Social Impact of Amniocentesis in America*. London: Routledge.

Rawls, J. (1972) *A Theory of Justice*. Oxford: Clarendon Press.

—— (1993) *Political Liberalism*. New York: Columbia University Press.

Reay, D. (1997) 'Feminist Theory, Habitus, and Social Class: Disrupting Notions of Classlessness'. *Women's Studies International Forum*, 20(2): 225–33.

Rich, A. (1986a) 'Compulsory Heterosexuality and Lesbian Existence', in A. Rich (ed.), *Blood, Bread and Poetry: Selected Prose 1979–1985*. London: Virago.

—— (1986b) *Of Woman Born*. London: Virago.

Riley, D. (1988) *Am I That Name? Feminism and the Category of 'Women' in History*. Basingstoke: Macmillan – Palgrave.

Robinson, V. and Richardson, D. (1996) 'Repackaging Women and Feminism: Taking the Heat Off Patriarchy', in D. Bell and R. Klein (eds), *op. cit.*

Roof, J. (1998) '1970s Lesbian Feminism Meets 1990s Butch-Femme', in S.R. Munt (ed.), *op. cit.*

Rorty, R. (1989) *Contingency, Irony, and Solidarity*. Cambridge: Cambridge University Press.

Roseneil, S. (1999) 'Postmodern Feminist Politics'. *European Journal of Women's Studies*, 6: 161–82.

Rothschild, J. (1983) (ed.) *Machina Ex Dea: Feminist Perspectives on Technology*. New York: Pergamon.

Rowland, R. and Klein, R. (1996) 'Radical Feminism: History, Politics, Action', in D. Bell and R. Klein (eds), *op. cit.*

Rubin, G. (1975) 'The Traffic in Women: Notes on the "Political Economy" of Sex', in R.R. Reiter (ed.), *Toward an Anthropology of Women*. New York: Monthly Review Press.

——(1993) 'Thinking Sex: Notes for a Radical Theory of the Politics of Sexuality', in H. Abelove *et al.* (eds), *The Lesbian and Gay Studies Reader*. London: Routledge.

Rubin, G. and Butler, J. (1998) 'Sexual Traffic', in M. Merck *et al.* (eds), *op. cit.*

Ruddick, S. (1990) *Maternal Thinking*. London: Women's Press.

Rudy, K. (1999) 'Liberal Theory and Feminist Politics'. *Women and Politics*, 20(2): 33–57.

——(2001) 'Radical Feminism, Lesbian Separatism, and Queer Theory'. *Feminist Studies*, 27(1): 191–222.

Saetnan, A.R. (1996) 'Ultrasonic Discourse: Contested Meanings of Gender and Technology in the Norwegian Ultrasound Screening Debate'. *European Journal of Women's Studies*, 3: 55–75.

——(1997) 'Standing One's Ground Requires Finding Some Ground to Stand On', in B. Berner (ed.), *Gendered Practices: Feminist Studies of Technology and Society*. Linkoping, Sweden: Department of Technology and Social Change, Linkoping University.

Said, E.W. (1993) *Culture & Imperialism*. London: Chatto & Windus.

Saussure, F.D. (1959) *Course in General Linguistics*. New York: McGraw-Hill.

Sawicki, J. (1991a) *Disciplining Foucault: Feminism, Power and the Body*. London: Routledge.

——(1991b) 'Foucault and Feminism: Towards a Politics of Difference', in C. Pateman and M.L. Shanley (eds), *op. cit.*

Saxton, M. (2000) 'Messages and Meanings of Prenatal Genetic Testing', in E. Parens and A. Asch (eds), *op. cit.*

Sayers, J. (1986) *Sexual Contradictions: Psychology, Psychoanalysis and Feminism*. London: Tavistock.

Scheman, N. (1993) *Engenderings: Constructions of Knowledge, Authority, and Privilege*. London: Routledge.

Schwarz, B. (2000) 'Actually Existing Postcolonialism'. *Radical Philosophy*, 104: 16–24.

Scott, A. (2001) '(In)Forming Politics: Processes of Feminist Activism in the Information Age'. *Women's Studies International Forum*, 24(3/4): 409–21.

Scott, J.W. (1988a) 'Deconstructing Equality Versus Difference'. *Feminist Studies*, 14(1): 33–50.

—— (1988b) *Gender and the Politics of History*. New York: Columbia University Press.

—— (1992) '"Experience"', in J. Butler and J.W. Scott (eds), *op. cit.*

Sedgwick, E.K. (1990) *Epistemology of the Closet*. Berkeley: University of California Press.

Segal, L. (1994) *Straight Sex: The Politics of Pleasure*. London: Virago.

—— (1997) 'Generations of Feminism'. *Radical Philosophy*, 83 (May/June): 6–16.

—— (1999) *Why Feminism?* Cambridge: Polity Press.

Seidman, S. (1997) *Difference Troubles*. Cambridge: Cambridge University Press.

Sevenhuijsen, S. (1998) *Citizenship and the Ethics of Care*. London: Routledge.

Shakespeare, T. (1998) 'Choices and Rights: Eugenics, Genetics and Disability Equality'. *Disability & Society*, 13(5): 665–81.

Shanley, M.L. and Pateman, C. (eds) (1991) *Feminist Interpretations of Political Theory*. Cambridge: Polity Press.

Sheldon, A. (1999) 'Personal and Perplexing: Feminist Disability Politics Evaluated'. *Disability & Society*, 14(5): 643–58.

Shelley, M. (1976) 'Confessions of a Pseudo-Male Chauvinist', in B. Grier and C. Reid (eds), *The Lavender Herring: Lesbian Essays from the Ladder*. Baltimore: Diana Press.

Sher, G. (1987) 'Other Voices, Other Rooms? Women's Psychology and Moral Theory', in E.F. Kittay and D.T. Meyers (eds), *op. cit.*

Shildrick, M. (1997) *Leaky Bodies and Boundaries*. London: Routledge.

Shiva, V. (1989) *Staying Alive: Women, Ecology, and Development*. London: Zed Books.

Silva, E.B. (2000) 'The Cook, the Cooker and the Gendering of the Kitchen'. *Sociological Review*, 48(4): 612–28.

Singer, L. (1992) 'Feminism and Postmodernism', in J. Butler and J.W. Scott (eds), *op. cit.*

Skeggs, B. (2001) 'The Toilet Paper: Femininity, Class and Mis-Recognition'. *Women's Studies International Forum*, 24(3/4): 295–307.

Smart, C. (1992) *Regulating Womanhood: Historical Essays on Marriage, Motherhood and Sexuality*. London: Routledge.

Smith, A.M. (1994) *New Right Discourse on Race and Sexuality*. Cambridge: Cambridge University Press.

Smith, D.E. (1987) *The Everyday World as Problematic: A Feminist Sociology*. Milton Keynes: Open University Press.

—— (1997) 'Comment on Hekman's "Theory and Method: Feminist Standpoint Theory Revisited"'. *Signs*, 22(2): 393–98.

Soper, K. (1993a) 'Postmodernism, Subjectivity and the Question of Value', in J. Squires (ed.), *op. cit.*

—— (1993b) 'Productive Contradictions', in C. Ramazanoglu (ed.), *op. cit.*

Spelman, E.V. (1988) *Inessential Woman: Problems of Exclusion in Feminist Thought*. Boston: Beacon.

Spivak, G.C. (1987) *In Other Worlds: Essays in Cultural Politics*. New York: Methuen.

Spivak, G.C. (1990) *The Post-Colonial Critic*. London: Routledge.

—— (2000) 'Poststructuralism, Marginality, Postcoloniality and Value', in D. Brydon (ed.), *op. cit.*

Squires, J. (1993) 'Introduction', in J. Squires (ed.), *op. cit.*

—— (ed) (1993) *Principled Positions*. London: Lawrence and Wishart.

—— (2001) 'Representing Groups, Deconstructing Identities'. *Feminist Theory*, 2(1): 7–27.

Stabile, C. (1994) *Feminism and the Technological Fix*. Manchester: Manchester University Press.

Stacey, J. (2001) 'The Empress of Feminist Theory is Overdressed'. *Feminist Theory*, 2(1): 99–103.

Stack, C.B. (1993) 'The Culture of Gender: Women and Men of Color', in M.J. Larrabee (ed.), *op. cit.*

Stanley, L. (1990) 'Recovering "Women" in History from Historical Deconstructionism'. *Women's Studies International Forum*, 13: 153–55.

—— (1997) 'Writing the Borders: Episodic and Theoretic Thoughts on Not/Belonging', in L. Stanley (ed.), *op. cit.*

—— (ed.) (1997) *Knowing Feminisms*. London: Sage.

Stanley, L. and Wise, S. (2000) 'But the Empress Has No Clothes!' *Feminist Theory*, 1(3): 261–88.

Stanworth, M. (1987) 'Reproductive Technologies and the Deconstruction of Motherhood', in M. Stanworth (ed.), *Reproductive Technologies: Gender, Motherhood and Medicine*. Cambridge: Polity Press.

Star, S.L. (1991) 'Power, Technologies and the Phenomenology of Conventions: On Being Allergic to Onions.' in J. Law (ed.), *op. cit.*

Stepulevage, L. (2001) 'Gender/Technology Relations: Complicating the Gender Binary'. *Gender and Education*, 13(3): 325–38.

Suchting, W. (1993) 'Reconstructing Marxism'. *Science and Society*, 57(2): 133–59.

Sum, N.-L. (2000) 'From the Politics of Identity to Politics of Complexity', in S. Ahmed *et al.* (eds), *op. cit.*

Sundin, E. (1998) 'Organizational Conflict, Technology and Space: A Swedish Case Study of the Gender System and the Economic System in Action'. *Gender, Work and Organization*, 5: 31–42.

Sybylla, R. (2001) 'Hearing Whose Voice? The Ethics of Care and the Practices of Liberty: A Critique'. *Economy and Society*, 30(1): 66–84.

Tancred, P. (1995) 'Women's Work: A Challenge to the Sociology of Work'. *Gender, Work and Organization*, 2: 11–20.

Taylor, C. (1991) *The Ethics of Authenticity*, London: Harvard University Press.

Thacker, A. (1993) 'Foucault's Aesthetics of Existence'. *Radical Philosophy*, 63 (Spring): 13–21.

The History Net (2002) 'Women's History'. http://womenshistory.about.com/library/qu/blquwesr.htm

Thompson, D. (2001) *Radical Feminism Today*. London: Sage.

Tong, R. (1998) 'The Ethics of Care: A Feminist Virtue Ethics of Care for Healthcare Practitioners'. *Journal of Medicine and Philosophy*, 23(2): 131–52.

Tronto, J.C. (1989) 'Women and Caring: What Can Feminists Learn About Morality from Caring', in A.M. Jaggar and S. Bordo (eds), *Gender/Body/Knowledge: Feminist Reconstructions of Being and Knowing*. London: Rutgers University Press.

—— (1993a) 'Beyond Gender Difference to a Theory of Care', in M.J. Larrabee (ed.), *op. cit.*

—— (1993b) *Moral Boundaries: A Political Argument for an Ethic of Care*. London: Routledge.

—— (1995) *Caring for Democracy*. Utrecht: Universiteit voor Humanistiek.

Turkle, S. (1988) 'Computational Reticence: Why Women Fear the Intimate Machine', in C. Kramarae (ed.), *Technology and Women's Voices*. London: Routledge.

Turkle, S. and Seymour, P. (1990) 'Epistemological Pluralism: Styles and Voices within the Computer Culture'. *Signs*, 16(1): 128–258.

UN (1995a) 'Fourth World Conference on Women: Beijing Declaration'.

—— (1995b) 'Fourth World Conference on Women: Platform for Action'.

Ungerson, C. (1987) *Policy is Personal: Sex, Gender, and Informal Care*. London: Tavistock.

UNICEF (1999) *Human Rights for Children and Women*. New York: UNICEF.

Vance, C.S. (1992) 'Pleasure and Danger: Toward a Politics of Sexuality', in C.S. Vance (ed.), *op. cit.*

—— (ed.) (1992) *Pleasure and Danger: Exploring Female Sexuality*. London: Pandora.

Veltmeyer, H. (2000) 'Post-Marxist Project: An Assessment and Critique of Ernesto Laclau'. *Sociological Inquiry*, 70(4): 499–519.

Vogel, L. (1995) *Woman Questions: Essays for a Materialist Feminism*. London: Pluto Press.

—— (2000) 'Domestic Labor Revisited'. *Science and Society*, 64(2): 151–70.

Volman, M. and Ten Dam, G. (1998) 'Equal but Different: Contradictions in the Development of Gender Identity in the 1990s'. *British Journal of Sociology of Education*, 4: 529–45.

Vuola, E. (2002) 'Remaking Universals? – Transnational Feminism(S) Challenging Fundamentalist Ecumenism'. *Theory, Culture and Society*, 19: 175–95.

Wajcman, J. (2000) 'Reflections on Gender and Technology Studies: In What State is the Art?' *Social Studies of Science*, 30(3): 447–64.

Walby, S. (1990) *Theorising Patriarchy*. Oxford: Blackwell.

—— (1992) 'Post-Post-Modernism? Theorising Social Complexity', in M. Barrett and A. Phillips (eds), *op. cit.*

—— (1997) *Gender Transformations*. London: Routledge.

Walker, L. (1995) 'More Than Just Skin-Deep: Fem(Me)Inity and the Subversion of Identity'. *Gender, Place and Culture*, 2(1): 71–7.

Walker, L.J. (1984) 'Sex Differences in the Development of Moral Reasoning'. *Child Development*, 55: 677–91.

Walker, R. (1999) 'Welfare to Work Versus Poverty and Family Change: Policy Lessons from the USA'. *Work, Employment and Society*, 13(3): 539–53.

Walters, S.D. (1996) 'From Here to Queer: Radical Feminism, Postmodernism, and The Lesbian Menace (or, Why Can't a Woman be More Like a Fag?' *Signs*, 21: 830–69.

Waters, K. (1996) '(Re)Turning to the Modern: Radical Feminism and the Post-Modern Turn', in D. Bell and R. Klein (eds), *op. cit.*

Way, S. (1998) 'Social Construction of Episiotomy'. *Journal of Clinical Nursing,* 7: 113–17.

Webster, J. (1996) *Shaping Women's Work.* London: Longman.

Weeks, J. (1991) *Against Nature: Essays on History, Sexuality and Identity.* London: Rivers Oram Press.

Weeks, K. (1996) 'Subject for a Feminist Standpoint', in S. Makdisis *et al.* (eds), *Marxism and Beyond Marxism.* New York: Routledge.

Weir, L. (1998) 'Pregnancy Ultrasound in Maternal Discourse', in M. Shildrick and J. Price (eds), *Vital Signs: Feminist Reconfigurations of the Bio/Logical Body.* Edinburgh: Edinburgh University Press.

Williams, B. (1985) *Ethics and the Limits of Philosophy.* Cambridge, Mass: Harvard University Press.

Williams, J.C. (1989) 'Deconstructing Gender'. *Michigan Law Review,* 87 (February): 797–844.

Willis, E. (1998) 'The "New" Genetics and the Sociology of Medical Technology'. *Journal of Sociology,* 34(1): 170–83.

Wilson, E. (1993) 'Is Transgression Transgressive?', in J. Bristow and A.R. Wilson (eds), *Activating Theory: Lesbian, Gay, Bisexual Politics.* London: Wishart.

Winner, L. (1980) 'Do Artifacts Have Politics?' *Daedalus,* 109: 121–36.

Wood, E.M. (1995) *Democracy against Capitalism: Renewing Historical Materialism.* Cambridge: Cambridge University Press.

Woolgar, S. (1991) 'The Turn to Technology in Social Studies of Science'. *Science, Technology and Human Values,* 16(1): 20–50.

Woolley, F. (2000) 'Degrees of Connection: A Critique of Rawls's Theory of Mutual Disinterest'. *Feminist Economics,* 6(2): 1–21.

Wright, E.O. *et al.* (1992) *Reconstructing Marxism: Essays on Explanation and the Theory of History.* London: Verso.

—— (1994) 'Communications. Historical Materialism: Theory and Methodology'. *Science & Society,* 58(1): 53–60.

Young, I.M. (1981) 'Beyond the Unhappy Marriage: A Critique of the Dual Systems Theory', in L. Sergent (ed.), *Women and Revolution: A Discussion of the Unhappy Marriage of Marxism and Feminism.* Boston: South End Press.

—— (1989) 'Polity and Group Differences: A Critique of Universal Citizenship'. *Ethics,* 99: 250–74.

—— (1990) *Justice and the Politics of Difference.* Princeton: Princeton University Press.

—— (1995) 'Gender as Seriality: Thinking About Women as a Social Collective', in L. Nicholson and S. Seidman (eds), *op. cit.*

—— (1997) 'Socialist Feminism and the Limits of Dual Systems Theory', in R. Hennessy and C. Ingraham (eds), *op. cit.*

Yuval-Davis, N. (1997a) *Gender and Nation.* London: Sage.

—— (1997b) 'Women, Citizenship and Difference'. *Feminist Review,* 57: 4–27.

Zalewski, M. (2000) *Feminism after Postmodernism.* London: Routledge.

Index